DEVELOPMENT
IN THE
THIRD WORLD

Michael Morrish

…ersity Press

Oxford University Press,
Great Clarendon Street, Oxford OX2 6DP

Oxford New York
Athens Auckland Bangkok Bogota Buenos Aires
Calcutta Cape Town Chennai Dar es Salaam
Delhi Florence Hong Kong Istanbul Karachi
Kuala Lumpur Madrid Melbourne Mexico City
Mumbai Nairobi Paris São Paulo Singapore
Taipei Tokyo Toronto Warsaw

and associated companies in
Berlin Ibadan

Oxford is a trade mark of
Oxford University Press

ISBN 0 19 913270 4
© Oxford University Press 1983

First published 1983
Eleventh impression 1998

Typeset by Western Printing Services Ltd,
Bristol
Printed in Hong Kong

Acknowledgements

We would like to thank the following for
permission to reproduce photographs:

African Business 1.4, 2.7, 4.1, 7.27, 8.3(2), 10.15,
10.16; J. Allan Cash 1.15, p. 22(1), 2.10, 2.11,
2.13, 2.14, p. 48(3,5,6,7), 3.16, 3.19, 4.6, 4.7,
4.22, 4.32, 5.8, 6.6, 7.3, 7.5, 7.17, 8.10, 9.1, 9.21,
10.13; Aspect/Mike Wells p. 22(3), 9.5; Associated
Press 5.24; Alan Band Associates 7.11, 7.13;
Camerapix 1.23, p. 22(6), 6.29, 8.21; Camera Press
p. 22(5), 2.12, 2.20, 4.9; Cavendish/Olivier 6.22,
8.15; Richard Costain Ltd. 5.22; Egyptian Embassy
2.35; Peter Fraenkel 8.9; Dora Gauss 2.22;
Geoslides p. 48(9), 9.2; Ghana Information Services
1.20; Richard Gozney 4.10, 6.25; Sally and Richard
Greenhill 4.43, 4.44, 6.20, 9.9; A. T. Grove 3.10;
John Hillelson/J. Kandell/NYT 3.14, /Gilles Peress
6.16, /Richard Melloul 9.14, /William Campbell
10.14, /Ernest Cole 10.18, /Faucon &
Weeder/Sygma 10.19; Hoa-Qui 1.2; Keystone Press
Agency 3.12, 3.15, 5.21, 6.15, 8.23; Mansell
Collection 6.12; Mepha/N. Westwater 1.24, 3.22,
J. Paul 4.23, 4.27, 4.37; Marion and Tony
Morrison p. 48(1), 3.8, 4.16, 4.38, 8.19; Margaret
Murray 1.13, 1.14, 1.18, 1.19, p. 22(2), 2.33, 4.5,
4.34, 4.35, 5.9, 8.13; National Film Board of
Canada p. 48(4,8), 4.4; A. M. O'Connor 7.30,
7.31; Christine Osborne 1.3; Oxfam 1.16, 2.27,
2.28, 3.23, 5.6, 5.20, 5.28, 6.6, 7.8, 7.12, 8.3(3,4),
8.10, 9.8, 10.13, 10.25; Papua New Guinea High
Commission/Chris Owen 4.13, /Veronica Williams
4.14; Popperfoto 5.31, 6.5, 6.7, 9.11, 10.1, 10.6,
10.7, 10.12; Rex Features 5.19, 6.1, 6.3, 10.5;
Dave Saunders 9.23; Sunday Times, London/Peter
Brookes 10.3; John Topham Picture Library 2.9,
p. 48(2), 4.8, 5.16, 6.11, 6.21, 7.24, 9.16; UAC
International 9.4; United Nations p. 22(4), 2.25,
2.30, 2.34, 3.18, 3.25, 3.27, 4.3, 4.21, 5.1, 5.4,
5.13, 5.29, 6.8, 7.26, 8.3(1), 9.6, 10.20, 10.21;
B. B. Whittaker 4.41; Mepha T. Noonan p. 5.

Cover photograph: John Hillelson/Georg Gerster.
It shows a road through the tropical forest in the
Brazilian State of Mato Grosso.

The author would like to acknowledge the
following:

Committee on Poverty and the Arms Trade for Fig.
10.8 by Mahood; Food and Agriculture
Organization of the United Nations, *Ceres* 1975 for
the interview on p. 82; Ronald Higgins, *The
Seventh Enemy*, Hodder & Stoughton (1982) for
Fig. 10.2; Macmillan, London and Basingstoke for
Fig. 7.16 from *The City in the Third World* (ed. D.
Dwyer); John Morris for Fig. 3.3 and the text on
p. 45 which appeared in *Classroom Geographer*,
December 1974; *Teaching Geography*, April 1979 for
the extract on p. 7.

330.91724/

Contents

Preface

Development issues are among the most vital that fall within the scope of geographical study. This book aims to provide a thorough grounding in Third World geography for students preparing for their first public examinations. Although the approach is basically systematic the wide range of regional examples will help students to link theoretical concepts to the real world. A strong emphasis has been placed on the use of exercises to teach and illustrate fundamental ideas. These exercises vary considerably in style and length so that the teacher can match the depth of analysis to the students' ability.

Use has been made of contemporary sources, including a number of newspaper and magazine extracts, to emphasize the topicality of the course content. Often when dealing with the Third World the reliability of available statistical information may be called into question, and teachers should therefore approach some of the data with caution. With the world situation changing so rapidly it is also hoped that teachers will incorporate current material into their course.

Any study of the Third World will raise questions of values and attitudes which invariably arouse differing opinions. I feel it is important to face these issues and discuss them, but teachers should be alert to the eurocentric bias that colours many attitudes and they should remind their students of this. As I also believe that the interdependence of the North and South should be made clear, I have considered a number of the social and political factors that influence international relations in order that their geographical impact may be assessed. Finally I hope that this book will demonstrate to students the relevance of development issues to the lives of ordinary people.

M.M.

Development in the Third World

Chapter **1** What is development?

How do you see the world?

No one can be expected to know about the whole world in detail, but it is surprising how distorted our views of other countries frequently are. Most people have a very limited knowledge of even the basic geography of other parts of the world. Answer Exercises 1 to 4 to see how good your knowledge of the world is.

Fig. 1.1 The location of thirty selected countries of the world

1 Look at the world map in Fig. 1.1.
   a How many of the numbered countries marked on the map can you name? Check your answers in an atlas; how many did you get right?
   b What was the average number of correct answers for the class?
   c Which ten countries did most people name correctly? Why do you think these were known best?

2 Without looking at an atlas rank the following countries in order of size (largest area first): India, Brazil, China, Saudi Arabia, Canada, Kenya, West Germany, Australia.

3 Name five cities in each of the following countries: France, USA, USSR, Japan, South Africa, Argentina.

4 Match the following six countries to their populations (in millions): New Zealand, Mexico, Nigeria, Indonesia, Colombia, United Kingdom (144, 79, 69, 56, 27, 3).

You may need to refer to an atlas to check your answers. The purpose of an atlas is to provide an easy reference source for information of this kind, but it is hard to get a proper impression of foreign places

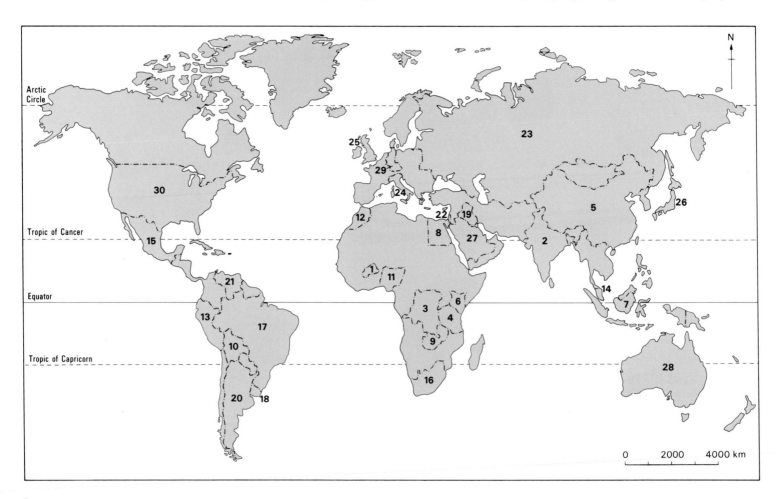

and their people without visiting them. Although you can read about them, study information and look at photographs, it is not the same as actually being there. You miss the sounds and excitement of different surroundings, the sensations of a strange climate and the surprises of a foreign culture. This is how one village in Africa impressed a schoolgirl from a British city on her first visit:

For myself it was the vastness, the feeling of space, that struck me first. Passing through Kissy Street in Freetown at the start of our journey I had been horrified by the dirty, cramped conditions under which people lived. Yet here the street was wide and open, houses sprawled either side. The atmosphere was relaxed. These people might not be rich, but they had an invaluable jewel—they had room, room to sit and talk, room to walk, and for the children, endless room to run and play.

Secondly, it was the people that I noticed. Though thin, few had distorted stomachs, which suggested that their meagre diet was adequate. Yet many, especially the young and the very old, had open infested sores. Modern medicine was obviously not freely available to them, as was rather painfully apparent when just before our departure an old man shuffled over to us. 'Have you something for pain, my back . . . pain', he muttered. Sadly, we had not, and he shuffled away—disheartened, and still in pain.

These people were friendly, smiling, full of life. We were welcomed and made to feel welcome, again sighs of relief—I for one had been worried about the reception we would receive, and whether we would be an unwelcome hindrance. The whole village, it seemed, had turned up for the arrival—it seemed to be as exciting to them as it was to us. At first the children were a little shy, but that wore off within moments, and soon they were fervently practising their English. Within moments of arrival I felt an overwhelming sensation of satisfaction and pleasure that I had made the trip.

Fig. 1.2 An everyday scene in a village in Sierra Leone

What is the Third World?

The Third World is a phrase that is often used to refer to the poor nations of the world, those that we might otherwise describe as less developed, developing, or even underdeveloped.

The term originated in the 1950s during the period of political tension known as the Cold War. At that time the Third World was used to indicate those countries which did not belong to the Western or to the Communist political blocs (the First and Second Worlds). Nowadays, however, many of these poorer countries have strong political links with the West, the USSR, or China. Other nations, particularly the Arab oil-exporters of the Middle East, have developed a powerful political status of their own. And of course, the long-standing hostility between the USSR and China has split the Communist world.

Although the term Third World has lost its original meaning, it is still used, but now reflects economic, rather than political, characteristics. A common characteristic of most less developed countries is the wide gap in incomes between the wealthy minority and the poverty-stricken majority. In some respects the major cities where this wealth is concentrated are not really part of the Third World at all. They are more like isolated outposts of the developed countries. The bulk of the poor are found in the neglected rural areas where hundreds of millions of people scrape a meagre living through agriculture.

The main thing to remember about the Third World is that it consists of an enormous variety of countries in Africa, Asia and Latin America, all with their own characteristics and problems. Of course, many people in Britain have never visited a developing country. A few of you may have been to one for a holiday while others may have spent some time abroad if your parents were working there. Your parents may come from a developing country, even though you have not been there yourself. Whatever your experience you are bound to see things from your own personal point of view. All our opinions and beliefs are based on the amount of knowledge we possess. Most of us have to rely on newspaper and television reports for information about the Third World. Therefore we must be aware of the limitations these sources of information have.

5 How many members of your class have some experience of developing countries? What are their impressions of life there?

6 Find a current news story that concerns a country or region in the developing world.
   a Collect as many newspaper reports and magazine articles as you can that refer to that story.
   b How does each paper report it? Does the emphasis vary? Is one report more factual than another?

Newspapers and magazines tend to include the news items that they think will interest their readers most. Naturally, the majority of these are connected with their home country. Stories from further away will usually be of international importance. Alternatively they may be concerned with a disaster or some other type of 'human interest' topic. Very often we only hear about a developing country if a dramatic event occurs.

Fig. 1.3   Street-dwellers in Bombay overlooked by high-rise flats for the wealthy

Rich and poor

The wealth of our world is not shared equally among us. The richest 10 per cent of the world's population consume 60 per cent of the goods produced, while an estimated 800 million people (about 20 per cent of mankind) live in absolute poverty. Millions more are engaged in a constant struggle to obtain the bare necessities of life. Just one piece of bad luck can spell disaster for a peasant in the less developed countries. Yet those of us living in rich, developed countries all enjoy a comparatively luxurious existence. How did we come to be so much better off? Why aren't the world's resources distributed more fairly? What are we doing to improve the situation, and is it enough?

These are very difficult questions to answer. They involve a large number of complex issues, many of which are highly political. President Nyerere of Tanzania has defined development as: 'the building of a society in which all members have equal rights and equal opportunities; in which all can live at peace with their neighbours without suffering or imposing injustice, being exploited or exploiting; in which all have gradually increasing basic levels of material welfare before any individual lives in luxury.'

Fig. 1.4 Julius Nyerere at a Third World conference

PRESIDENT OF
UNITED REPUBLIC OF
TANZANIA

Fig. 1.5 Hours of work needed to earn the price of the same basket of goods

City	Primary teachers	Bus drivers	Bank tellers	Secretaries
New York	7	13	12	15
Sydney	9	17	13	14
London	18	20	18	20
Tokyo	26	28	17	30
Mexico City	22	36	23	31
Hong Kong	20	63	38	26
Istanbul	36	64	46	39
Bogota	38	70	49	29
Sao Paulo	31	115	35	21
Bombay	110	118	76	99

7 What do you think are the main points President Nyerere is making? Do you agree with him? Can you suggest any other ways in which development could be judged?

A country's level of development is usually measured in terms of its wealth. The poorest countries are the least developed. Poverty influences every aspect of life, and there are a large number of problems associated with it. The standard of living is low and most people live on a hand-to-mouth basis. Because of this they are unable to save and invest money to improve their conditions. The less developed countries cannot afford elaborate educational and health services; therefore people are more prone to disease, which makes them weaker and less productive. Impure water supplies and inadequate sewage systems make the situation worse. Because the standard of living tends to be higher in the cities of these countries, people are leaving the countryside to find work in urban areas. Since jobs there are limited this leads to a high level of unemployment. Industries find it difficult to expand owing to a lack of expertise and capital. Transport systems are usually outdated and inappropriate to current requirements. In rural areas any form of adequate road system is hard to find.

Many less developed countries rely on a few economic activities, normally associated with the production and export of raw materials. The prices for these goods are constantly changing so that the income from them is highly unpredictable. Consequently these countries find it very difficult to plan ahead. Natural environments can also work against them, where rainfall is low or unreliable and high temperatures encourage disease.

8 Study Fig. 1.5. The figures have been adjusted to take account of variations in tax levels, hours worked, and food prices from place to place.
   a Locate each city on a world map.
   b Which of the cities listed would you classify as being in the developing world?
   c What is the overall pattern revealed by the data?
   d Which are the worst paid and best paid occupations?
   e Why might this data give a misleading impression of standards of living in cities in the developing world?

Using statistics to measure development

Since the countries of the world vary so much geographers must find ways of collecting and showing information as simply as possible. To do this it is necessary to use statistics. These are usually collected by the governments of the countries concerned and then gathered together by organizations like the United Nations and the World Bank. This information can be used by international agencies to decide on development programmes and by private firms to choose sites for future investment. The accuracy of the information can vary a great deal and much of it may be out of date or incomplete. Some countries may provide false information for political purposes; many of the poorer nations have neither the finance nor the organization to carry out comprehensive surveys, even for something as basic as a population census.

Fig. 1.6 gives basic information about thirty countries which range from the very rich to the very poor, and vary considerably in terms of their natural environments and population density. Data are given for each country on eight factors (A to H) which summarize its level of development:

A *Gross national product per head.* A country's gross national product (GNP) is the total value, expressed in money, of all the goods and services produced in that country in a year. When that figure is divided by the total population of the country it gives the GNP per head. The GNP figures for developing countries are often misleading since a large percentage of the population may be involved in subsistence agriculture. This means that they produce most of their own requirements and sell very little. Since GNP takes no account of the goods people consume themselves the standard of living appears to be lower than it actually is. On the other hand, since GNP per head is a measure of the *average* wealth of the population it can conceal marked differences in income. In developing countries wealth is often concentrated in a few hands.

Fig. 1.6   Basic information about thirty selected countries

Country	A	B	C	D	E	F	G	H
1 Upper Volta	160	1·6	1880	42	83	30	9	5
2 India	180	2·0	2020	51	74	180	22	36
3 Zaire	210	2·7	2270	46	76	70	34	15
4 Tanzania	230	3·0	2060	51	83	70	12	66
5 China	230	1·6	2470	70	62	810	25	n/a
6 Kenya	330	3·3	2030	53	79	140	14	40
7 Indonesia	360	1·8	2270	47	60	280	20	62
8 Egypt	390	2·2	2760	54	51	460	45	44
9 Zambia	480	3·0	2000	48	68	470	38	39
10 Bolivia	510	2·6	1970	52	51	370	33	63
11 Nigeria	560	2·5	1950	48	56	110	20	n/a
12 Morocco	670	2·9	2530	55	53	290	41	28
13 Peru	740	2·7	2270	56	39	650	67	72
14 Malaysia	1090	2·7	2610	67	50	720	29	60
15 Mexico	1290	3·3	2650	65	39	1380	67	76
16 South Africa	1480	2·7	2830	60	30	2990	50	n/a
17 Brazil	1570	2·8	2560	62	41	790	65	76
18 Uruguay	1610	0·3	3040	71	12	1050	84	94
19 Iraq	1860	3·3	2130	55	42	633	72	n/a
20 Argentina	1910	1·3	3350	71	14	1870	82	94
21 Venezuela	2910	3·3	2440	66	20	2990	83	82
22 Israel	3500	2·7	3140	72	7	2360	89	88
23 USSR	3700	0·9	3460	70	17	5500	65	99
24 Italy	3850	0·7	3430	73	13	3230	69	98
25 United Kingdom	5030	0·1	3340	73	2	5210	91	99
26 Japan	7280	1·2	2950	76	13	3830	78	99
27 Saudi Arabia	7690	3·5	2620	53	62	1310	67	n/a
28 Australia	7990	1·6	3430	73	6	6620	89	100
29 West Germany	9580	0·1	3380	72	4	6020	85	99
30 United States	9590	0·8	3580	73	2	11370	73	99

A: Gross national product per head (US dollars)
B: Population growth rate (percentage)
C: Daily food supply per head (calories)
D: Life expectancy at birth (years)
E: Labour force employed in agriculture (percentage)
F: Energy consumption per head (kilograms of coal equivalent)
G: Urban population (percentage)
H: Adult literacy rate (percentage)

Also workers in the cities, where industry is concentrated, earn far more than the peasants in rural areas. One final point to remember is that since the price of essential goods may be lower than in developed countries, a smaller income would go further in some developing countries.

B *Population growth rate.* This is the percentage by which a country's population is growing each year. It reflects the natural increase of the population, which is the difference between the birth-rate and the death-rate (expressed per thousand of the population). For example, if a country's birth-rate is 42 per 1000 and its death-rate is 22 per 1000, then the natural increase is 20 per 1000 (or 2 per cent) a year.

C *Daily food supply.* This is measured in calories and indicates the energy value of an average diet in a country. It is calculated by dividing the available food supply by the total population.

D *Life expectancy at birth.* This indicates the average number of years a new-born baby could be expected to live. In developing countries the infant mortality-rate is usually high and this lowers the overall life expectancy, along with generally poor health among adults.

E *Labour force employed in agriculture.* Expressed as a percentage of the total workforce, this is a good guide to a country's level of development. In developed countries highly scientific and mechanized farming methods make labour requirements very small. The more traditional methods of the developing countries require a large percentage of the workforce to be involved in agriculture.

F *Energy consumption.* The wealthier nations consume the bulk of the world's energy since they need vast amounts of fuel for their industries, transport systems, and homes. Energy consumption is measured in kilograms of coal equivalent: the amount of power that can be derived from a kilogram of coal, whether it is produced by oil, gas, wood, nuclear fuels, or any other means.

G *Urban population.* This is simply the percentage of a country's population which lives in urban areas (settlements over a certain size). Difficulties arise over the definition of what size of settlement should be regarded as urban.

H *Adult literacy rate.* This shows the percentage of the adult population who can read and write. It is a useful indication of the amount of education in a country.

9 For this exercise you will need to work in groups of eight. Each member of the group should choose a different factor (A to H) from those given in Fig. 1.6. (Each country has been given a number which shows its position on Fig. 1.1.) On a copy of Fig. 1.1 shade in each of the thirty countries according to the categories listed below for your chosen factor. The colour scheme should range from a dark colour for the highest value to a light colour for the lowest value.

A 0–500, 501–1500, 1501–3000, over 3000
B under 1, 1–1·9, 2–2·9, 3 and over
C 0–2000, 2001–2500, 2501–3000, over 3000
D 0–50, 51–60, 61–70, over 70
E 0–25, 26–50, 51–75, 76–100
F 0–500, 501–1000, 1001–3000, over 3000
G 0–25, 26–50, 51–75, 76–100
H 0–40, 41–60, 61–80, 81–100

When all the maps are completed (don't forget to include a title and key) put them all together and compare them. Each person should briefly describe the pattern of their map to the rest of the group.
a Which factors do you consider to be the best indicators of development?
b Which countries appear to be i) most developed, ii) least developed?
c Generally speaking, between which lines of latitude are the less developed countries concentrated?
d Two of the maps should have a pattern that is the opposite of the other six. Which factors do these two illustrate? Why would you expect them to be different?
e Are there any countries which seem to be developed according to some factors but not others?

The maps that you produced for the previous exercise are called choropleth maps. They use different colours or shadings to show the distribution of groups of values.

By comparing one map with another we can see if there is any similarity between the two patterns. If two maps seem to match quite closely it suggests that the factors they illustrate may be linked in some way. For example, since the maps of daily food supply and life expectancy are similar it would be reasonable to suggest that one affects the other. In other words, there is a relationship between the two factors. However, at this stage we cannot be certain that this is the case. We can put forward this relationship as a theory that can be tested by other methods. Such a theory or idea is known as a hypothesis.

One way of testing a hypothesis is to plot the values of two different factors on a graph. Fig. 1.7 is such a graph relating GNP per head to energy consumption (A and F respectively on Fig. 1.6). Each country is represented by a single cross at the coordinate of the two values. The crosses for all thirty countries make up a scatter of points, which is why this type of graph is known as a scattergraph. The pattern of points indicates the strength and nature of the relationship between the two factors. If the points are grouped so that they run from the bottom left to the top right corners of the graph, then this indicates a positive relationship. This means that as the value of one factor increases so the value of the other increases as well. The nearer the points come to forming a straight line the closer the relationship between the two factors.

When dealing with two factors which have a very wide range of values it is necessary to use a graph with logarithmic scales on each axis. These scales compress the range so that the points will still form a straight-line relationship if the factors are linked. Fig. 1.7 is this type of graph.

To plot the remaining factors in Fig. 1.6 against GNP per head it is better to use graph paper with only one logarithmic scale (the vertical scale), which should be used for GNP. Fig. 1.8 is an example of this semi-logarithmic type of graph which has been used to compare GNP per head with the percentage of the labour force employed in agriculture. In this case the points run from top left to bottom right, indicating a negative relationship. This means that as the value of one factor increases so the value of the other decreases. If the pattern of the points is very widely scattered, showing no clear trend in any direction, then the two factors are not related.

On Fig. 1.8 there is a single point which is plotted well away from the main line of points: this is known as a residual. The country that this point represents is Saudi Arabia and its position on the graph indicates that it has a much higher GNP per head than the percentage employed in agriculture would normally suggest.

10 a Working in groups of five, so that each person does one graph, plot GNP per head against each of the five other factors listed in Fig. 1.6, i.e. population growth rate, daily food supply, life expectancy at birth, urban population, and adult literacy rate. Compare the patterns shown by the five graphs.

b On a copy of Fig. 1.9 fill in the top line of the matrix to summarize the relationship between GNP and each of the other seven factors, using the following abbreviations: SP (strong positive), WP (weak positive), SN (strong negative), WN (weak nega-

tive), NO (no clear relationship).

c Think carefully about the likely relationships between the other factors and on the basis of your estimates fill in the remainder of the matrix using the same abbreviations. How do your conclusions compare with those of other members of the class?

d You may want to check some of these by plotting scattergraphs for other pairs of factors. These can be done on ordinary millimetre graph paper unless the graph includes energy consumption which requires one logarithmic scale as in Fig. 1.8.

Fig. 1.7 GNP per head and energy consumption for thirty selected countries

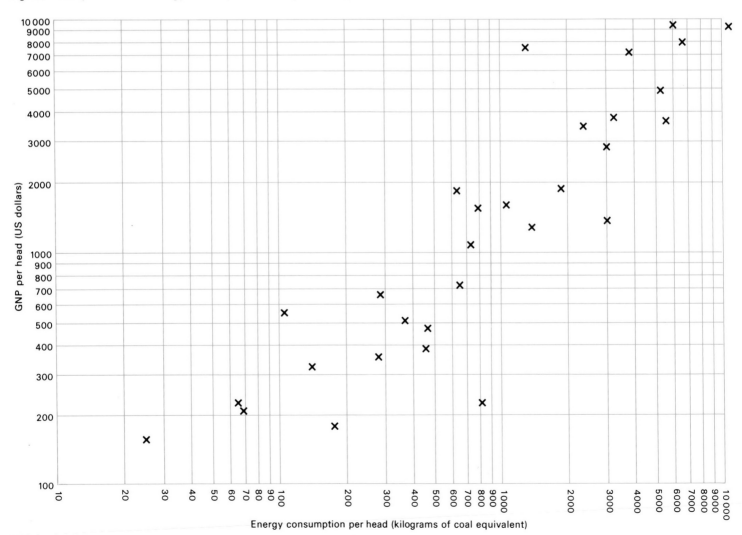

The procedure which you carried out when comparing your graphs or maps is known as visual correlation. If two factors are closely related then it can be said that they correlate well. The correlations you have discovered so far should have given you a clearer idea of the state of development of the thirty countries.

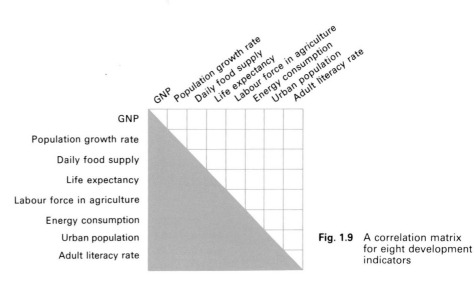

Fig. 1.9 A correlation matrix for eight development indicators

Fig. 1.8 GNP per head and labour force employed in agriculture for thirty selected countries

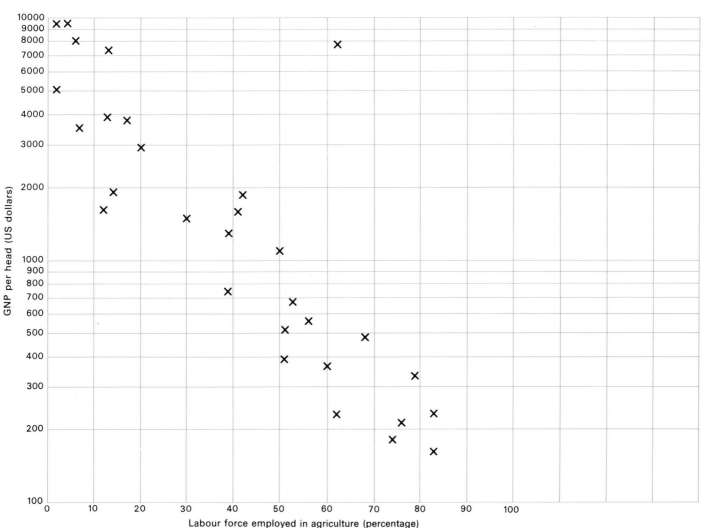

Statistical correlation

Although maps and graphs can give a clear general impression of relationships they are not precise. Statistical analysis offers an exact method of studying the relationship between two sets of data; it tells us not only if a correlation exists but also how strong the link is. A fairly straightforward way of doing this is to use Spearman's rank correlation test. This is usually known as Spearman's R for short.

To show how the test is carried out we will follow a worked example (Fig. 1.10). In this case the average life expectancy and GNP per head are compared for ten countries. The steps involved are as follows:

1 Rank the countries in descending order on each of the two factors that are being tested. The country with the highest value is ranked 1, that with the next highest is ranked 2, and so on. If two countries have the same value then they are each classified according to the average of the two ranks they occupy.

2 Work out the difference (d) between the two ranks for each country.
3 Square the differences (d²).
4 Add up the squares of the differences to find Σd^2 (Σ means 'the sum of').
5 Now insert this value into the formula to find Spearman's R:

$$R = 1 - \left(\frac{6 \times \Sigma d^2}{n^3 - n} \right)$$

where n = the number (of countries).

The value of R will lie somewhere between 1 and −1. A result which falls between 0·7 and 1 indicates a strong positive correlation. Likewise a result falling between −0·7 and −1 indicates a strong negative correlation. Values closer to nought indicate progressively weaker correlations (negative for minus numbers and positive for plus numbers). A value of nought indicates no correlation whatsoever. A value of 1 or −1 indicates a perfect positive or negative correlation respectively. In the case of our worked example the final result of 0·89 suggests a very strong positive correlation.

11 Refer to Fig. 1.6 to find the statistics for daily food supply and the percentage of the labour force in agriculture for the same ten countries that appeared in the worked example.
   a Carry out a Spearman's R test on this data, filling in a table in the same way as is shown in Fig. 1.10.
   b What type of correlation does your result indicate?
   c Is the correlation stronger or weaker than that shown in the worked example between life expectancy and GNP per head in Fig. 1.10?

12 a Look again at the matrix you filled in for Exercise 10 and choose a pair of factors that you thought would have a strong negative correlation.
   b Carry out a Spearman's R test on these two factors for the same ten countries in Fig. 1.10, taking the necessary data from Fig. 1.6.
   c Is the correlation between the factors as strong as you expected?

Fig. 1.10 A worked example of Spearman's R correlating GNP per head and life expectancy at birth

Country	(a) GNP per head (dollars)	Rank (a)	(b) Life expectancy (years)	Rank (b)	Difference (d) between ranks a & b	Difference squared (d²)
West Germany	9580	1	72	3	2	4
Japan	7280	2	76	1	1	1
United Kingdom	5030	3	73	2	1	1
USSR	3700	4	70	4	0	0
South Africa	1480	5	60	6	1	1
Mexico	1290	6	65	5	1	1
Nigeria	560	7	48	9	2	4
Bolivia	510	8	52	7	1	1
Indonesia	360	9	47	10	1	1
India	180	10	51	8	2	4

$$\Sigma d^2 = 18$$

$$R = 1 - \left(\frac{6 \times 18}{1000 - 10} \right)$$

$$= 1 - \left(\frac{108}{990} \right)$$

$$= 1 - 0·11$$

$$= 0·89$$

Datoyili in northern Ghana

So far we have been taking a worldwide view of development. Now we shall go to the other extreme by considering one single location, a small village in Ghana called Datoyili. The following description of life there will give you some idea of the day-to-day existence of poor rural people in the Third World. There is no such thing as a 'typical' village—life is much too varied for that—but this case study does tell you about the importance of traditional ways and the resourcefulness of the villagers.

Life in Datoyili has not changed much over the years. The modern world has had very little impact on the ways of the villagers. They still provide most of their everyday needs themselves. Virtually everything they require is obtained locally, either from the village's own resources or from the nearby market town.

13 a Look at the plan of Datoyili (Fig. 1.11). What does it tell you about the lives of the people who live there?

b Write down your impressions and then compare them with other members of the class. What were the most common observations?

Datoyili is situated in the flat savanna lands of northern Ghana. The savanna consists of a carpet of grasses dotted with short, widely spaced trees. The soil is a reddish loam, a well-drained mixture of sand and clay; it is not particularly fertile but is extensively farmed where it occurs thickly.

The village lies 10 km south-west of Tamale, close to the road that leads to the market town. The settlement itself consists of a cluster of sixteen family compounds; it has no focal point and even the chief's compound is not located centrally. A compound is a group of single-storey huts, each one linked by a two-metre-high wall. Every family builds its own, after gaining permission from the chief, and uses methods that have been handed down from one generation to the next. Hut walls are made of

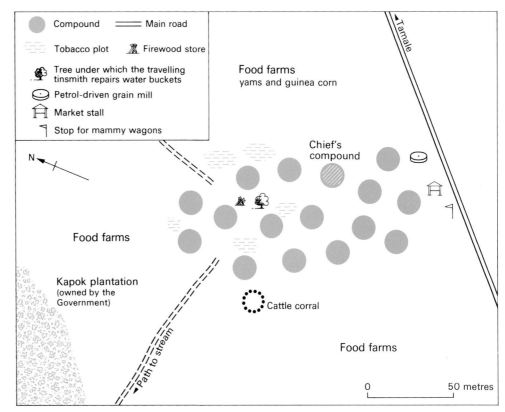

Fig. 1.11 A plan of Datoyili

Fig. 1.12 A plan of the chief's compound

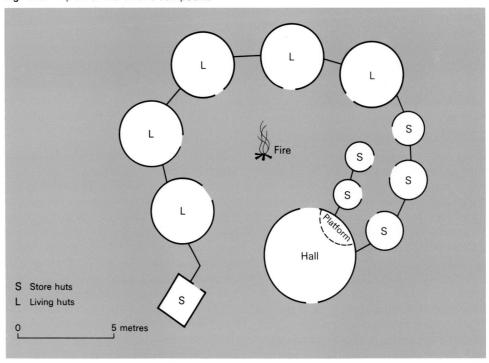

Fig. 1.13 Family compounds in the savanna belt of West Africa

sticky clay or mud which is built up layer by layer and dries as hard as brick. The conical roof is supported by wooden rafters set into the mud walls and is thatched with guinea-corn stalks. Building and repairs are carried out during the dry season. Unless the huts are maintained annually they will not last for more than five years.

A plan of the chief's compound is shown in Fig. 1.12. Like most compounds it consists of a series of huts for the chief and his wives, with several smaller huts for storing food. All the huts face into a central court-yard which is the focus of family life and contains the communal fireplace. Inside the huts it is dark and cool, the only light coming through a small doorway. The floors are smooth, hard clay and apart from the occasional wooden stool or woven basket there is no furniture. Cooking pots and other clay pots containing food are stacked neatly against the walls. There is no electricity in the village, so light is provided by hurricane lamps or by burning a wick in oil.

The inhabitants of Datoyili are all subsistence farmers, growing crops and rearing livestock chiefly to supply their own food. The farming operations are governed by the climate, which clearly reflects the village's location in the tropics.

14 Study the two graphs in Fig. 1.17.
  a Compare the pattern of temperature and rainfall for Tamale and London.
  b What problems would the climate present to farmers in each location?

All farming land in Datoyili is leased from its owner, the chief. The land near the compounds is manured and permanently cultivated, while land further away has to

Fig. 1.14 Harvesting groundnuts

Fig. 1.15 Yam mounds

Fig. 1.16 A field of sorghum

Fig. 1.17 Average monthly rainfall and temperature for Tamale and London

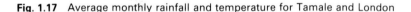

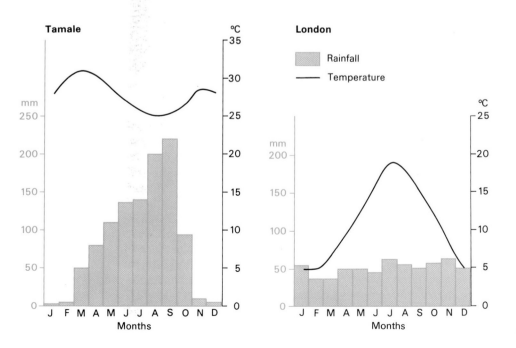

be left fallow for several years to recover its fertility. In this part of the savanna the rainy season lasts from March to October and is followed by a period of intense drought. Consequently, agriculture is restricted to livestock rearing and the cultivation of crops that can be grown during the rainy season or are unaffected by the drought. The main food crops are yams (a starchy potato-like vegetable) and guinea corn or sorghum (a tall-growing grass with reddish seeds). The seed is either ground into flour or cooked whole while the leaves are used as cattle fodder. The grain is also used to make beer.

Groundnuts are grown both as a food crop and as a source of oil. The oil is used mainly for cooking in Datoyili but it can also be made into margarine or soap. Some groundnuts are raised as a cash crop and sold in the local market: so is tobacco, though the villagers usually dry the leaves and store them until they can get a good

17

Fig. 1.18 The grain store in a family compound

price. A variety of animals is kept, including cattle, chickens, goats, and sheep. Cattle are a sign of wealth and are sold only when absolutely necessary; mostly they are kept for their milk. Nowadays the cattle are inoculated to protect them from rinderpest and diseases spread by the tsetse-fly.

Although Datoyili does possess some farming machinery left over from a co-operative farming scheme, the most commonly used implement is a digging tool. This is a simple broad-bladed hoe with a short wooden handle which can be put to a variety of uses. As one would expect, farmers work very hard in Datoyili but their standard of living remains low. When the harvest is completed in December many men travel south to find work in the cocoa plantations where they stay for about three months.

The women of the village are responsible for all the domestic work. The senior wife in each family supervises the household activities which are carried out co-operatively by the wives and children. Each wife takes it in turn to cook for the whole family. This is done over a wood or charcoal fire set into a hardened clay framework that supports the round metal pots. Every few days firewood must be collected from around the village and stacked by the side of one of the huts until it is needed. The women have to fetch water to supply the needs of the compound, which means that each wife must go to the stream four times daily. In the rainy season water is plentiful nearby but during the dry season the nearest stream is 2·5 km away. The water is collected in metal buckets that the women carry on their heads.

Trading in Tamale market is also done by the women. They are lucky that Datoyili is so close to this large centre and is connected by an all-weather road. If they can afford it the women travel into Tamale by mammy wagon, privately operated lorries that serve as the local buses. If not they have to walk the 10 km carrying their produce on their heads.

Tamale has the nearest secondary school but not many villagers can afford to send their children there. However, primary education in Ghana is free and every day a government teacher comes to the village from Tamale. Since Datoyili has no school buildings the lessons have to take place outside in the shade of a tree. There are no medical services in the village and the nearest doctor is at Tamale. The nearest post office is also in the market town.

Fig. 1.19 Carrying water back to the village

Fig. 1.20 Yams for sale in the local market

For the most part modern life has passed Datoyili by. The villagers are chiefly concerned with getting enough to eat. Food may well run short in the difficult time towards the end of the dry season. Many of the children in Datoyili have swollen stomachs caused by undernourishment and malnutrition. The necessities of life are not guaranteed as they are in our welfare state: in Datoyili most people's time is devoted to providing them. If conditions work against this, the villagers have no option but to do without.

15 a Read through the account of Datoyili again and note down all the main aspects of life there; for example housing, food, water supply, work, public services, entertainment, etc.
  b Now compare this with your own family life and home. How many luxuries and services do you rely on that the people of Datoyili manage to do without?
  c Make a list of all the differences in styles of living between Datoyili and your neighbourhood. What are the advantages and disadvantages of living in each place?

There are usually very good reasons for traditional ways of life. They have developed over many centuries as a practical way of dealing with a particular environment. When modern practices are introduced they tend to upset the balance. We will now look at the effect of change on two everyday things: how people dress and their homes and offices.

Life in the Sudan

The Sudan, a desert country in north-east Africa, has a very hot climate. The traditional way of life in the Sudan is well adapted to minimize the discomfort of the environment. Styles of building, clothing, and personal behaviour are all designed to combat the heat. However, temperatures are not constantly high. Like all desert areas the Sudan has a wide daily temperature range, with hot days and cold nights. There are also considerable seasonal variations in temperature, rainfall, humidity, and wind.

16 Study the climate graph for Khartoum (Fig. 1.21), the capital city of the Sudan.

   a When is the hottest time of the year?

   b Which months would you consider to be Khartoum's winter? What is the lowest temperature during these months?

   c Measure the temperature range for each month. What is the average for the year? Which months have the highest and lowest ranges in temperature?

   d Humidity is highest during the rainy season. Which months does this cover?

   e How long does Khartoum's dry season last? How do temperatures vary as the dry season progresses?

   f Write a paragraph comparing Khartoum's climate with that of London given in Fig. 1.17.

Between May and July the Sudan comes under the influence of southerly winds, which bring very hot, dry conditions and occasional fierce dust storms. During the rainy season from July to September there is less wind, giving rise to high humidity, although maximum temperatures are lower. The winter months have the lowest temperatures, as northerly winds from the Mediterranean bring clear skies and very low humidity.

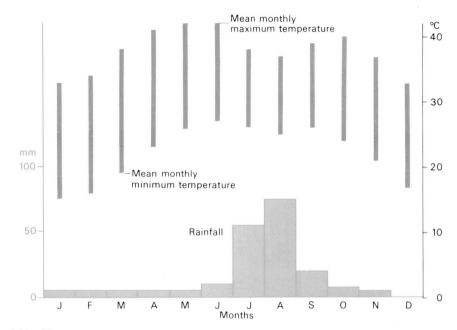

Fig. 1.21 Climatic graph for Khartoum

Fig. 1.22 A traditional Sudanese house

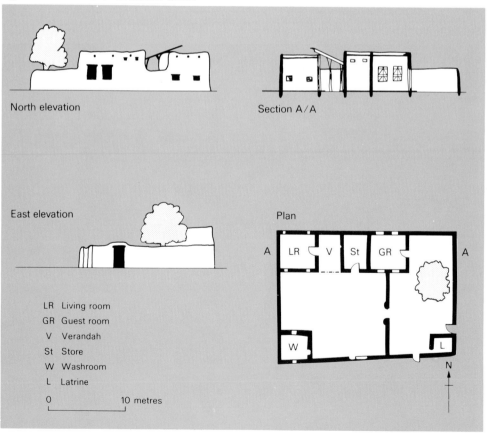

20

The traditional buildings in the Sudan have developed so that they are suited to all the climatic conditions that occur. Fig. 1.22 shows the main features of a Sudanese house. It is constructed entirely from materials that are available locally. The design follows the traditional Arab style of rectangular buildings with flat roofs. The walls are made of dried mud, which is either built up in layers or shaped into bricks for greater strength. Because timber is scarce in desert areas its use in construction is limited: most wood has to be used as fuel for cooking. It is essential though for beams to support the heavy clay roofs and these are usually made from split palm-tree trunks. The houses have very small windows which are fitted with timber shutters.

Since these clay buildings contain a lot of heavy material it takes a long time for them to heat up or cool down. Houses are often painted white to reflect the sun's rays. Consequently the houses remain cool during the heat of the day but retain warmth for the cold desert night. In the summer, when the houses would be uncomfortably hot during the night, people usually sleep outdoors. Meanwhile, the shutters are opened so that the night breeze can cool the house in preparation for the next day.

Daily routine is geared to the climatic conditions, so that all work and trade is carried out during the cooler parts of the day. In the middle of the day, when temperatures are at their highest, people stay indoors where it is still relatively cool. During the evening, however, when the houses have warmed up, people gather in the cooling breeze of the open courtyard. In fact the Sudanese house is not strictly a building: it is really a walled private area which contains both enclosed and open spaces.

17 a Make a copy of the drawings of the Sudanese house (Fig. 1.22). Add a series of labels which point out the main features of its construction and how they reflect local conditions.

   b Make a simple drawing or plan of your own house and label its main design features. How are they adapted to our temperate climate? Can you suggest any improvements to the design?

Fig. 1.23 Traditional and modern buildings in central Khartoum

21

1

2

3

4

5

6

Fig. 1.24 Sudanese men wearing djallabiyas

Adaptation to climate is also reflected in Sudanese clothing. The men wear a long, loose-fitting cotton robe called a 'djallabiya'. The female equivalent is a long strip of thin cotton that is wound round the body like an Indian sari. Both are very light and made from white material to reflect the sun. They allow air to circulate freely around the body which helps to evaporate sweat and keep the person cool. When walking along the street the Sudanese tend to move slowly to avoid making themselves hot; they instinctively seek out patches of shade where possible.

Since the Sudan's independence in 1956 there has been a marked change in the lifestyle of the more affluent Sudanese. Like many other Third World countries the Sudan has chosen to develop along the lines of the industrial West. This has led to the adoption of many western standards and forms of behaviour. For example, the suc-cessful man in Khartoum now wears a white shirt and tie, with dark trousers and lace-up shoes. For formal occasions he will dress in a dark suit. Since these clothes were designed for people living in a temperate climate to prevent loss of body heat, they are totally unsuitable for a desert environment.

In the modern world businessmen like to move around briskly as a sign of efficiency. When someone acts like this in the tropics he makes himself hotter still. If his office building is made of glass and concrete it will get hot far more quickly than a traditional building. All this means that some system of artificial cooling has to be installed. It may be simple electric fans to create a breeze, but is more likely to be full air-conditioning. Once people are used to working in a cool environment they will want this for their homes as well and, if they can afford it, their car. Consequently, their families also come to expect air-conditioning wherever they go and the demand for it spreads.

Air-conditioning is very pleasant for the privileged minority who can enjoy its benefits, but it has many drawbacks. Air-conditioned buildings pump heat into the outside air, raising the temperature. The machinery involved also creates heat. For a country like the Sudan, which has no coal or oil, the cost of fuel to run this machinery is high. The fuel has to be paid for out of earnings from the Sudan's exports. This money could be put to use in more productive ways, but as long as people feel the need to dress in western clothes air-conditioning will be considered a necessity.

18 Look at the photographs on the opposite page.
   a What aspects of the modern world do they represent? How might these have altered traditional life in a developing country? What are their disadvantages?
   b What do you think persuades people to abandon their traditional ways?

Summary

In this chapter we have considered different ways in which development can be judged. Development is not simply concerned with wealth, but with many other aspects of life such as health, education, housing, and employment. Statistics measuring these factors should be treated carefully, since their reliability is by no means certain. Though countries in the Third World face common problems, each country has its own unique situation to handle. Many people, chiefly in the rural areas, still live in a traditional fashion, having little contact with the outside world. However, the effect of the western world is spreading and bringing with it major changes in the lifestyle of the ordinary people.

Chapter **2** The pressure of population

Patterns of population growth

Every day the world's population increases by 200 000 people. This represents an annual increase of over 70 million people, or the addition of a country with as many people as, for example, Mexico or Nigeria. It took sixteen hundred years to double the world's population as it stood in the first century A.D. It will take only forty years to double the present world total. This is the pattern of the population explosion, but no one can be certain what will happen in the future.

The population of a country is always changing, with some people dying and others being born. This causes a continual alteration of the individuals who make up the population. Births and deaths are normally expressed in rates per thousand people living at a particular time. The rates are calculated on an annual basis by relating the number of births and deaths recorded to the total population. For example, a country of 50 million people which had 1 million births and 0·5 million deaths during the year would have a birth-rate of 20 per thousand and a death-rate of 10 per thousand. These are referred to as crude rates because they are not adjusted to take account of the proportion of the population that falls into the child-bearing age group.

The difference between the birth-rate and death-rate indicates the natural increase or decrease of the population. In most countries of the world there are more births than deaths, giving rates of increase that vary considerably from region to region. These increases are usually expressed as a percentage of the total population, again measured on an annual basis. So, using the example above, the natural increase is half a million during the year, which represents 1 per cent of the total population

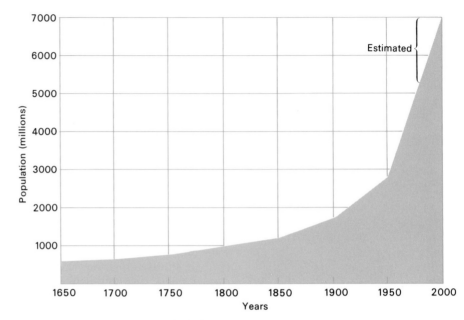

Fig. 2.1 World population growth, 1650–2000

Fig. 2.2 The growth of population in major regions of the world (millions)

Year	Europe and USSR	North America	Oceania	Asia	Latin America	Africa
1650	103	1	2	292	10	100
1750	144	1	2	456	10	98
1800	192	6	2	596	21	95
1850	274	26	2	698	33	98
1900	423	81	6	886	63	130
1950	576	167	13	1384	162	207
1980	733	239	22	2287	326	413

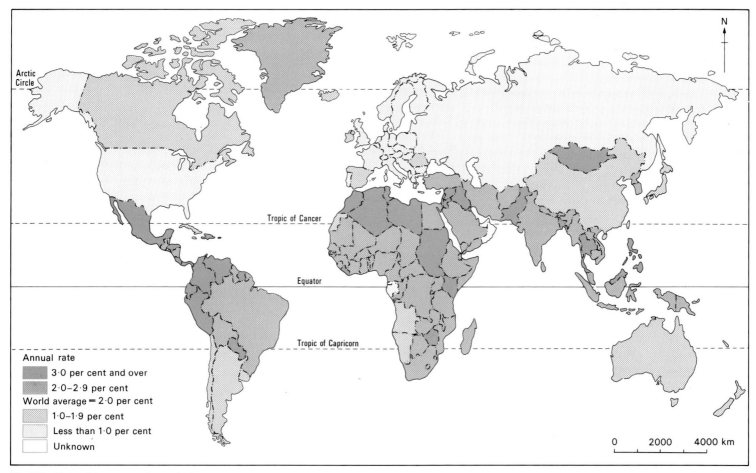

Fig. 2.3 Natural increase of population

Annual rate
- 3·0 per cent and over
- 2·0–2·9 per cent

World average = 2·0 per cent
- 1·0–1·9 per cent
- Less than 1·0 per cent
- Unknown

of 50 million. Currently the world population is growing by about 2 per cent a year. However, the rates of increase for individual countries range from as much as 4 per cent to only 0·1 per cent. In fact a few countries in the developed world, including the UK, have experienced a slight decrease in their total population in recent years.

Fig. 2.1 shows the pattern of the increase in world population since 1650. Present estimates suggest that the world total will reach 7000 million people by the year 2000.

1 Study Fig. 2.1.
  a When did the world population reach 1000 million?
  b How many years did it take to double to 2000 million?
  c How long did it take to double again to 4000 million?

2 **a** Study Fig. 2.3 carefully and write a few sentences describing the general pattern that it reveals.
  b Which parts of the world have the highest and lowest rates of increase?
  c Use an atlas to identify five countries in each of the four categories and list them as examples.

3 **a** Use the data given in Fig. 2.2 to plot six lines on a single graph showing population growth for the main regions of the world.
  b How does your graph match up to your comments on the rates of increase considered in Exercise 2?

The cycle of population change

By plotting the birth-rate and death-rate for any country on a graph it is possible to see when the greatest natural increase has taken place. Most developed countries have accurate records of births and deaths that go back at least a hundred years. Unfortunately, information for less developed countries is much harder to come by and can be unreliable.

Fig. 2.4 shows the relationship between birth-rates and death-rates in the developed and less developed countries. In the case of the developed countries improvements in medicine and hygiene have led to a gradual decrease in the death-rate since the early eighteen hundreds. This has been accompanied by a fall in the birth-rate since the late nineteenth century due to the introduction of contraception and a move towards smaller families. As people become more affluent they tend to have fewer children so that they can maintain their standard of living. In the less developed countries, however, the birth-rates and death-rates remained high until well into the twentieth century. Since the Second World War these countries have benefited greatly from improved medicine and the death-rate has dropped sharply. On the other hand birth control has only had a marginal effect so that their populations are increasing rapidly. This is indicated by the wide gap between the two lines.

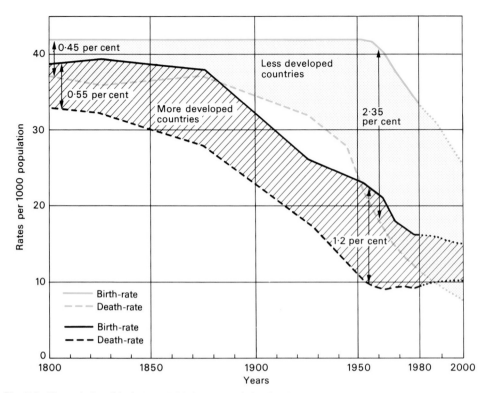

Fig. 2.4 The relationship between birth-rate and death-rate

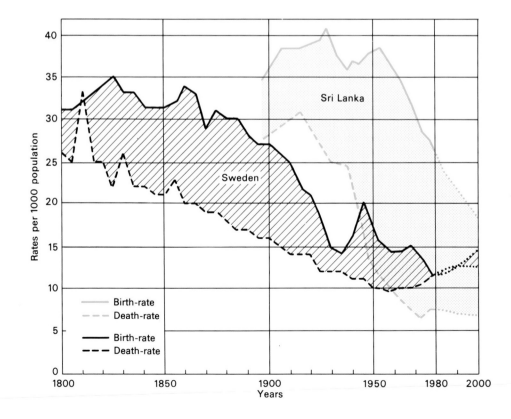

Fig. 2.5 A comparison of Sweden's and Sri Lanka's birth-rate and death-rate

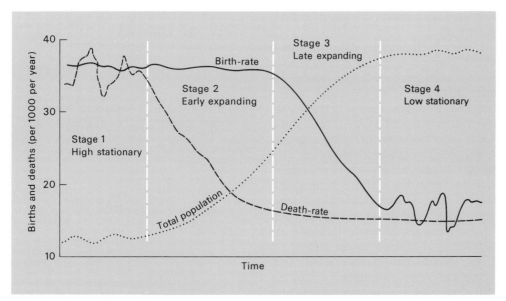

Fig. 2.6 Stages of population growth

Fig. 2.7 Advertising and reality

4 Fig. 2.6 is a diagram suggesting the way in which population growth can change over time. Study the diagram and then copy out the following paragraph, filling in the gaps with the words provided.

In the first stage the . . . . . .-rate tends to fluctuate more than the . . . . . .-rate, but because both rates are high, the population remains fairly . . . . . . During the second stage improvements in . . . . . . and . . . . . . lead to a . . . . . . death-rate, although the birth-rate remains . . . . . . This produces a rapid . . . . . . in the overall population. In stage three the death-rate stabilizes at a . . . . . . level, but the birth-rate . . . . . . due to improved . . . . . . and the use of . . . . . . However, the population continues to . . . . . . until the beginning of stage . . . . . . In this final stage both rates are low, though the birth-rate tends to . . . . . . more. Since the two rates are relatively . . . . . . they cancel each other out and the population . . . . . .

Missing words: *increase, birth, four, hygiene, equal, drops, standards of living, high, fluctuate, death, medicine, rise, constant, contraception, low, falling, stabilizes.*

5 Fig. 2.5 shows the pattern of births and deaths for a developed country, Sweden, and a developing country, Sri Lanka.
  a Measure the difference between the birth-rate and the death-rate for every ten years for each country. This tells you the natural increase per thousand. Now plot these two sets of values as lines on a graph using the same axes as Fig. 2.5.
  b Mark in the various stages of growth. What pattern do they show?

27

Population distribution

The distribution of population over the earth's surface is very uneven. In the first place only 30 per cent of the surface area is land, the majority of which is situated in the northern hemisphere. Much of the land is uninhabited and further large areas support only a very sparse population. A mere 20 per cent of the continents offer conditions that are attractive for human settlement. Man is limited by several important factors in his choice of areas for occupation, for example extremes of temperature and humidity. While it is possible to create artificial conditions to avoid these (through air-conditioning and heating) the expense involved inevitably limits the population in very hot or very cold areas. Most people live in areas that are naturally tolerable all the year round.

Another factor is man's ability to support himself through agriculture. The regions with the most fertile soils and suitable climates have been occupied for several thousand years. Ten per cent of the world's land area is currently used for the cultivation of crops and a further 6 per cent provides good grassland for raising animals. Another 10 per cent consists of poor grassland that provides useful but unreliable pastures. It has been claimed that these proportions could be increased considerably but there are still many technical and environmental problems to be solved.

The developed world relies on both agriculture and industry to support its population. Countries like Britain, which only grows half its food requirements, use the

Fig. 2.9 The Canadian wheatlands	**Fig. 2.10** The Arctic
Fig. 2.11 A Himalayan valley	**Fig. 2.12** An English orchard

Fig. 2.8 World population distribution

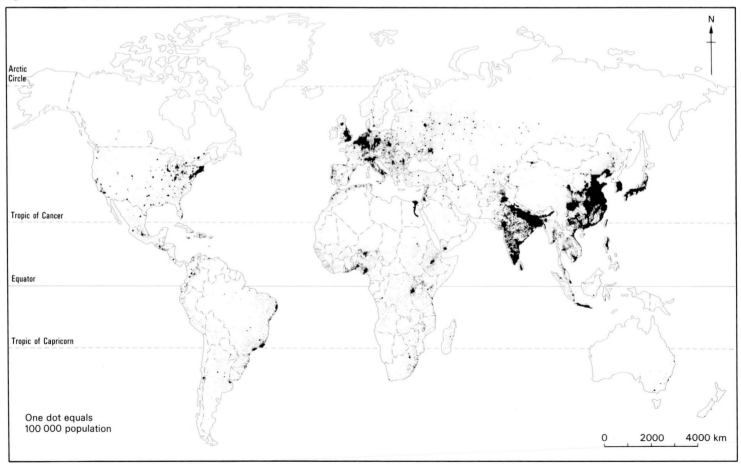

Arctic Circle

Tropic of Cancer

Equator

Tropic of Capricorn

One dot equals
100 000 population

N

0   2000   4000 km

Fig. 2.13 The Sahara desert

Fig. 2.14 Tropical forest in Nigeria

income from their industries to pay for imported farm produce. Yet the rapid consumption of raw materials by such industries has led man to explore difficult environments for new supplies. If the demand for these natural resources is great enough then man will find ways to live there and extract them.

Which are the hostile environments that have largely repelled man? The hot deserts of the world cover 20 per cent of the land area but support only 4 per cent of the human population. Their soils are poor and shallow and there is little opportunity for irrigated farming. The savanna grasslands that lie next to the deserts have a population density of only 5 people per km². Although they can have quite high rainfall it is unevenly distributed and unreliable. Their infertile and badly drained soils are vulnerable to severe erosion. The tropical rain forests cover 10 per cent of the land area and support 6 per cent of the population, most of whom live in Indonesia and Malaysia. Regions like the Amazon basin have a population density of only 1 person per km². The rain forest climate is very hot and humid, encouraging a wide variety of pests and disease; if the trees are cleared for farming then the soils are rapidly destroyed.

Twenty per cent of the world's land area has winter temperatures that stay far below freezing. Even in summer these tundra areas barely thaw out and below the surface their soils remain permanently frozen. A final 20 per cent of the land is too steep for farming and possesses thin mountain soils that are easily carried away.

As the world population increases, more and more pressure is being put on the favourable regions of the world. The stresses which arise vary considerably between the developed and less developed countries, but they are evident in all heavily populated areas.

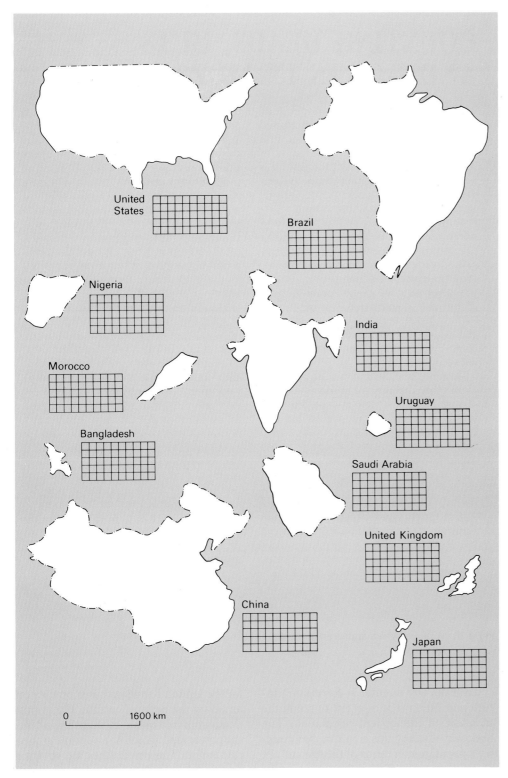

Fig. 2.15 Outlines for use in Exercise 8

6 Study the photos on pages 29–30 which show some hospitable and inhospitable environments.
  a For each photo write down four adjectives that summarize its characteristics. Try not to use the same adjective twice.
  b Which adjectives were used most commonly by members of the class?

7 Refer to Fig. 3.6 on page 47.
  a Using this as a basis mark on an outline map of the world the areas that you would consider to be too high, too cold, too hot or too barren to support a sizeable human population.
  b Now mark in a bright colour the areas that you would expect to be most densely populated. What are your reasons for choosing these areas?
  c When you have finished compare your map with Fig. 2.8. How closely do they match?

8 a Make a tracing of the country outlines and boxes in Fig. 2.15. Using the table of population densities given below shade in the appropriate box for each country. For every 10 people per km² one small square should be shaded.

	Population per km²		Population per km²
Bangladesh	500	Nigeria	90
Japan	310	Morocco	40
UK	230	United States	20
India	190	Brazil	10
Uruguay	160	Saudi Arabia	5
China	90		

  b Divide the countries into those that you consider are developed and those that are less developed. Do the less developed tend to have higher population densities?
  c Why can the average population density figure be misleading?

Population structure

Every country needs basic information about its inhabitants so that the government can plan effectively. This data can be collected in two ways. Firstly, a census can be conducted to find out the size and characteristics of the current population. Since the population is continually changing, censuses are usually taken at regular intervals of about ten years. Secondly, to provide continuous information about the change in the population it is necessary to register all births, deaths, and migrations. This is known as vital registration.

A large number of developing countries have only inadequate or unreliable census information. During World Population Year in 1974 the United Nations helped thirty nations to hold a census, twenty for the first time. There are many practical difficulties involved in carrying out a census. First of all they are very costly: many developing countries prefer to allocate funds to more pressing matters. In countries where few people can read, census officials have to travel round and collect information verbally. They are often regarded with suspicion, resentment, and at times open hostility. People may give false statements about their age, occupation, and possessions for reasons of status. Frequently language differences or local dialects make communication a problem. Some sections of the population may be missed entirely if they live in inaccessible areas or have a nomadic way of life.

9 Read the article about Mozambique's census (Fig. 2.16).
- **a** Explain how the census was organized.
- **b** What practical problems arose when it was being carried out?
- **c** What information did the census collect? How might the Mozambique government use this information?

COUNTING HEADS, HUTS AND GOATS IN MOZAMBIQUE

Village festivals and street parties took place throughout Mozambique yesterday to mark the opening of the first census since independence.

The precise population of Mozambique is not known. During colonial times the census was linked to hut tax and forced labour, so many people ran into the bush to escape the census-takers. The Portuguese estimated the population at 9 million during independence, but in the vaccination campaign several months later the new government processed 11 million people.

The census is the biggest organizational effort that Mozambique has conducted. About 20 000 census-takers, mostly teachers and students, had to be trained, deployed across the country, and provided with food and lodging.

Despite more than a year of planning, there have been some serious organizational difficulties. Students have arrived in several villages to find no food and lodging. In Vilanculos the census-takers went without transport for a week because no one would take responsibility for giving them their bicycles, which remained locked in a warehouse. In many areas there is a serious shortage of transport. This exercise would stretch the transport capacities of any developing country, but there is a special problem here. Because of the government's failure to approve the import of spare parts, thousands of vehicles are now off the road.

In many areas, however—especially in communal villages, set up since independence, where there is a high level of political organization—local officials have done considerable advance planning.

Yesterday's festivities were not merely celebrations. They also served a practical purpose. There are many migrant workers here and polygamy, although frowned on, is still legal, so men sometimes have homes in more than one town. To avoid double counting, people were therefore registered in the place where they spent Thursday night.

The census will try to establish fertility and child mortality by asking women how many children they have had and how many died. People will be asked what their native language is, if they can speak Portuguese, and if they can read. They will also be asked what their house is built of, if they have electricity, and if they have a latrine. And they will be asked if they have a radio, and how many cattle and goats they have.

The census itself will be vital to planning the country's development, especially health and veterinary services, and education. But, to many people, the most useful aspect of the census will be the amount of organization it has required, which has given people useful experience and shown up clearly the weak points in local administration.

Fig. 2.16 A report which appeared in the *Guardian* newspaper, August 1980

To make any attempt at forecasting future population it is essential to study the structure of the current population. The basic way of doing this is to analyse a country's population in terms of the age and sex of its inhabitants. This information can be shown diagrammatically by a population pyramid. Fig. 2.17 is a population pyramid for the United Kingdom based on data collected by the national census. The population is split into males and females and then the percentage in each five-year age group is calculated. The percentages are shown as horizontal bars drawn out from a central axis.

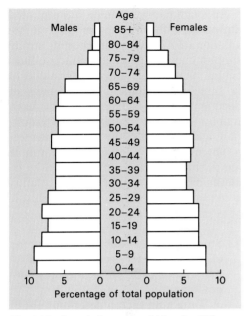

Fig. 2.17   Population pyramid for the UK

Fig. 2.19   Five simplified population pyramids

Fig. 2.18   The structure of the Moroccan population

Age groups	Males (per cent)	Females (per cent)
85+	1	0·5
80 – 84	1	1
75 – 79	1	0·5
70 – 74	2	2
65 – 69	1	1
60 – 64	2	2
55 – 59	2	1
50 – 54	3	3
45 – 49	3	3
40 – 44	5	5
35 – 39	5	6
30 – 34	5	7
25 – 29	5	7
20 – 24	7	7
15 – 19	10	9
10 – 14	15	13
5 – 9	16	16
0 – 4	16	16

10 Study Fig. 2.18.

a   On graph paper draw a population pyramid for Morocco to illustrate this information. Remember that your horizontal axis will need to extend to at least 16 per cent on both the male and female sides.

b   Compare the pattern shown with that of the UK in Fig. 2.17. What are the main differences and similarities between the two pyramids? Can you suggest any reasons for the variations?

c   How might the pyramids reflect the relative development of the two countries?

11 Fig. 2.19 shows five different types of national population structure. By studying each pyramid carefully you should be able to predict the way in which its population is changing. Make a copy of each one and match it up to the appropriate caption from the list of five below:

a   A country with low birth-rates and death-rates.

b   A country which has experienced a marked and rapid decline in its birth-rate.

c   A country where death-rates have begun to fall, particularly in the 0–5 age group, while birth-rates remain high.

d   A country with high birth-rates and death-rates.

e   A country which has experienced a considerable period of time with low birth-rates and death-rates, but is now increasing its birth-rate.

Much of the work in this chapter has been rather theoretical. To demonstrate how some of these theories can be applied in practice we will now consider three countries in detail. Two of them, China and India, have the largest populations in the world. Yet the success they have had in controlling population growth is very different. The third example is Egypt, a much smaller country, but one where the pressure on resources is equally critical.

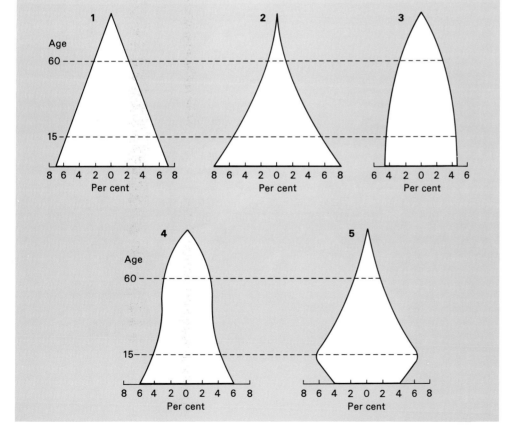

China

At least one-fifth of all mankind lives in China. Though recent estimates put the country's population at over 1 billion there is no way of knowing how accurate this figure is. China's last official census was in 1953 and since then the government has had difficulty in monitoring population growth. The collection of statistics has been disrupted by social and political upheaval, especially during the Cultural Revolution. However, it is clear that birth-rates have dropped fast since the early 1960s due to widespread family planning. The target population growth rate for 1981 was less than 1 per cent.

Despite China's solid achievements since the Communists came to power it is still very much a developing country. Population control is vital in making the most of China's modest agricultural and industrial growth, yet the policy on birth control has changed several times in the last thirty years.

12 Read the two following quotations. What is the reasoning behind their opposing viewpoints?

Chairman Mao (1949): 'It is a very good thing that China has a big population. Even if China's population multiplies many times, she is fully capable of finding a solution; the solution is production.'

Shao Li-tzu, a deputy to the First National People's Congress (1954): 'It is a good thing to have a large population, but in an environment beset with difficulties, it appears that there should be a limit set.'

Although family planning was neglected during the difficulties of the Cultural Revolution, the 1970s saw it receiving strong support once again. There are active campaigns to encourage late marriage and two- or three-child families. China's barefoot doctors (medical auxiliaries with basic training) promote contraception, sterilization, and abortion in the rural communes.

Three-quarters of the Chinese people live in the countryside, but they are by no means evenly distributed. The population is concentrated in the areas that are capable of intensive cultivation.

13 Study Fig. 2.21. Compare the pattern of population density with an atlas map showing the physical geography of China.

    a Write a paragraph describing the ways in which the two patterns seem to be linked.

Fig. 2.20 A grandfather sits with young children while their parents are at work

b Name the regions which are most densely and least densely populated.

c Identify each of the million cities marked on the map. In which parts of the country are most of the large cities situated?

Population densities in the most highly cultivated regions can reach 800 people per km². This is particularly true of the crowded deltalands around Guangzhou (Canton) and Shanghai, where rich river deposits offer excellent conditions for agriculture. In general eastern China is most favourable for settlement, especially on the coastal lowlands and along the river valleys that penetrate the highlands. Western China is very sparsely populated and holds little hope for extensive colonization: its dry, unreliable climate makes cultivation extremely hazardous.

China's strategy for coping with its growing population lies in improving the productivity of existing agricultural areas. So far the Communists' system of communes has managed to keep pace with the population increase. The disastrous famines that occurred in the 1920s and 1930s have not been repeated. Techniques such as elaborate water control schemes, the terracing of hillsides, and the increased application of fertilizer have achieved significant advances in food production. Nevertheless the rural standard of living will depend for many years yet on luck with the weather.

During the Cultural Revolution several hundred thousand young people from the cities were sent into the countryside to work on the land. In recent years many of them have moved back to the cities, bitter at what they regard as lost time on the communes. However, city jobs are hard to find and consequently, frustrated unemployed youths now pose a serious problem for the Communist authorities. The authorities are also concerned that China's large urban population enjoys a privileged lifestyle in comparison with the rural peasants.

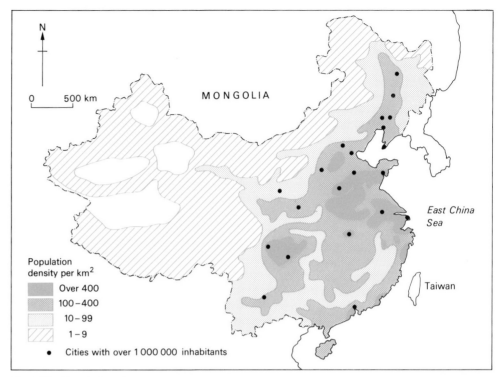

Fig. 2.21 Population density in China

Fig. 2.22 Gele commune, Sichuan: terracing to make maximum use of the land

India

In population terms India is the second largest country in the world after China. Yet its growth rate is considerably higher than that of China. According to the 1981 census India's population has reached 684 million, an increase of over 100 million since the census of 1971. If current trends continue the country's total population will reach 1 billion by the end of the century. The main reason for this rapid and accelerating growth is that while death-rates have fallen dramatically, birth-rates have remained high. Life expectancy has improved from about twenty years (on average) in 1900 to fifty in the late 1970s. This has prolonged the periods of child-bearing for a greater number of women.

The Indian government has been much more successful in reducing health hazards than in encouraging people to limit the size of their families. Infant mortality has been cut dramatically in the last twenty years, leading to a high proportion of the population being under the age of fifteen. National programmes have significantly curbed the effects of diseases like malaria, trachoma, leprosy, and tuberculosis. Schemes to improve the quality of drinking-water supplies have limited the spread of water-borne diseases. Deaths from famines have been lessened by the more efficient distribution of food and supplies from abroad.

14 Refer to Fig. 2.23.
  a What was the birth-rate and the death-rate in 1900, 1940, and 1980?
  b What was the rate of natural increase in these three years?
  c When did India enter the second stage of the population cycle? Has it entered the third stage?
  d What does the population pyramid (Fig. 2.24) suggest about the pattern of population growth in India?
  e What percentage of the Indian population is under fifteen?
  f How does the Indian population pyramid compare with those of the UK and Morocco on page 33?

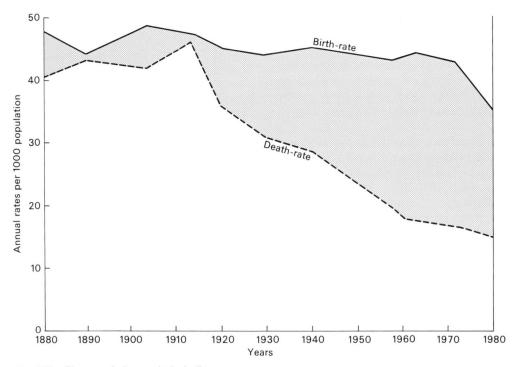

Fig. 2.23 The population cycle in India

Fig. 2.24 Population pyramid for India

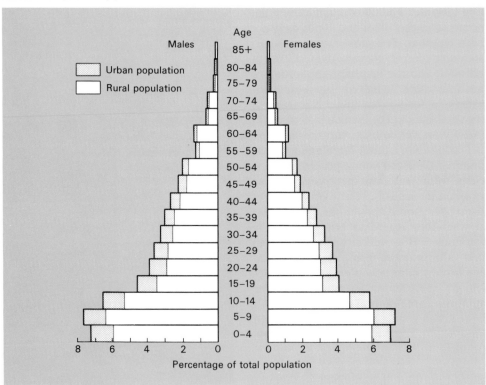

There has been government-backed family planning in India since 1930, but it did not become a major campaign until the mid 1960s. When other methods of contraception proved ineffective the government decided to concentrate on sterilization, which involves a fairly simple operation. In the early 1970s a massive publicity drive offered gifts and money to people who would volunteer for sterilization. Large camps were set up where mass operations could be carried out. Between April 1972 and March 1973 over 3 million people came forward to be sterilized. But the number of people who were willing to have this done was rapidly exhausted: before long there was a marked shortage of volunteers.

In June 1975 a state of emergency was declared in India. Under its sweeping powers the government launched an intensified campaign of sterilizations, often forcing people to be treated. Here is the story of one couple during the emergency:

Shanti Devi is a poor dishwasher who used to live in a slum next to a posh Delhi colony. That proximity made it easy to eke out her existence. Then India's government—armed with its emergency powers—bulldozed her house and threw her miles out of the city. The government also gave her a piece of land, but there was a snag. Either she or her husband had to produce a sterilization certificate before she got the lease papers. Having lost six out of nine children and left with three daughters, she was keen to have another pregnancy in the hope of getting a son. Meanwhile, the municipal garden where her husband was working stopped his monthly salary as he was not producing his sterilization certificate. He plodded on with his work for about two months hoping he would get paid; he couldn't obviously leave his job—where would he get another? In the ensuing hardship, the wife started insisting that he look for overtime work in some private gardens, which the underfed man could not do. After an altercation with

his wife, he left her for good. Soon pressures began to build up upon her also and lest she be thrown out of her little piece of land, she was forced to get herself sterilized—a voluntary sterilization, according to official records.

(from a report by Anil Agarwal in *New Scientist*, May 1977)

15 Refer to the passage above to answer the following questions:
   a What class of people did the husband and wife come from?
   b Why were they particularly vulnerable to government pressure?
   c Why did they resist the idea of sterilization?
   d What finally forced the woman to be sterilized?

Fig. 2.25 A young couple discusses family planning with a social worker

In 1976–7, when the 'terror' was at its height, 8·3 million sterilizations took place in one year. But the anger and resentment that was caused by the family-planning campaign led to the defeat of the government in the 1977 national elections. The new ruling-party banned compulsory sterilizations. However, serious damage had already been done to India's long-term hopes for birth control. Large sections of the population were hostile to any form of family planning while government officials were confused and demoralized. In 1977–8 there were only 0·8 million sterilizations, the lowest total for twelve years. Overall, it now seems that the emergency campaign has had no significant effect on the decline in India's birth-rate.

There are considerable regional differences in the rates of population increase. For example, the north-western states of Punjab and Rajasthan have the highest birth-rate and the lowest death-rate, resulting in the fastest natural increase in the country. In contrast, the southern states of Andhra Pradesh, Tamil Nadu, Kerala, and Karnataka have the lowest birth-rate and a relatively high death-rate, giving the slowest natural increase nationally. The highest death-rates are found in the states of Uttar Pradesh and Madhyar Pradesh, but a high birth-rate leads to an average natural increase.

Of course, these regional increase rates apply to populations of very different size. Population pressure is not necessarily greatest in the regions with the fastest rates of growth. The sheer weight of numbers, as in the two most populous states of Uttar Pradesh and Bihar, can present overwhelming problems when resources are stretched to their limit. Similarly, thinly populated states like Rajasthan can suffer from overpopulation if their low carrying capacity is exceeded.

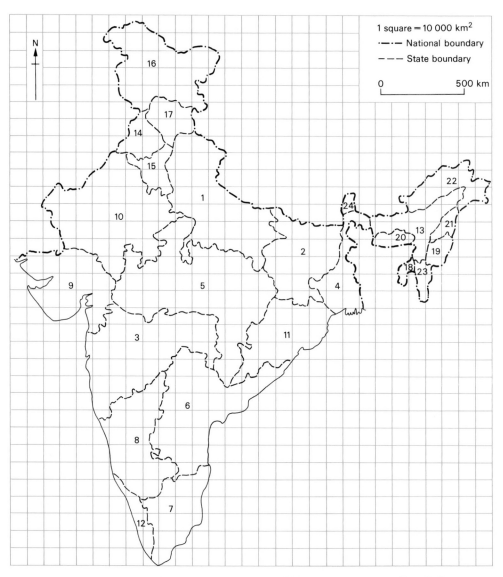

1 square = 10 000 km²
—·— National boundary
— — State boundary

0 _____ 500 km

State	Population (millions)		State	Population (millions)
1 Uttar Pradesh	100		13 Assam	19
2 Bihar	64		14 Punjab	16
3 Maharashtra	60		15 Haryana	12
4 West Bengal	53		16 Jammu & Kashmir	5
5 Madhya Pradesh	50		17 Himachal Pradesh	4
6 Andhra Pradesh	50		18 Tripura	2
7 Tamil Nadu	47		19 Manipur	1
8 Karnataka	34		20 Meghalaya	1
9 Gujarat	32		21 Nagaland	1
10 Rajasthan	31		22 Arunachal Pradesh	n.a.
11 Orissa	26		23 Mizoram	n.a.
12 Kerala	25		24 Sikkim	n.a.

Fig. 2.26 The states of India and their population

16 a Use the printed grid in Fig. 2.26 to calculate the approximate area of each state in India by counting up the number of squares. When more than half a square is enclosed by a state count it as one; where less than half is included do not count it. Draw up a table listing each state and enter its population (given in Fig. 2.26) and its estimated area in squares.

b Divide the population figure for each state by the number of squares it covers and then multiply by 100. This will give you the population density (in persons per km²) which you should enter in another column of the table.

c On a copy of Fig. 2.26 shade in each state according to the following categories of population density, measured in people per km²: under 100, 100–199, 200–299, 300–399, 400 and over.

d Compare your finished map with an atlas map of India's physical geography. Which types of land are most densely populated?

Population distribution in India remained remarkably constant for a long time, but now population pressure is leading to important changes. Whereas in the past people were strongly tied to their local community, recent developments have broken down these old patterns. The main movement has been to the largest cities, particularly Calcutta, Bombay, Madras, and Delhi. India's urban population quadrupled between 1901 and 1971, and now represents 20 per cent of the national total. This may seem a low percentage but it is very significant in terms of absolute numbers. The massive influx of rural migrants has put the cities under great strain, taxing public services and employment opportunities to breaking-point.

Economic development of rural areas is essential to remove pressure from the cities. This will rely largely on the revitalization of agriculture. Traditionally Indian farmers have coped with population pressure by

Fig. 2.27   A farmer considers his failed crop

Fig. 2.28   Home is a concrete pipe for this family in Calcutta

expanding the area of cultivated land. This can be done either by increasing the total area under cultivation or by growing more crops on existing farmland. Between 1950 and 1966 India increased its total farmed area from 132 million to 155 million hectares. Six million hectares of this was due to multiple cropping, the remaining 17 million hectares was the result of extending the cultivated area. Since the late 1960s the emphasis has switched to the introduction of new crops and modern farming techniques. This has become known as the 'green revolution'.

The initial success of the green revolution staved off the population problem for a while, but further advances in agriculture are proving more costly and difficult. The danger of severe famine, as occurred in Bihar in the mid 1960s, will be present in India for many years yet.

Egypt

Egypt owes its existence to the River Nile. The country's population clings to its valley and delta, where water for irrigation and fertile soils make farming possible. Without the Nile Egypt would be a sparsely peopled desert country like its neighbours. In fact Egypt has a population of over 40 million and is the homeland of one-third of all Arabs.

The Egyptian population is increasing at a rate of 2·5 per cent each year and this is expected to accelerate during the 1980s. Its rapid expansion began in the late 1940s when the death-rate dropped dramatically. Like many less developed countries Egypt benefited from advances in medical knowledge and techniques that greatly reduced the risk of disease. However, birth-rates have remained high in spite of long-established family-planning campaigns. Religious objections to contraception and a tradition of early marriage continue to undermine the government's efforts. With nearly half its population under the age of fifteen Egypt cannot escape another large population increase as these people enter child-bearing age.

This daunting growth requires heavy expenditure on imported food supplies and the provision of housing, hospitals, and schools. But the major problem facing Egypt is a severe shortage of land. Less than 4 per cent of the country's land area supports 99 per cent of the population, three-fifths of whom still rely on farming for their livelihood. By the end of the century rural Egypt will have to find room for another 15 to 20 million people. Already densities are very high and many land holdings are too small to provide a decent standard of living. In addition there are large numbers of landless labourers who suffer from persistent underemployment. Agricultural productivity is at a high level thanks to the many improvements that have been introduced so far: new crop types, better rotation systems, multiple cropping, and extensive use of fertilizers. Virtually all Egypt's farmland is irrigated.

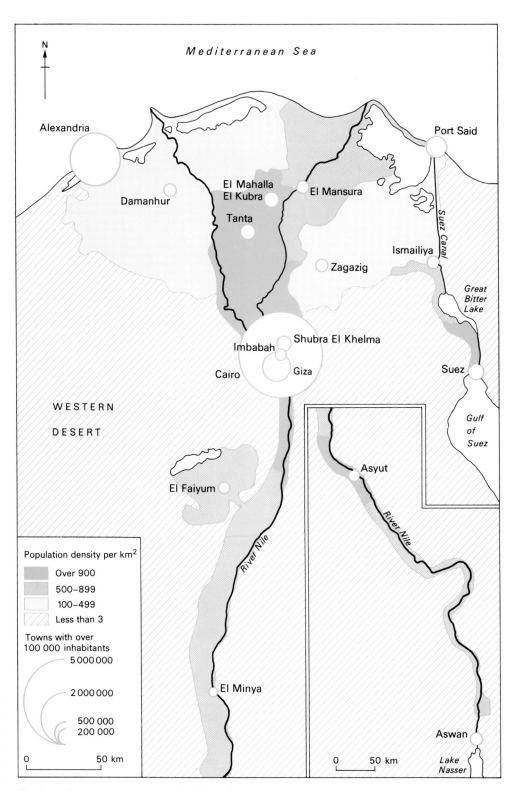

Fig. 2.29 Population density in the Nile valley

In effect there is little scope left for increasing yields from the existing cultivated land area.

17 Find the area shown in Fig. 2.29 on an atlas map of Egypt and compare it with the rest of the country.

  a The total area of Egypt is over 1 million km²: what is the approximate area of the Nile delta?

  b How far is it from the Aswan dam to the Mediterranean Sea?

  c What is the pattern of population density shown in Fig. 2.29?

  d Which are Egypt's major cities and where are they situated?

18 Study Fig. 2.30.

  a What types of crop are being produced in the fields?

  b Why do you think there is a line of taller plants surrounding the fields?

  c How can you tell the land relies on irrigation?

  d What purpose might be served by the bank in the background where the village is situated?

  e How wealthy would you expect the farmer to be?

Fig. 2.30 A farmer tends his irrigated fields in the Nile valley

Fig. 2.31 Cultivated land and cropped area in Egypt, 1820–1980

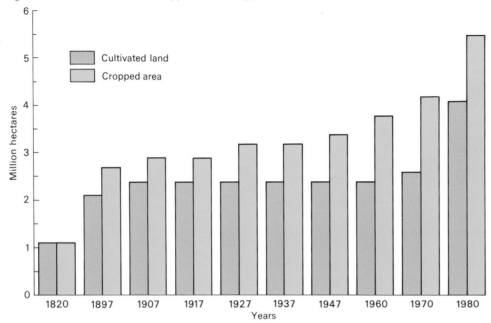

Fig. 2.32 Cultivated land and cropped area in Egypt (hectares per head of rural population)

Year	Cultivated land	Cropped area
1820	0·57	0·57
1897	0·25	0·36
1907	0·25	0·34
1917	0·21	0·32
1927	0·19	0·32
1937	0·17	0·30
1947	0·19	0·30
1960	0·15	0·23
1970	0·15	0·21
1980	0·15	0·21

Fig. 2.33 A modern sprinkler system is used to irrigate the desert

19 Look at Fig. 2.31. The cropped area takes account of multiple cropping made possible by all-year-round irrigation.
   a Describe the pattern shown by the graph.
   b Use the information given in Fig. 2.32 to draw a similar bar graph showing the number of hectares per head of the rural population over the same period.
   c How does your graph reflect Egypt's rising population?
   d Compare the two graphs for the period 1960 to 1980: how do they show that the situation is getting worse?

The only way of increasing the area under cultivation is by major land reclamation schemes. During the 1970s Egypt established fourteen of these along the Nile, all dependent on irrigation, using water stored behind the High Dam at Aswan. They were designed to add about 0·6 million hectares to the previous cultivated area of 2·6 million hectares. It was also planned to reclaim another 0·9 million hectares in the Western Desert, using natu-

Fig. 2.34 Crowded pedestrian walkways in Cairo

Fig. 2.35 New housing in Suez

ral reservoirs of groundwater. Unfortunately the soils in this area are very sandy and far inferior to the rich silt of the Nile valley. Yet even these ambitious schemes, extensive as they are, cannot keep pace with the increase in rural population.

A partial solution may lie in Egypt's cities. Forty-five per cent of the Egyptian population live in urban areas and half of these people are concentrated in the two major cities of Cairo and Alexandria. They are the centres of Egypt's expanding industries and have attracted many migrants from rural districts. The government sees further industrial development as a way of coping with increasing demands for employment. There is considerable scope for expansion in the towns along the Suez canal, which has been re-opened as part of a large-scale development scheme.

It is ironic that Egypt finds among its neighbours many thinly populated Arab states which have become rich through oil-exporting. Egypt will need their assistance if it is to tackle successfully the problems arising from population pressure.

Summary

The world population is rising fast. The highest rates of increase are found in the developing countries, while in most developed nations the population is growing very slowly. World population distribution is highly uneven and reflects the suitability of the environment for occupation by man. Low-lying areas with a favourable climate and fertile land are most densely peopled. International trade allows countries to exceed their carrying capacities by importing extra food and resources. Changes in population are monitored by censuses and vital registration. These are very costly and difficult to organize, making it impossible for many developing countries to carry them out effectively.

Chapter **3** Managing the natural world

Ecosystems and man

Man cannot be separated from his natural surroundings. No matter how much he may insulate himself against his environment, he is still a part of it. All man's activities affect the natural world and cause changes in it. Equally, both short-term and long-term changes in the environment have a profound effect on man. Everything is linked in such a complex fashion that scientists are only just discovering the full extent of man's impact on the earth. The patterns of interlinked elements in the natural world are known as ecosystems.

1 Make a list of the activities given below and then write next to each, one way in which it alters the natural environment. Collect everyone's answers together to see how many different effects were mentioned for each activity.

Farming, fishing, mining, forestry, industry, transport, building cities, leisure, generating power, collecting water.

Fig. 3.1 An asbestos mine: one example of man's impact on the landscape

To understand the effects man has on the earth it is necessary to consider the workings of nature. The part of the earth where life exists is called the biosphere. It incorporates the lower part of the atmosphere (gases), the oceans (liquids), and the world's land surfaces (solids). These three elements are linked by flows of energy, water, and chemicals. The biosphere can also be divided into two interrelated parts: the biotic (living) world and the abiotic (non-living) world. The biotic and abiotic elements of any area together make up an ecosystem, the main working unit of nature. Ecosystems can exist on any scale up to world level: for example, the continent of Africa and a pool of water can each be considered as ecosystems.

All the organisms that make up the biotic world must have energy, water, and chemical compounds to survive. Every organism, plant or animal has its own particular role to play in its natural community. The organisms in a community must exist in balanced proportions so that food chains and chemical cycles can operate properly. Accordingly, an ecosystem undergoes constant change as substances and energy leave and enter the system, while organisms are born, grow and die.

All ecosystems are powered by energy from the sun. Energy can exist in a variety of ways: as heat, as light, or it can be stored in plants or in the muscles of animals. Sunlight is trapped by plants which use its energy to produce food. The food is made from carbon dioxide, water, and minerals through the process of photosynthesis. This process also releases oxygen which replenishes the atmosphere. Plants are the producers of food and animals are the consumers. The lowest level of consumers are herbivores, which only eat plant material. Above them are various levels of carnivores, which eat other animals, and omnivores, which eat both plants and animals. The top carnivore or omnivore in any ecosystem is the one that is not preyed upon by any other animal. On a world basis man is the top omnivore. As you work up from the plants through the herbivores to the different levels of carnivore you can trace a food chain (Fig. 3.2), as each animal becomes the prey of another.

Farming, of any type, may be thought of as the conversion of inputs of energy—from

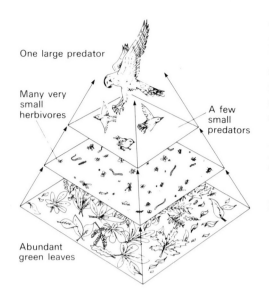

One large predator

Many very small herbivores

A few small predators

Abundant green leaves

the sun, from farm labour, and from fuels—into outputs of food through the 'work' of plants and animals. Such a system (Fig. 3.3) is working all the time under natural conditions with sun, plants, and animals each forming part of the ecosystem of an area.

In cultivating an area a farmer ideally tries to ensure, by working the land by hand and with the help of energy from

Fig. 3.2 An example of a food chain

machines and animals, that full use is made of the sun's light and heat. This energy, together with the area's soil cover and rainfall, helps to produce a given mass of plants (level 1 in the system). Some of this plant material supports a very much smaller mass of herbivores (level 2). These are in turn preyed upon by the carnivorous animals and birds, of which there is a very small mass in any one area. Farming which aims to produce animal and plant products for human consumption brings man into the system (level 3).

At each of the stages or levels in the ecosystem much energy is used up and so is lost to the next level. However, waste materials can be returned to the soil by the action of bacteria, decomposing these wastes into re-usable materials.

Fig. 3.3 Farming as an ecosystem

Outputs of plant and animal material

Level 1 Plants	Level 2 Animals: Herbivores	Level 3 Animals: Omnivores

Inputs of energy

Energy lost

Water from rainfall and the soil

Energy lost

Energy lost

Energy from the sun (light and heat)

Plants grow using the sun's energy, water and minerals

Herbivores live by eating plants

Omnivores eat plants and animals

Energy from the farmer and his animals

Minerals from the soil

Energy from fuels used to run machinery

Wastes decomposed and returned to the soil

Major environmental zones

Throughout the world there is an enormous variety of vegetation and climate. Yet it is possible to identify a series of zones which have broadly similar environmental characteristics. These are listed in Fig. 3.4 which also gives a general picture of their vegetation, rainfall, temperature, population, and how far man has modified the landscape. Of course, in some parts of the world man has completely replaced the natural vegetation, mainly through farming.

The areas occupied by each environmental zone are shown in Fig. 3.6. In reality there are no distinct borders between the zones and the environment changes gradually as one merges into another. There are also considerable variations within each zone, especially where mountain ranges create their own climatic conditions.

2 On Fig. 3.6 there are eight locations, each one in a different environmental zone. Match up each climatic graph in Fig. 3.5 to its correct location. The climatic characteristics listed in Fig. 3.4 will help you do this.

Fig. 3.4 The world's major environmental zones

Zone	Land area (%)	Vegetation	Impact of man on vegetation	Population density	Rainfall	Temperature
Equatorial forest	8	Broadleaved, evergreen forest; wide variety of trees	Very variable	Low to very high	High, 1000 mm +; spread throughout year	High throughout year; little seasonal variation
Temperate forest	7	Broadleaved, deciduous and mixed forests	Extensive clearing and cultivation	Medium to high	Moderate, 750–1000 mm; spread throughout year	Cool to warm; seasonal range increases inland
Boreal forest	14	Needleleaf, evergreen forest; small number of tree types	Limited clearing	Very low	Low, 250–500 mm; mainly in summer	Short, cool summers; large annual range
Savanna	24	Ranges from open, tall grassland to tropical woodland towards the equator	Burning, grazing, variable clearing and cultivation	Generally low	Variable, 250–1000 mm; mainly in spring and summer	High throughout year; small seasonal variations
Mediterranean	1	Evergreen drought-resistant trees and shrubs	Extensive clearing and cultivation	Variable	Low to moderate, 500–750 mm; pronounced summer drought	Warm summers, cool winters; moderate annual range
Temperate grassland	9	Varies from tall grass prairie to short grass steppe as rainfall decreases	Grazing	Low	Low to moderate, 300–600 mm; throughout year with spring or summer maximum	Warm summers, cool winters; marked seasonal variation
Hot desert	21	Scattered drought-resistant shrubs; sand and rock deserts	Little impact	Very low	Very low, 0–250 mm	Very hot summers; variable seasonal range
Tundra	5	Herbs, mosses and lichens	Little impact	Very low	Low, 100–400 mm; late summer or autumn maximum	Very cold; short, cool summers; very large annual range
Polar	11	Ice caps; no plants	No impact	Nil	Low; little data available	Extremely cold

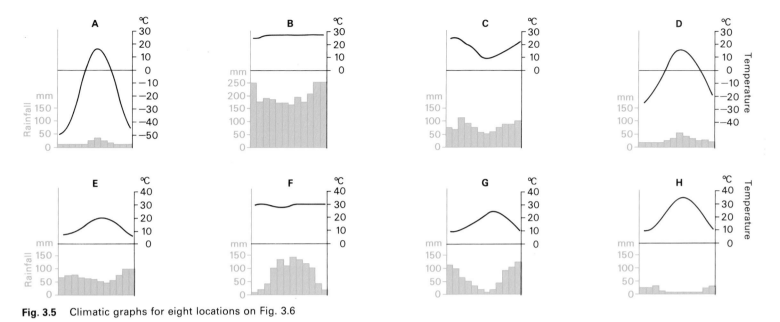

Fig. 3.5   Climatic graphs for eight locations on Fig. 3.6

Fig. 3.6   The location of the world's major environmental zones

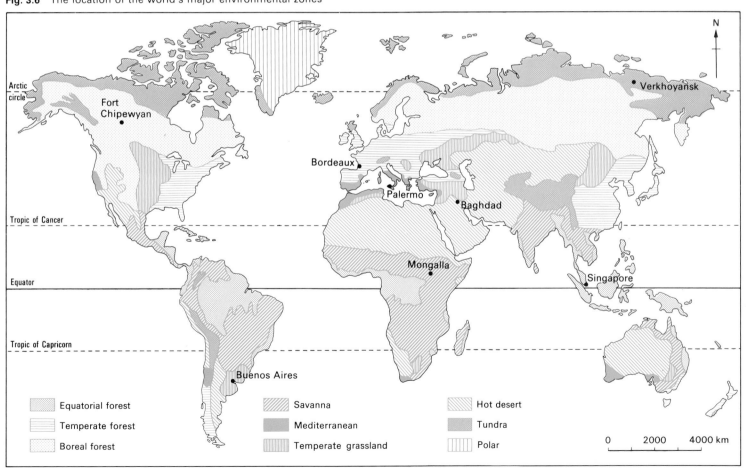

3 The nine photographs on this page each show the natural vegetation of one major environmental zone. Again referring to Fig. 3.4, work out which photograph illustrates each zone.

1

2

3

4

5

6

7

8

9

Tropical forests

The ecology of the tropical rain forest is the richest and most delicately balanced in the world. Its climate has no seasons, hot, humid conditions prevailing throughout the year. Rainfall is heavy with an annual total of about 2500 mm which supports an abundance of vegetation. But the lush appearance of the forest is misleading. The tropical soils that lie beneath it are thin and infertile. The forest survives because it has created the conditions it needs over millions of years.

The tallest trees, which can reach 50 metres in height, provide a sheltering canopy that filters the rain and absorbs the sunlight. Beneath their crowns the interior of the forest is dark and luxuriant (Fig. 3.7). The tree trunks are laced with a bewildering variety of creepers, ferns, and parasitic plants, all climbing upwards as they compete for light. At ground level there is little undergrowth around the thick tree roots and only a small layer of leaf litter covers the forest floor. Plants grow very fast and an enormous number of species has developed.

In the past scattered human tribes inhabited the forest without causing any disruption to the natural system. Their numbers were limited and they led a wandering life. They understood the complexities of the forest and exploited it carefully through hunting, gathering, fishing, and simple farming. Since the 1950s though the tropical forests have come under increasing pressure from man. They are now being cut down at a rate of 20 hectares per minute. If this continues the entire stock, representing more than half the world's forests, will be exhausted within fifty years.

The main cause of this destruction is the clearance of land to grow food. This is chiefly carried out by people who support themselves through shifting cultivation. These farmers clear patches of the forest, burn the trees to provide a fertilizer, and then cultivate the land for one or two years. After a few crops the soil is exhausted and the people must move on to new areas. The

Fig. 3.7 Vegetation layers in tropical forest

Fig. 3.8 A tree crusher at work in the Amazon rain forest

cleared land should then be left for at least ten years while the forest grows back. In large parts of Asia and Africa this system has broken down due to the pressure of population: at least 200 million people are engaged in shifting cultivation. Because of the increased demand for food a larger and larger area of land is under cultivation at any one time. Farmers are forced to return to previously used patches before they have fully recovered their fertility. Consequently the structure of the soil is destroyed and crop yields are very poor. Before long the land becomes useless for agriculture and has to be abandoned completely.

4 Draw a simple diagram to show the sequence of operations involved in shifting cultivation. Then modify your diagram to indicate the changes that occur when the population increases sharply.

Commercial livestock rearing is another type of farming that poses a threat to tropical forests. Large multinational firms are clearing vast areas of the Amazon basin to establish pastures for cattle ranching. They are mainly interested in cheaper methods of meat production and have little interest in maintaining the quality of the land. International timber firms are also eager to exploit the forests for their valuable hardwoods such as teak, mahogany, and rosewood. At present tropical forests supply only 15 per cent of the world trade in timber. Countries like Brazil and Indonesia want to benefit from the income that increased timber exports would bring.

For whatever reason the clearance of the forest has a disastrous effect on the environment. When the trees are felled the ground is exposed to the full effects of the tropical climate. Without the protection of the top canopy the thin layer of humus covering the soil is rapidly washed away. The absence of trees means that less water can be trapped by the ground or vegetation when it rains. This, in turn, means that less moisture passes back into the atmosphere through evapotranspiration, causing a reduction in rainfall. Both these factors can lead to the onset of drought conditions. The soil is also baked hard and cracked by the intense heating of the sun, which makes it very easy to erode. When rain does occur most of the water sweeps across the hard ground surface, carrying away the precious topsoil. Lower down in the river basin the increased surface runoff can result in severe flooding. Crops are ruined and the sediment carried by the floodwaters chokes reservoirs and irrigation works. The damaged soil in the forest area can support little plant growth and since the nutrients have been washed away it is very difficult for any trees to re-establish themselves.

Fig. 3.9 The effects of deforestation in a tropical area

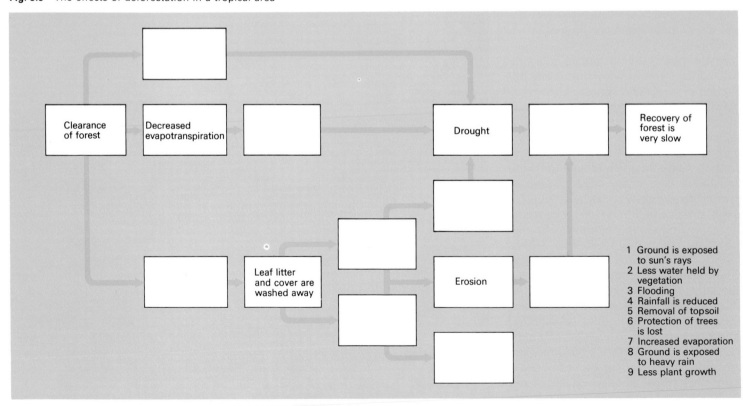

1 Ground is exposed to sun's rays
2 Less water held by vegetation
3 Flooding
4 Rainfall is reduced
5 Removal of topsoil
6 Protection of trees is lost
7 Increased evaporation
8 Ground is exposed to heavy rain
9 Less plant growth

5 Make a copy of Fig. 3.9. Using the paragraph above for guidance, complete the diagram by putting each factor listed in its appropriate box.

The destruction of the tropical forests could have worldwide environmental effects since burning the trees creates large amounts of carbon dioxide in the atmosphere. Tree burning is doubly dangerous because the forests act as a giant lung for the earth's atmosphere. They take in carbon dioxide and convert it into oxygen by the process of photosynthesis. Careful measurement of the carbon dioxide level in the atmosphere indicates that it rose by 5 per cent from 1958–76. Experts believe that if the level continues to increase it will lead to a worldwide rise in temperature. This is because carbon dioxide in the atmosphere prevents radiation from the earth escaping into space.

The tropical forests also represent an invaluable reserve of biological species. It is thought that half the world's species occur only in this particular ecosystem. They are essential for medical research and the development of new agricultural strains. There is a desperate need to set aside substantial areas of forest as natural reserves; at present only 1·5 per cent is protected in this way.

6 The extent of tropical deforestation varies considerably from place to place. Fig. 3.11 lists the countries affected, classified according to the seriousness of the problem.
Critical means that lowland forests are mostly gone, hill forests are now under attack or dwindling, and the natural system is breaking down. Life: 10 years at most.
Established means that destructive shifting cultivation and logging are now in full swing. Life: 15–20 years on average.
Developing means that logging has not yet or has only just started. Shifting cultivation is not yet a problem.

Fig. 3.10 Severe gully erosion resulting from forest clearance

Fig. 3.11 Countries affected by tropical deforestation

Critical	Established	Developing
Thailand	Sabah	West Irian
Philippines	Sarawak	Papua New Guinea
Malaysia	Sumatra	Sierra Leone
India	Kalimantan	Liberia
Australia (Queensland)	Brazil	Congo
Ghana	Venezuela	Zaire
Nigeria	Mexico	Gabon
Panama	Honduras	Peru
Guatemala		Colombia
West Indies		Ecuador
Ivory Coast		Cameroon

a Use an atlas to find the countries in the table. On an outline map of the world number each country and add a key. Then shade in each country according to its classification. Use a dark colour for *critical*, a medium colour for *established*, and a light colour for *developing*.

b By referring to your map write a short paragraph describing which parts of the world are in most danger from tropical deforestation. Which regions are least damaged at present?

The threatened Amazon

The amount of forest clearance differs from one part of a country to another. For example, some areas in the extensive rain forest of Brazil have already been reduced to virtually desert conditions while others remain untouched. We will now consider the case of the Amazon basin in greater detail since this represents the best example of the way in which man is attacking the tropical forests.

The Amazon basin in South America is the world's largest continuous belt of rain forest. It covers two-fifths of the continent. For centuries it remained an unknown wilderness inhabited only by scattered Amerindian tribes. In 1500, when the Portuguese first began to colonize Brazil, the Indians numbered about 1 million. But over time their numbers were drastically reduced by contact with the Europeans, particularly through disease. The Indians had no natural immunity to European infections such as measles, smallpox, and influenza.

Throughout colonial times the fringes of the forest were exploited in a small way for sugar plantations and cattle ranching, and the Indians were forcibly pressed into work as labourers. In the late nineteenth century the Amazon experienced an economic boom as areas of the forest were tapped for natural rubber. However, this prosperity was short-lived since Brazil could not compete with the new rubber plantations that were developed in Malaya after 1900. From then until the 1960s the Amazon was largely ignored in terms of economic development.

Now the situation has changed dramatically. The pressure of Brazil's rapidly increasing population encouraged the government to exploit the country's vast untapped resources. The Amazon basin was seen as an enormous storehouse of minerals for industry and land for agriculture. Foreign companies were eager to prospect for raw materials and establish large-scale ranching operations. Brazilian firms also wanted to buy land in the rain forest and benefit from commercial developments there. During the 1960s, as private business interests moved into the Amazon, thousands of Indians were massacred to gain possession of their land. Now, there are as few as 50 000 Indians surviving in the Amazon.

Even at this time though the sheer size of the Amazon basin and the difficulty of access protected it from major exploitation. The turning-point came in 1970 when the Brazilian government announced a hastily prepared plan to build a network of long-distance roads across the area. This was prompted by a severe drought in north-east Brazil, a poverty-stricken region which contains a quarter of the country's population. The government wanted to open up the forest for settlement and subsistence farming to relieve pressure on the north-east.

Fig. 3.12 Indians, until recently untouched by the modern world, beg for food on the new highway

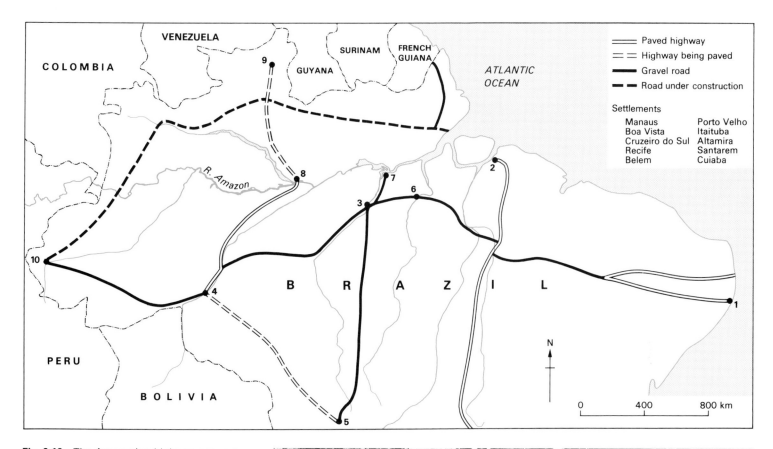

Fig. 3.13 The Amazonian highway network

Key:
— Paved highway
‒ ‒ Highway being paved
▬ Gravel road
▬ ▬ Road under construction

Settlements
Manaus   Porto Velho
Boa Vista   Itaituba
Cruzeiro do Sul Altamira
Recife   Santarem
Belem   Cuiaba

7 a Make a tracing of Fig. 3.13. Use an atlas to identify the towns and cities numbered 1 to 10. Their names are listed in the key.
b What is the approximate area covered by the map in km²?
c How long is the road between town 1 and town 10?
d Roughly how long is the total system of roads?

Fig. 3.14 Workers take a break from road building in Brazil

53

Construction of the main east-west route began in September 1970, just three months after the scheme was made public. Over the following decade the network was gradually extended, opening up large areas of the forest for colonization and development. Although some sections have been paved the majority of the road system has a surface of local gravel or hard-baked clay. A strip 100 km wide on either side of the highway comes under government control for farming exploitation. Each settler is given 100 hectares of land, 1 hectare of which has been cleared. Early reports of the settlement programme have not been encouraging. The settlers, some of whom had never farmed before, have found it very difficult to establish their crops. Soils are infertile and yields declined sharply after a few harvests. The humid climate encourages the spread of diseases such as malaria which are rarely found in virgin rain forest. Living conditions in the settlements are also poor, with makeshift housing of mud, wood and palm leaves, and unreliable water supplies.

Worst of all, the growth of farming is causing severe damage to the environment. Here is an eye-witness account of the effect deforestation is having on a small part of the Amazon basin.

We flew at about 300 metres over the limitless spread of trees, having from this height the appearance of sparkling moss. Across this the BR 174 highway was a red line, ruled to the horizon. Immediately beneath, the road was close enough for the erosion to be visible, biting into its margins, and there were swamps created in its making, bristling with dead trees and gaudy with stagnation. Fires appeared as blue smudges here and there, and there were never less than a half-dozen in sight, and many charcoal scrawls and flourishes showed on the green pages of the jungle where others had burnt out.

Such clearances were often the work of rich businessmen running plantations as a sideline, or hobby farmers from the city. Land here costs too much to attract ranchers thinking in terms of 20 000 to 30 000 hectares, whose operations would show up on a satellite photograph. Close to Manaus

Fig. 3.15 Settlers on one of the government farming schemes in Brazil

Fig. 3.16 A village on the *varzea* by the Amazon

it was a matter of 100 hectares here and 200 there, but it was sad to think just how many small fires must have been alight all over the Amazon basin on a fine day like this.

What our bird's-eye view made so startlingly clear was that the process the scientists call 'desertification' was even more rapid than we had been led to expect. In many places where patches of forest had been left, strewn with ash to await replanting or cultivation, the arid ochre of the subsoil already showed through. There were old, abandoned fields too, now totally eroded, and from them the new desert spread like a creeping tide in all directions.

(from 'The Rape of Amazonia' by Norman Lewis, *Observer Magazine*, April 1979)

8 Read the extract above carefully and answer the following questions:
  a Why has the construction of highways encouraged the destruction of the forest?
  b What is the main method of clearing the trees?
  c Who is responsible for this?
  d What do they use the land for?
  e Why is the desertification spreading?
  f Why would you expect the region surrounding Manaus to be exploited more than most?

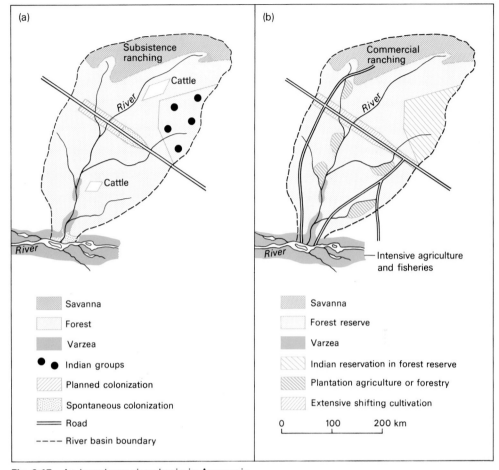

Fig. 3.17 An imaginary river basin in Amazonia

If many of the problems encountered in the Amazon basin support the arguments of the environmentalists, the question remains: what is the best way to develop it? The simplest answer seems to be 'don't'. Nevertheless, there are small areas that could be exploited effectively, each forming a distinct ecosystem that is separate from the main body of the forest. About 2 per cent of Amazonia consists of rich *varzea*, seasonally flooded land along the edge of the rivers. Subsistence agriculture could be carried out on these rich alluvial soils where the annual flooding restores the land's fertility. Surveys of the forest also suggest that there are islands of fertile soil scattered throughout the more fragile rain forest. These would be able to sustain limited agriculture. Although they may only amount to 1 per cent of the Amazon

area, they would still add up to an enormous 50 000 km².

As for the vulnerable forest itself, any exploitation should be carefully considered and extremely limited. It is essential that the tree canopy remains intact and that nutrients are not allowed to be leached out of the soil. The natural checks which limit the number of pests in the environment must be maintained. This effectively restricts development to the collection of forest products and selective timber cutting. Forest products cover a wide range of flowers, nuts, fruits, seeds, and barks as well as the tapping of resins, saps, and rubber latex. Probably the most valuable and long-term commercial activity would be the production of fish. This hardly exists at present but could become a thriving industry.

9 Study Fig. 3.17. Diagram (a) indicates the pattern of exploitation found at the present time. Diagram (b) suggests how that exploitation could be modified to preserve the tropical forest.
  a Roughly how large is the area of the river basin?
  b What hazards would arise from the current pattern of exploitation?
  c List all the changes that would have to be made if the plan in diagram (b) were put into action.
  d Can you suggest any drawbacks that might be associated with this plan?

Desertification

The borders of the world's deserts are never static. In the semi-arid lands which lie on the desert margins rainfall is highly variable and unpredictable. Desert conditions advance in times of drought and retreat during wetter periods. But over the past thousand years more and more land has been lost to the desert. There has been a slow but steady decline in land quality that turns forest into savanna and savanna into barren, unproductive scrub. This progressive downgrading is known as desertification. How far this is the result of a change in climate is not known. What is certain is that man has hastened the process by his misuse of the land.

For centuries nomadic herders have grazed their animals on the savanna grasslands. Farmers have burnt and cleared areas of forest to cultivate crops. Forested areas around settlements have been cut down to provide fuel. On the whole the impact of these activities was relatively small until recently, when population pressure has greatly increased the demand for land. This has forced some farmers to cultivate marginal areas which are easily eroded once the natural vegetation is removed. Nomads have increased the size of their herds and pastures have been worn out through overgrazing. Irrigation schemes have dried out the land by lowering the water table in the collection areas. Fields which rely on irrigation have been ruined by the build-up of a salt crust due to waterlogging and evaporation.

The ill-effects of man's activities are made much more serious when a lengthy drought occurs. During the drought in the Sahel area of West Africa between 1968 and 1973 the Sahara desert was advancing southwards at a rate of 10 km a year. Some scientists have suggested that this indicates a long-term climatic change. They believe that the sub-tropical belts of warm descending air, which produce desert conditions, have shifted permanently southwards. Others disagree and argue that droughts are natural variations in what is

Fig. 3.18 These women have walked several kilometres to collect firewood

Fig. 3.19 Ruins of the ancient city of Mohenjo-Daro

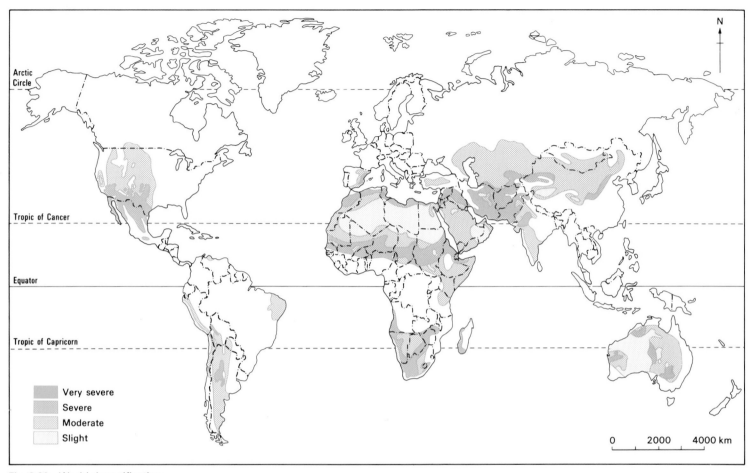

Fig. 3.20 World desertification

basically an unchanging climatic pattern.

However, between 5000 and 15 000 years ago some desert regions experienced long spells of a much wetter climate. The Sahara was covered by extensive areas of savanna grassland, trees grew on the mountains, and big game were hunted by the sizeable human tribes that lived there. Similarly, the Indus valley was the granary of north-west India 4000 years ago and supported a thriving civilization in cities like Mohenjo-Daro. Was the decline of these cultures the result of a change of climate or did man bring about his own downfall through over-exploitation of the land? No one can be certain.

It seems likely that man's actions can aggravate drought conditions and worsen their effects. Where vegetation has been

lost due to overgrazing a greater proportion of the sun's rays are reflected back from the earth's surface. This cuts down the convection currents in the atmosphere which produce rainfall and so conditions become drier still. The situation is not helped by the tendency to increase livestock numbers and the area under cultivation when drought strikes. In 1973, at the height of the Sahel drought, the number of grazing animals was twice the carrying capacity of the region.

Desertification happens most rapidly in times of drought, but goes on during more favourable climatic conditions as well. The degree of desertification varies a great deal from place to place. Fig. 3.20 shows the affected areas divided into four categories, reflecting the severity of the problem:

Slight. In these areas man's activities have barely damaged the vegetation or soils. True deserts such as the Sahara and Atacama fall into this category because the plant life is so sparse that man can do little to make matters worse. You cannot desertify what is already a desert.

Moderate. At this stage there has been a significant fall in the quality of the plant cover. Wind and water erosion have been accelerated to produce small gullies and sandy hummocks. Soil salinity may be reducing crop yields by as much as a quarter.

Severe. This indicates that productive grassland has been largely replaced by useless herbs and shrubs. Alternatively the topsoil has been eroded to such an extent that most vegetation has disappeared or crop yields have been cut by more than half. In some areas soil salinity is so serious that sustained crop production is impossible.

Very severe. This category covers those small, scattered areas where desertification is irreversible. The land has been totally destroyed by deep gullies, salt crusts, or large shifting sand dunes and has become desert.

10 Look at Fig. 3.20. By consulting an atlas make a list of twenty countries that are suffering from severe desertification. How many of these are less developed countries?

11 Use the data given in Fig. 3.21 to draw a divided bar graph showing the degree of desertification of each continent. What factors might explain the differences between the continents shown by the graphs?

The total area affected by some degree of desertification is about 50 million km², which represents an enormous loss of agricultural land. Technically it would be possible to reclaim much of this and return it to full productivity. As always the main problem is cost. Moderate desertification can be solved fairly cheaply and simply, but land in the severe category needs much more time and investment to achieve a full recovery.

In 1977 the United Nations held a conference on desertification in Nairobi, Kenya. Unfortunately the outcome of the conference gave no clear guidance on the ways in which desertification could be prevented. The problem is much too complicated to allow any easy solutions.

Fig. 3.21 Desertification of arid lands

Continent	Degree of desertification	Per cent	Continent	Degree of desertification	Per cent
Africa	Slight	28	North America	Slight	2
	Moderate	35		Moderate	61
	Severe	36		Severe	36
	Very severe	1		Very severe	1
Asia	Slight	7	South America	Slight	4
	Moderate	66		Moderate	87
	Severe	27		Severe	8
				Very severe	1
Australia	Slight	42	Europe (Spain)	Moderate	80
	Moderate	46		Severe	20
	Severe	12			

Fig. 3.22 Nomadic herdsman at a water hole in the Sahel

Water

Water is an essential part of our daily lives: indeed, 65 per cent of our bodies consist of it. A clean, fresh water supply is a necessity for good health and hygienic living conditions, and virtually all man's economic activities, agricultural and industrial, rely on adequate water resources. Their use or misuse has fundamental effects on the natural environment. As world population increases so does the demand for water, yet at present many nations, particularly in the developed world, use water in a wasteful and irresponsible manner.

Of all the water in the world only $2\frac{1}{2}$ per cent is fresh and of that only 1 per cent is freely available to man. Fresh water is produced through the hydrological cycle, by which water is evaporated from the earth's surface into the atmosphere and then falls as rain or snow. Much of this is absorbed by vegetation and the soil or is trapped in ice-sheets and glaciers. Some collects underground in the pores of the rock: man can tap this by sinking wells. The remainder flows back to the sea via rivers and lakes and it is these which provide man with his main source of water.

In theory there is ample water to support a population several times larger than the current world total. The problems arise from its distribution and the cost of storing and transporting it. Rainfall varies from region to region, from year to year, and from season to season. Since most developing countries lie within the tropics their climates often have marked wet and dry seasons. During the dry season lack of water threatens people's health and the agriculture they depend on. Fetching water is a time-consuming and exhausting task for hundreds of millions of people in developing countries. But even where water is available it may not be clean. Fifteen hundred million inhabitants of the Third World have no access to safe water supplies (Fig. 3.23).

ICE COLD LAGER available over counter 35p

WARM STAGNANT WATER available at drinking hole after 4-hour walk in 100°F.

In parts of Africa, women and children often have to walk in the blistering heat for water that is too frequently stagnant and polluted.

Yet all we have to do is turn on the tap for clean, pure drinking water.

Helping to provide safer drinking water in poor countries is one of Oxfam's most important priorities.

We'd like to send you more information about Oxfam's work and explain how even small donations can be of great help.

It could help you appreciate that ice-cold lager even more.

I'm interested. Please send me more information about Oxfam's work in the poor countries.

Name

Address

I enclose a donation of £_____ in the meantime.
Room X, Oxfam, 274 Banbury Rd., Oxford OX2 7DZ.

Fig. 3.23 A charity appeal for funds to improve water supplies

12 a Estimate how much water your family uses each day. Compare this with the information given in Fig. 3.24. How economical are you?

b How does your family pay for its water? How much does it cost a day?

c How could your family economize if there was a water shortage?

There are six main issues associated with the world's water resources:

1 *Health.* A report by the World Health Organization suggests that 80 per cent of the world's diseases are caused in some way by contaminated water. These include cholera, typhoid, malaria, bilharzia, and leprosy. In all nearly 500 million people suffer from water-borne diseases.

Simple preventive measures can achieve dramatic reductions in the occurrence of disease. Since communal wells represent the greatest danger of infection improvements there are most effective. The lining of the well shaft with stones or concrete and the construction of a headwall both prevent pollution of the water supply. The well should also have a cover and a surrounding apron to drain away excess water.

2 *Agriculture.* Four-fifths of all the water used by man is consumed in farming. Since the introduction of new high-yield crops during the green revolution there has been an increasing demand for water on Third World farms. The new varieties require even more irrigation and there is an urgent need to introduce more economic techniques, such as trickle or drip irrigation, and to develop less thirsty crop strains.

3 *Environment.* It is now realized that decisions taken over water supplies can have far-reaching effects on the environment. In semi-arid lands, where drought is a recurring problem, the provision of new water-holes often encourages overgrazing. This in turn leads to the stripping of pastureland and the onset of desertification. The clearance of tropical forests, particularly in Asia, has led to wasteful and destructive flooding.

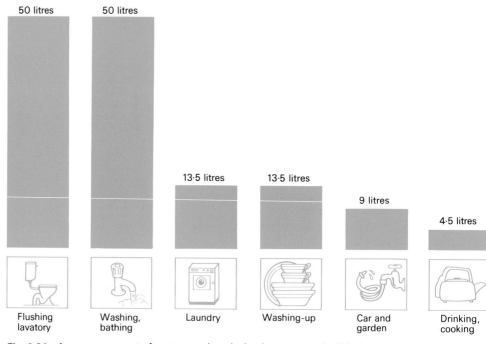

Fig. 3.24 Average amount of water used each day by a person in Britain

Fig. 3.25 The only water supply for this squatter settlement is kept in old oil drums

4 *Technology*. In the past there has been a concentration on expensive, large-scale schemes that carry a lot of prestige. These include large dams, sometimes with hydro-electric power installations, and ambitious irrigation networks. Usually these have been funded by developed nations in return for profitable construction contracts and trade deals with Third World countries. Now there is a strong feeling that development should be concentrated at the village level. This would involve smaller-scale programmes aimed at providing such necessities as pit latrines and communal water pumps. However, for these to be successful machinery must be adequately maintained.

5 *Politics*. As water resources become increasingly important, countries find themselves in competition for their use. This can happen where countries share a river as a frontier or where a river flows from one country to another. In such cases there has to be agreement over how much water each country can take out. Water conflicts have occurred between India and Pakistan over the Indus, between India and Bangladesh over the Ganges, between Syria and Iraq over the Tigris-Euphrates, and between Sudan and Egypt over the Nile. A more difficult problem concerns the use of underground water. This builds up in porous rocks over thousands of years and must therefore be regarded as a limited resource. Where it lies under several countries they must decide the rate at which it will be exploited.

6 *Money*. At the United Nations Habitat conference in 1976 it was suggested that all settlements should have clean water by 1990. Fig. 3.26 shows the position in 1970, though these figures are almost certainly optimistic. To reach the UN target roughly £2 would have to be spent each year for every man, woman, and child in the developing countries. In comparison the world arms budget represents £70 spent each year for every member of the developing countries. But the likelihood of that £2 being found is very slim indeed.

Fig. 3.26 Percentage of population with access to safe water

	Urban	Rural	Total
Africa (south of Sahara)	67	11	21
Latin America	76	24	54
Eastern Mediterranean	86	18	33
North Africa	73	44	55
South East Asia (including India)	53	9	17
Western Pacific (including China)	75	21	40

Fig. 3.27 Villagers using a new mechanical pump at a well in Upper Volta

We will now look at an example of water use in Mexico. The traditional farming methods in the Oaxaca valley have been fundamentally altered by new developments, as you will see from Fig. 3.28 and the following extract:

In the hot sunlight of the valley of Oaxaca, in Mexico's southern highlands, a Zapotec farmer peers into the hand-dug well in the centre of his small plot of land. For several hours he has drawn up buckets of water and poured them over his pepper plants; now the well is dry, and he will have to wait until tomorrow to tend the last few rows—if they survive another day of desiccation in the heat.

Shading his eyes with his hand, the farmer looks across his plot to the fields of a neighbour who has drilled a deep well and bought a diesel-powered pump. Water flows wastefully in the furrows between his plants. The mechanized pump saves labour, but it lowers the water table more quickly, so that all the shallow wells in the area run dry within a few hours.

Hand irrigation of crops is a three-thousand-year-old tradition in the valley of Oaxaca. This ancient method indirectly regulated the use of water and maintained a long-term balance between farmers and their resources. But new irrigation practices, which have yet to come under social or legal controls, require a new kind of response, a different social order.

(from 'Oaxaca's spiralling race for water' by Susan Lees in *Ecologist*)

13 Study Fig. 3.28 and the extract above.

a Make a list of all the changes that have occurred in the Oaxaca valley since the introduction of new methods of irrigation.

b Draw a flow diagram to show the way in which the Oaxaca valley is shifting from a traditional to a modern way of life. What effect is this having on the social system in the valley?

c What problems are farmers likely to face in the future if this pattern of change continues?

	Traditional	Modern
Farming system	Small-scale subsistence farming. Main crops: maize and beans. A few cash crops for sale at local markets: wheat, fruit, vegetables, flowers. Self-contained rural life. Little contact with outside world.	Increasing emphasis on commercial farming. Introduction of modern technology. Development of dairy farming to supply growing urban markets with milk products. Large areas of land given over to alfalfa, the main fodder crop for dairy cattle.
Irrigation methods	Stone and brushwood dams block streams and catch floodwaters. Water diverted to fields by narrow earthen canals and simple aqueducts. Shallow wells, 3–6 m deep. Water raised and spread by hand.	Concrete dams and reservoirs built on streams in piedmont zone. Much more water stored and distributed to dry areas. Wells, up to 45m deep, built with technical assistance from government. Water raised by diesel pumps.
Effects	Irrigation requires intensive hand labour so water is used economically over small area of land. Farmers limit their crops according to water available. Simple lifestyle based on customs of local community. Little regard for material wealth. Restricted use of natural resources maintains environment and water supply.	Abundant water provided with small labour input. Much water wasted or lost through evaporation. Farmers increase crops based on irrigation: continual rise in demand for water. Village traditions break down due to impact of modern world. Farmers in competition for material gain. Pressure on them to adopt modern techniques. Greater use of water causes drop in level of water table. Shallow wells dry up quickly. Pumped wells must be sunk ever deeper.

Fig. 3.28 The impact of irrigation in the Oaxaca valley

Summary

This chapter has looked at some of the world's natural resources and the ways in which man affects them. The biosphere, where all living things exist, can be divided into functional units called ecosystems which can be identified at all scales. Because ecosystems are very complex and closely interrelated, man's actions can have widespread and often unexpected consequences. We have seen how the clearance of tropical forests can lead to a disastrous breakdown of environmental processes. Man is also encouraging the spread of the world's deserts by the destruction of vegetation through poor farming practices. Water is a vital resource that needs to be managed with much greater care: modern irrigation methods can be extremely wasteful.

Chapter 4 Improving agriculture

The development of farming

Like all living things, man must have food to survive. Yet man is different from other creatures because he has the ability to increase his food supply. He does this by the organized growing of crops and rearing of animals: in other words, by farming.

If there were no farming, the population would be limited to those people who could support themselves by hunting wild animals and eating wild plants. They are known as hunter-gatherers. For hundreds of thousands of years man was a hunter-gatherer: his only concerns were to find food, shelter, and warmth.

There are still some people who live in this fashion today, such as the Eskimoes, Pygmies, Aborigines, and Amazonian Indians. Because they understand their natural environment so well they can find a rich and varied food supply even in unpromising surroundings. For instance, Australian Aborigines living in semi-desert lands have a diet involving about 350 different types of food. Hunter-gatherers are few in number, however, and their primitive lifestyles are being destroyed by contact with the modern world.

1 How many different types of food does your family's average weekly menu include? Make a list of all the types of food that you eat regularly: how many are there? How does this compare with other members of the class? Which are the twenty most commonly mentioned foods?

Over time man began to understand the movements of the herds of animals he hunted and he learnt how to follow them throughout the year. From this it was a logical step to controlling the herds' move-

Fig. 4.1 Threshing barley by the traditional method in Ethiopia

ment and regarding them as his possessions. People who drive herds of animals for their own use are called nomads. The animals provide most of the nomads' requirements of food and materials. Examples of nomadic people today are the Bedouin and Tuareg of the Sahara, the Fulani of West Africa, and the Kirghiz of Central Asia.

When people discovered where there were areas of reliable pasture they stayed in one place with their herds. They gradually learnt how to increase the pasture by sowing extra seeds of the wild grasses. This was the start of true farming. The next major discovery was that by digging the soil and planting seeds, crops could be made to grow in new areas. Consequently, man began to alter significantly the natural pattern of vegetation. For the first time farmers were in a position to produce more food

than they needed immediately, so that surplus food could be stored away to guard against times of shortage.

From then on farming areas were able to support more people, and as the population increased so groups of people moved to other areas. They discovered and settled fertile new lands in Africa, Asia, and Europe. The food surplus was also used to support people who were not actively involved in farming. These included craftsmen who developed new tools and techniques to make farming more efficient. The earliest cities grew up in areas where a food surplus was available, notably in the Tigris-Euphrates valley in the Middle East. The exchange of food for goods and services led to the development of trade between the cities and the countryside and eventually between one country and another.

Types of farming

It is difficult to classify each type of farming exactly but some broad divisions can be made (Fig. 4.2).

The most obvious distinction is the difference between growing crops and raising animals. Crop cultivation is called arable farming and usually occupies the better quality land, that which is flatter and more fertile. Livestock rearing, or pastoral farming, is normally carried out in the less fertile areas, since animals are more tolerant of difficult conditions. Sometimes mixed farming is practised, which involves both crops and animals. This is more common in the developed countries.

Another distinction is between shifting and sedentary agriculture. Shifting agriculture involves movement from one area of land to another. The farmers have to move on after a year or two because the soil becomes exhausted: shifting pastoralists may need to move to new pastures every day. Because only a small proportion of the land can be used at any one time shifting agriculture can only support a low density of population. As soon as population levels begin to rise sedentary farming, or the long-term occupation of one area, becomes essential. Sedentary farmers have to use crop rotation, fertilizers, and seed selection to maintain the quality of their land.

A further important split is the difference between subsistence and commercial agriculture. A subsistence farmer produces only enough food for himself and his family: it is a hand-to-mouth existence, with everyone going hungry if the harvest is bad. In a particularly good year the farmer may have a surplus to sell at the local market, but this is regarded as an unexpected bonus. Commercial agriculture is concerned with making a profit through the regular sale of produce. The money gained from this is essential in keeping the system going, since it must be used to pay for future farming operations.

One particular type of commercial farming is monoculture, in which a single product is produced in large quantities. This makes the operation cheaper and more efficient, but also more vulnerable to the dangers of disease, bad weather, and falling prices. In the less developed countries monoculture is associated with tropical plantations which were established through European colonization.

Fig. 4.2 World farming types

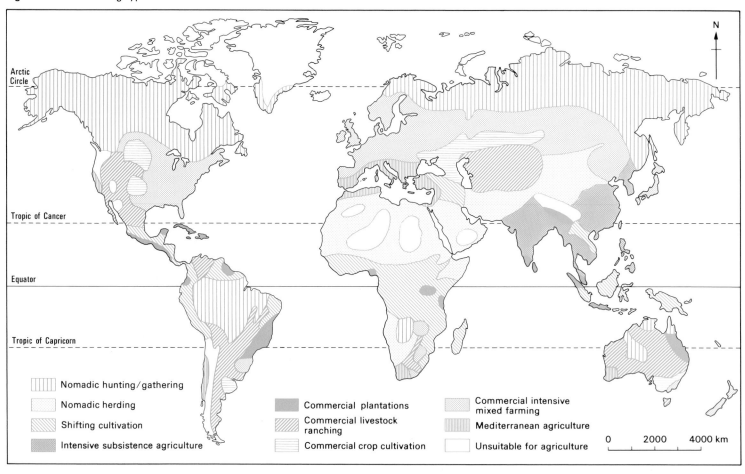

Fig. 4.4 Wheat farming

Fig. 4.6 Nomadic sheep and goat herding

Fig. 4.3 Rice farming

Fig. 4.5 Cattle herding

Fig. 4.7 Sheep rearing

Fig. 4.8 Banana plantation

Fig. 4.9 Market gardening

Fig. 4.10 Shifting cultivation

Agriculture can also be classified as either intensive or extensive. Intensive farming aims to be highly productive by using large amounts of labour, chemicals, or equipment per unit of land. It is found in areas where the population density is high and therefore land is scarce. Some crops will only show a profit if grown in this way. Extensive agriculture aims to get maximum production from each unit of manpower. Although yields are low and some land may be wasted the returns are high compared to the amount of effort put in.

2 Make a copy of the table in Fig. 4.11 and complete it by ticking the appropriate four characteristics of each of the eight farming types listed below. These are illustrated in Figs. 4.3 to 4.10.

1 Rice farming in South-East Asia
2 Wheat farming in North America
3 Cattle herding in West Africa
4 Nomadic sheep and goat herding in the Sahara
5 Sheep rearing in Australia and New Zealand
6 Banana plantations in Central America
7 Market gardening in north-west Europe
8 Shifting cultivation in Indonesia

3 Fig. 4.12 lists the twenty-five most important crops in terms of world production.

a Cover up the final column of the table and see if you can guess which region of the world each crop originates from.
b Check your answers against the table and then use the information to produce a map of crop origins. On a copy of a world map write the name of each crop against the appropriate region or regions.
c Use the data in Fig. 4.12 to draw a bar graph showing the production of the top twenty-five crops in the world. What proportion of the total production of these crops is contributed by the top seven?

Fig. 4.11 The characteristics of eight farming types

	1	2	3	4	5	6	7	8
Arable								
Pastoral								
Sedentary								
Shifting								
Commercial								
Subsistence								
Intensive								
Extensive								

Fig. 4.12 Top of the crops chart

Crop	Annual production (million tonnes)	Origin
1 Wheat	360	Middle East
2 Rice	320	South East Asia, Africa
3 Maize	300	Central America
4 Potato	300	South America
5 Barley	170	Middle East
6 Sweet potato	130	Central America, South America
7 Cassava	100	Central America, South America
8 Grapes	60	Middle East, Europe, Central Asia
9 Soybean	60	China
10 Oats	50	Europe
11 Sorghum	50	Africa
12 Sugar cane	50	South Pacific, South East Asia
13 Millets	45	Central Asia, Africa
14 Banana	35	South East Asia
15 Tomato	35	Central America
16 Sugar beet	30	Europe
17 Rye	30	Europe
18 Oranges	30	South East Asia
19 Coconut	30	South Pacific
20 Cottonseed oil	25	South America, Africa
21 Apples	20	Middle East
22 Yam	20	Africa
23 Peanut	20	South America
24 Watermelon	20	Africa
25 Cabbage	15	Europe, China

We are now going to look at a number of farming types found in the Third World. Although they are specific examples they demonstrate many general features of agriculture in developing countries.

Shifting cultivation in Papua New Guinea

Shifting cultivation is a traditional form of agriculture that is found in many areas of tropical rain forest and wooded savanna. Locate and identify them on Fig. 4.2. There are many different names for the technique, including bush fallowing, slash and burn, and swidden. Similarly, there is a wide variety of farming systems associated with it.

The Maring people are primitive subsistence farmers living in the mountainous rain forests of Papua New Guinea. Each group of Maring, numbering between 100 and 1000 members, occupies a territory of a few square kilometres. Within this area they cultivate small 'gardens' which are used for a year or two and then abandoned.

Every year each gardening pair, usually man and wife, clears the forest for a garden, rarely larger than half a hectare in size. After cutting down the undergrowth the trees are felled and their branches lopped off. Some logs are used to make fences and then the remainder of the wood is burnt. Burning not only disposes of all the leaf-matter but also releases all the goodness from the cut vegetation into the soil. Since the soil which underlies the forest is only 5 cm thick these nutrients are essential for the growth of the crops. A wide range of plants is sown—bananas, sweet potatoes, yams, sugar cane, beans, and many more. Although they seem to be planted in a haphazard fashion the Maring are expert at arranging them for the best results.

The hot, wet climate ensures rapid growth and the gardeners' main task is weeding. However, they are very careful not to remove the shoots of the new forest trees. The Maring realize that their livelihood depends on the forest's healthy recovery. In fact they call the growing trees 'nduk mi', which means 'mother of garden'. After two years or so the trees will have developed sufficiently to make any cultivation very difficult. The gardeners then abandon the remaining crops to their

Fig. 4.13 Tending a well-fenced garden in the highlands

Fig. 4.14 A couple carry a dead pig as an offering for a village celebration

i) In a forest most of the plant foods are above the soil in the trees. In this picture the green dots show us where the plant foods are.

ii) When we clear the forest and burn it the plant foods lie in the surface of the soil.

iii) If we leave the soil bare the rain will soon wash the plant foods out of the soil.

iv) If we grow a crop, the plants will take up some of the plant foods and hold them safe.

v) If we dig the old crop into the soil, the humus holds the plant foods safe for the next crop.

vi) But if we burn the old plants, the plant foods are left in the soil for the rain to wash away and the soil is then ruined.

Fig. 4.15 How a tropical 'garden' should be cultivated

pigs for a few days. The pigs soften and turn over the soil in their search for food and also thin out the tree seedlings. After this, secondary forest takes over completely and is left for between ten and forty years, depending on the altitude. By this time the land has recovered enough to be cultivated again.

The Maring get nearly all their food directly from their gardens and their pigs. The pigs are fed on garden produce and also go foraging through the forest. The gardens are highly productive and it takes only one-tenth of a hectare to feed an adult for a year. It must be remembered though that shifting cultivation only works effectively with a low population density. If numbers increase then pressure on the land is too great

and forest areas are returned to cultivation too early.

The type of farming practised by the Maring has no long-term ill effect on the environment. Because they understand their surroundings so well their gardens blend in with the natural processes of the forest. Fig. 4.15 is a series of diagrams from a textbook designed for tropical farmers. It demonstrates the right technique for cultivating a forest garden. Unfortunately, not all shifting cultivation is carried out with such concern for the environment. Sometimes settlers with little knowledge of the forest cultivate it in a very damaging way. This has been one of the major problems arising from settlement schemes in the Amazon basin.

4 Study Fig. 4.15 carefully.
   a What mistakes might an ignorant farmer make when cultivating a forest clearing?
   b What effects would these mistakes have on the natural environment?
   c How can they be avoided by sensible farming?
   d Why are textbooks likely to be of limited use in educating farmers?
   e Draw a set of diagrams like Fig. 4.15 to illustrate the sequence of farming followed by the Maring people of New Guinea.

Subsistence farming in the Andes

The village of Uchucmarca is situated in a mountain valley in northern Peru. It has a population of less than one thousand. The inhabitants call it a *pueblo olvidado*, meaning a 'forgotten town'. They are not exaggerating its isolation. The only way to reach the village is on foot or by horse. It is eight hours from the nearest road and five hours from the nearest light bulb. Its closest market town, Celendin (with a population of 9000), is a twelve-hour journey away. The few goods Uchucmarca imports from the outside world are carried in on men's backs so the village has to be as self-sufficient as possible.

The main activity in the valley is farming. The peasants cultivate land ranging from 800 m to 4300 m in height. This difference in height leads to a wide variety of climate on the mountain side. There are six distinct zones recognized by the villagers, each with its own type of farming:

1 *Temple* (1250–1500 m). This is the lowest and hottest zone. Cash crops such as sugar cane, sweet potatoes, and bananas are grown intensively and all cultivation has to be irrigated.

2 *Kichwa fuerte* (1500–1900 m). A steeply sloping zone which often suffers from drought. With sufficient rainfall wheat and maize can be grown. Dense clumps of trees and shrubs provide firewood for the village.

3 *Kichwa* (1900–2500 m). At this height rainfall is more reliable and no irrigation is necessary. There is more farmland than lower down and wheat and maize are the main crops. Beans, barley, and some fruits are also grown.

4 *Templado* (2500–2800 m). This is a temperate zone with fairly steep slopes. It can support a wide variety of crops that are also found in other zones. However, lentils and peas are two crops which occur only in this zone.

5 *Jalka* (2800–3500 m). This is the highest agricultural zone of the valley. Above

Fig. 4.16 A village scene in the Peruvian Andes during the barley harvest

this level the danger of frost is too great. The angle of slope is gentler here and this represents the main potato-growing area. Ocas, a potato-like plant, are also cultivated.

6 *Jalka fuerte* (3500–4300 m). The land steepens again in this zone. It represents the chief area of communally owned pastures, where animals are reared for sale. Sheep are also kept for their wool.

5 Make a larger copy of Fig. 4.17. Mark in each of the six zones listed above by drawing in their height limits and naming them. Then add labels to indicate the main crops grown in each zone.

Each household in Uchucmarca has access to at least four or five of the farming zones. Types of tenure include ownership, sharecropping, and working as day labourers for produce. Land rights and labour

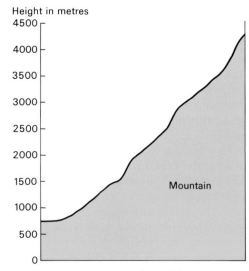

Height in metres

Fig. 4.17 Cross-section of the Uchucmarca valley

Fig. 4.18 Monthly farming operations in the Uchucmarca valley

JANUARY

Potatoes: *harvesting*
Upper maize: *weeding*
Lower maize: *planting*
Lower wheat: *ploughing*
Peas: *ploughing*
Barley: *ploughing*
Broad beans: *weeding*
Lentils: *planting*

FEBRUARY

Potatoes: *harvesting*
Lower maize: *weeding*
Lower wheat: *planting*
Peas: *planting*
Barley: *planting*
Broad beans: *weeding*

MARCH

Potatoes: *harvesting*
Ocas: *harvesting*

APRIL

Potatoes: *breaking turf*
Ocas: *harvesting*

MAY

Potatoes: *breaking turf*

JUNE

Potatoes: *ploughing*
Lower maize: *harvesting*
Lower wheat: *harvesting*
Ocas: *ploughing*

JULY

Potatoes: *planting*
Upper maize: *harvesting*
Upper wheat: *harvesting*
Peas: *harvesting*
Barley: *harvesting*
Broad beans: *harvesting*
Lentils: *harvesting*

AUGUST

Potatoes: *planting*
Upper maize: *harvesting*
Upper wheat: *harvesting*
Peas: *harvesting*
Ocas: *planting*
Barley: *harvesting*
Broad beans: *harvesting*

SEPTEMBER

Potatoes: *weeding*
Ocas: *weeding*

OCTOBER

Potatoes: *weeding*
Upper maize: *ploughing*
Broad beans: *ploughing*

NOVEMBER

Potatoes: *weeding*
Upper maize: *planting*
Upper wheat: *ploughing*
Peas: *ploughing*
Ocas: *weeding*
Barley: *ploughing*
Broad beans: *planting*

DECEMBER

Potatoes: *harvesting*
Upper maize: *weeding*
Lower maize: *ploughing*
Upper wheat: *planting*
Peas: *ploughing*
Ocas: *weeding*
Lentils: *ploughing*

Fig. 4.19 Calendar of farming operations in the Uchucmarca valley

Crop	JAN	FEB	MAR	APR	MAY	JUN	JUL	AUG	SEP	OCT	NOV	DEC
Potatoes												
Upper maize												
Lower maize												
Upper wheat												
Lower wheat												
Peas												
Ocas												
Barley												
Broad beans												
Lentils												

Farming operations: ☐ Breaking turf ☐ Ploughing ☐ Planting ☐ Weeding ☐ Harvesting

commitments are normally passed on from father to son and are also exchanged through marriage. The major land reform programme in Peru has had little effect on Uchucmarca, although it is now officially recognized as a *comunidad campesina* (peasant community). Its day-to-day government is carried out by a committee elected by the villagers.

All farming in the valley is completely unmechanized and no chemical fertilizers, weedkillers, or pesticides are used. But the peasant farmers do have an intimate knowledge of the Uchucmarca valley and the crops that they grow. A few tools serve a multitude of purposes. Initially the iron parts for these tools are bought, but they are reforged countless times to keep them serviceable. The teeth for the simple ploughs are made from old car springs and then fitted to hand-made wooden frames.

As with all subsistence farming a great deal of labour is required. The complex calendar of activity in the valley reflects the very wide range of crops that is cultivated. Each crop goes through a cycle of production that normally includes ploughing, planting, weeding, and harvesting. The land for potatoes also has to be prepared by breaking up the hard turf before ploughing can take place.

6 Use the information in Fig. 4.18 to fill in a copy of the calendar in Fig. 4.19. You should choose a different colour for each of the five farming operations and then shade the appropriate squares for each crop. The division of maize and wheat into upper and lower crops reflects the varying timetables in different height zones. When you have completed your calendar, answer the following questions:
   a In which months would the farmers be i) most busy, ii) least busy?
   b Which crops require i) the most labour, ii) the least labour?
   c Which crops require the most i) ploughing, ii) weeding, iii) harvesting?

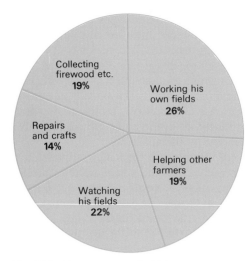

Fig. 4.20 How a peasant in Uchucmarca divides his time

Fig. 4.21 Breaking turf with a wooden hoe and bare hands

A peasant's work in Uchucmarca involves more than just tending his crops (Fig. 4.20). Only a quarter of his time is spent labouring on his own land. This is because all the farmers help each other during busy periods, particularly when maize and potatoes need weeding or the cereal crops are being harvested. A peasant must also devote a fifth of his time to guarding his land. Fences cannot keep out wild animals or thieves, so families have to watch their fields, which are usually spread throughout the valley. Near harvest time whole families may leave the village to go and live close to the fields.

Since Uchucmarca has no specialist craftsmen every farmer must spend time doing his own repair and construction work. He must also put in about one day's work each month on communal projects for the benefit of the whole village. The other major call on a peasant's time and energy is collecting firewood. Since most of the wood near the village has been used up it now involves a full day's work, including travelling time, to collect enough fuel for ten days.

Uchucmarca is too poor and isolated to have adopted any modern farming methods, but the traditional subsistence farming appears to support its inhabitants quite adequately.

7 The following figures show the amount of time devoted to each crop in the Uchucmarca valley: potatoes 35%, maize 25%, wheat 21%, peas 6%, barley 6%, ocas 5%, broad beans 2%.
   a Draw a pie diagram to illustrate this information. If you multiply each percentage by 3·6 this will give the number of degrees in the circle for each crop.
   b Does the pattern shown by the diagram reflect the details of the farming calendar you produced for Exercise 6?

8 Study Figs. 4.16 and 4.21.
   a What evidence is there in the photos of the self-sufficient existence of peasant farmers in the Andes?
   b Write a short description of each photo explaining how the natural environment influences farming operations and the people's lives.

Commercial irrigated farming

The purpose of irrigation is to move regular amounts of water from a lake, river or well to areas of cultivated land. Any irrigation scheme will be designed to do this as efficiently and cheaply as possible. There are many different ways of irrigating farmland, some of which date back thousands of years; Fig. 4.22 shows one of these traditional methods, the sakia, which is still commonly used in developing countries.

9 a Study Fig. 4.22 and write an explanation of the way in which the sakia works.
b What are its merits and drawbacks as a system of supplying water for irrigation?

When it is necessary to irrigate large areas there are two main methods: gravity flow irrigation and overhead irrigation. Gravity flow irrigation, as the name suggests, uses the natural slope of the land to distribute the water, and is most effective on gentle slopes with relatively non-porous soils. It is an expensive system to construct since it involves a network of carefully graded channels and usually a controlling dam to create a head of water. The flow is controlled by the use of strategically positioned sluice gates. Where the land is porous concrete channels have to be provided to prevent the water soaking away. Once installed, however, a gravity flow system is very cheap to run and simple to operate.

Overhead irrigation relies on a system of pipes and sprinklers to spray water onto the crops from above. This method requires pumps to force the water through the pipes and out of the sprays. Although it is costly to install it is less expensive than the major engineering works needed for gravity flow irrigation. But running costs are considerable since pumping engines require fuel and skilled labour for maintenance work.

Fig. 4.22 Raising water with a sakia

Fig. 4.23 A gravity flow irrigation system

In operation overhead irrigation has several distinct advantages over gravity flow methods. Sprinklers give a more even coverage of the ground surface and wet the whole plant, rather than just the roots. There is little soil movement because the water falls directly where it is absorbed, rather than flowing across the ground surface. Undulating land composed of porous, sandy soils can only be irrigated by overhead methods. When water from gravity flow irrigation is released onto a field soil movement is inevitable and the areas farthest from the entry point receive much less water than those nearby.

10 a Using Fig. 4.24, list the layouts in order of preference according to i) the efficiency of water distribution, ii) the cost of construction.
  b Which layouts would the farmer find easiest to use?

11 Look at the new system of irrigation shown in Fig. 4.25.
  a Explain how the system works.
  b Why is it likely to be more economic with water than other systems?
  c Can you suggest any disadvantages with this system?

One major drawback of irrigation is the build-up of salt in the soil as a result of repeated inundation and evaporation. A thin, but lethal, white crust of salt develops on the ground surface, making it useless for farming. A United Nations survey in the mid 1970s estimated that salt had damaged 20 per cent of Pakistan's Indus plain, the world's largest irrigated area. A similar degree of damage was recorded for irrigated areas in China, India, Syria, Argentina, Brazil, and Mexico.

The Gezira scheme in the Sudan was one of the earliest modern agricultural developments based on irrigation (Fig. 4.29). Planned in 1904, it was opened in 1925 and has been extended several times since then. The word Gezira means 'island' and refers to the area of land between the channels of the Blue and White Niles. It was chosen by the Sudanese government as the site for the

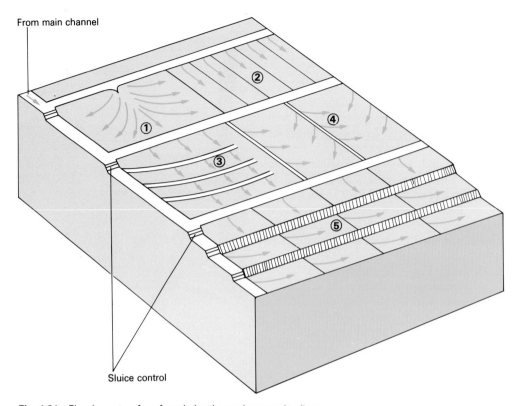

Fig. 4.24 Five layouts of surface irrigation using gravity flow

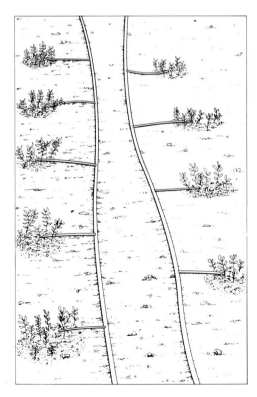

production of cotton as a major export crop. As the area lies on the southern edge of the Sahara desert and has a dry climate which makes it very marginal for farming, none of the development would have been possible without the construction of an extensive irrigation network.

12 Find the location of the Gezira scheme on an atlas map showing the physical geography of Africa.
  a How far does the Blue Nile drop from its source in the Ethiopian highlands to the Gezira?
  b Compare the climatic graphs for Addis Ababa, Wad Medani, and Cairo (Fig. 4.26). How does the climate alter as you move downstream?

Fig. 4.25 A modern irrigation system

Cairo (height 41 m)
Total annual rainfall 10 mm

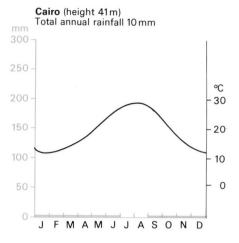

Wad Medani (height 410 m)
Total annual rainfall 410 mm

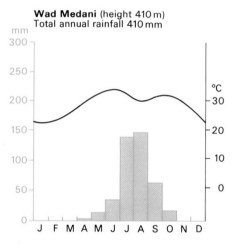

Addis Ababa (height 2400 m)
Total annual rainfall 1200 mm

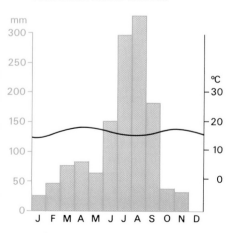

Fig. 4.26 Climatic graphs for three places in the Nile valley

Fig. 4.27 Sugar cane cultivation on irrigated land in the Sudan

13 Study Fig. 4.28.
a How does the overall flow of the River Nile vary throughout the year?
b What is the difference between the contributions made by the Blue Nile and the White Nile?
c Why would it be more sensible to dam the Blue Nile rather than the White Nile for water storage?
d What factors might be responsible for the White Nile's more even pattern of flow?

Between 1913 and 1925 a dam was constructed on the Blue Nile at Sennar. The purpose of this barrage is to trap and store some of the annual floodwaters that descend from the Ethiopian highlands. When the lake behind the dam has reached a certain level sluice gates can be opened to release water into the main irrigation canal. From this canal a complex system of smaller channels distributes the water to individual farming plots.

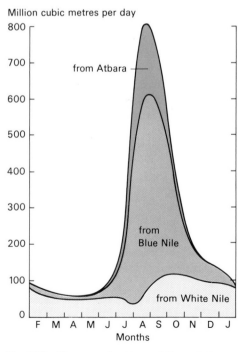

Fig. 4.28 The annual pattern of flow of the River Nile

75

The land of the Gezira is ideal for irrigation. Its surface slopes gently but consistently, allowing water to be distributed by gravity. The slope also allows water to drain easily, so there is no danger of waterlogging during the rainy season. The soils consist chiefly of impervious clay which avoids the need for expensive concrete drainage channels. And of course, the Blue Nile ensures a regular, if seasonal, supply of water.

There are about 100 000 tenant farmers in the Gezira scheme, who rent their land from the Sudan Gezira board. Each year a farmer is allocated an area of land to cultivate and is told by an inspector what crops he has to grow. Besides cotton, these include a variety of commercial and subsistence crops. The inspectors manage the blocks of land into which the Gezira is divided. They control the distribution of tenancies, the flow of irrigation water, the distribution of seeds, fertilizers and sprays, and the collection of cotton. This system is being altered now by the establishment of village councils and marketing co-operatives to give the farmers more say in managing their land. A farmer receives about 50 per cent of the income from his cotton, while the remaining money goes to the government and the board.

Generally speaking the Gezira tenant is regarded as a privileged person in the Sudan and is well off in comparison with other Sudanese farmers. The Gezira also relies on the work of a million landless labourers who are not so lucky. Most earn as little as 35p per day or about 2p for every kilo of cotton they pick. About half of these workers live in the Gezira all year round, while the rest travel long distances from the Sudan's western provinces and stay only for the four months of the cotton-picking season. They are contracted to work for an individual farmer, whose responsibility it is to provide food and housing. Their temporary homes are bare grass huts in the middle of the fields, without any basic facilities. The irrigation canals are their only source of water for drinking and washing, and these are infested with snails that carry a disease called bilharzia (page 100).

The Gezira is now being used as a model

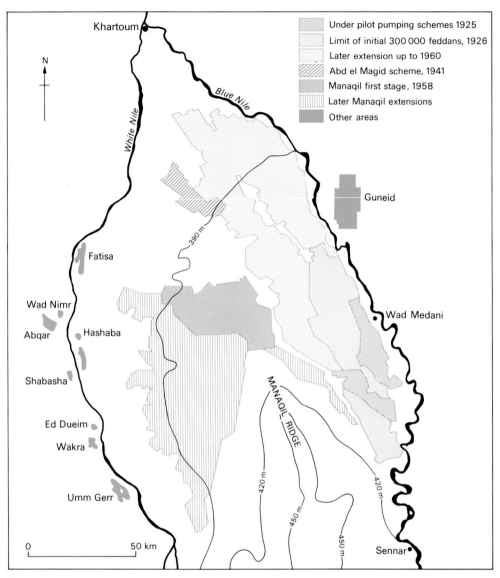

Fig. 4.29 The Gezira scheme: government irrigation areas

for further ambitious irrigation schemes in the Sudan. The environmental effect of taking more water from the Nile is unknown, though Egypt is naturally unhappy at the prospect of a reduced river flow in the lower Nile valley. The main part of the Gezira is beginning to suffer from soil exhaustion and the land has to be left fallow every fourth year. However, the Gezira's importance to the Sudan cannot be denied, and the country's hopes of future development are clearly pinned on further irrigation.

14 Study Fig. 4.29.
  a Roughly how large is the total irrigated area of the Gezira?
  b How has the Manaqil ridge affected the layout of the scheme?
  c How many different stages were there in the development of the Gezira? Why do you think they followed the sequence shown?
  d If there was a further extension of the irrigated land, where would you expect it to be?

The green revolution

There are two ways in which agricultural production can be improved. The first is by increasing the area of land under cultivation. In densely populated regions like South-East Asia most of the suitable land is already being farmed while in Africa and South America there is plenty of land, but enormous problems have to be solved in order to use the land properly. The second method is to increase the yield from existing farmland. This is done by the development of more productive crops and by the use of chemical fertilizers and pesticides.

In the early twentieth century developed countries in temperate areas made remarkable gains in productivity. It is only recently, however, that the less developed countries have benefited from concentrated agricultural research. Early successes in the improvement of tropical and sub-tropical agriculture led to the term 'the green revolution'. As we shall see later subsequent developments suggest that there may not be as dramatic a change as was first hoped.

A major aspect of the green revolution has been the introduction of hybrid cereal crops. In particular, rice, wheat, and maize have undergone breeding programmes to produce high-yield varieties. This is not to say that traditional strains are inferior or that tropical farmers are backward. Far from it: the traditional varieties have adapted themselves perfectly to the features of their local environment and the farmer understands their particular requirements.

The main limiting factor on the yield of traditional strains is the fertility of the soil. Crops grow tall and fast to outpace the weeds which compete for sunlight and soil nutrients. Because of this they cannot be grown too close together or they would shade each other from the sunlight. They have extensive root systems to collect the maximum goodness from the soil. If chemical fertilizers are applied they grow too large and tend to fall over, destroying some of the grain.

Fig. 4.30 Rice plants

In comparison the high-yield varieties are designed to make maximum use of fertilizers and pesticides. They have been bred from dwarf strains to produce a plant that has a short, stiff stem and small, upright leaves. This means that they can support a full head of grain without falling over. Also they can be sown closer together without blocking the sunlight to neighbouring plants. Their root systems are smaller since the fertilizer provides all the goodness that they need.

The first major research along these lines started in Mexico in 1943. A small team of scientists developed high-yield strains of wheat that were suitable for tropical conditions. By 1970 they were producing yields four times as high as those of the early 1940s. In 1960 the International Rice Research Institute was established in the Philippines with similar aims to the Mexican wheat programme. The initial high-yield strains were released in 1966 and were widely adopted in lowland Asia. IR8 was a very successful variety that gave high yields in a wide range of natural conditions. Its short growing season of 120 days (compared with 160 for traditional rice) meant that farmers could grow two crops a year.

While the high-yield varieties are an important aspect of the green revolution, so is the provision of modern agricultural supplies and services. Without the necessary irrigation, fertilizers, pesticides, and storage facilities the high-yield crops are of little use. Schemes also have to provide farmers with credit to pay for these new developments.

Although remarkable progress has been made in some areas the effects of the green revolution have not all been good. In India particularly the pattern of land ownership is such that unless government loans are available, tenant farmers remain in the power of the large landowners.

The practical problems of educating the farmers in new agricultural methods cause considerable difficulty. The high-yield varieties need precise doses of fertilizer and weedkiller at specific times and will not grow so well if they are dosed incorrectly. Weeds must also be kept in check and the water supply needs careful monitoring. The rising price of oil has led to sharp increases in chemical prices which the less developed countries can ill afford.

The green revolution has been accompanied by the introduction of complicated agricultural machinery such as tractors, rotary cultivators, and irrigation pumps. These need careful maintenance and skilled mechanics to repair them if they break down: understandably such people are in short supply in rural areas. The cost of importing spare parts for these machines is rising constantly, as is the cost of fuel to run them, and poor countries simply cannot afford the extra expense.

15 Fig. 4.30 shows two types of rice plant: one is a traditional strain, the other is a high-yield variety.
  a Which plant is which? How can you tell?
  b Make copies of the plants and label each one clearly to show its distinguishing characteristics. Underneath each drawing list out the advantages and disadvantages of that type of plant.

Rice farming in India

The impact of the green revolution is shown best by looking at the situations of two farmers in India. The first is a subsistence rice farmer working in the traditional fashion. The second is a farmer who has taken advantage of the new developments. The rice farmer's year is shown in Fig. 4.31.

The subsistence rice farmer is often a tenant. He pays for the use of the land by giving the landowner a portion of his crop, which may be as much as half his total production each year. Since the landowner normally has several tenants paying him he is frequently a wealthy man. In addition, the landowner is the farmer's only source of credit. When he needs cash he borrows it from the landowner at high rates of interest; when he comes to repay the loan he sells part of his crop to the landowner at the landowner's price.

The farmer must feed his family with what is left of his crop, but even that may be reduced if his grain store is affected by damp, rats, or other pests. Many other aspects of the tenant farmer's operations are inefficient. He is only able to grow one crop of rice each year (planted during the kharif or rainy season) which gives a relatively low yield. The cattle that he uses to raise water for irrigation and to plough his fields are likely to be underfed and overworked. Their dung is used as fuel for cooking rather than as valuable manure for the fields. During the harvest the farmer relies on landless labourers who are only employed for this short period. At other times of the year there is simply not enough work to go round.

16 Study Fig. 4.33 and make a list of all the disadvantages that the farmer suffers from.

By contrast the second farmer owns his own land, which he has bought with the help of a government loan. Consequently all the crops he produces are his own. Since he does not require his entire crop to feed

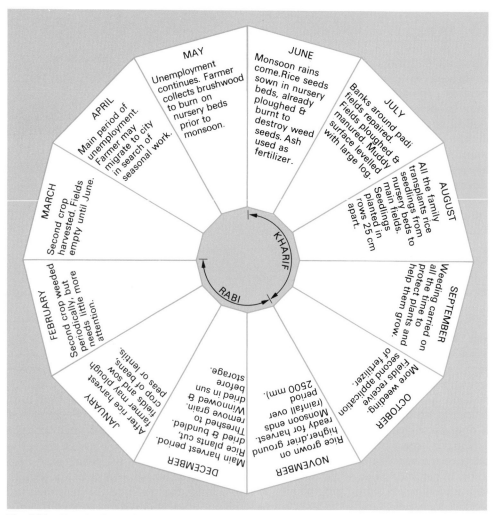

Fig. 4.31 The rice farmer's year

Fig. 4.32 Using oxen to plough the padi fields

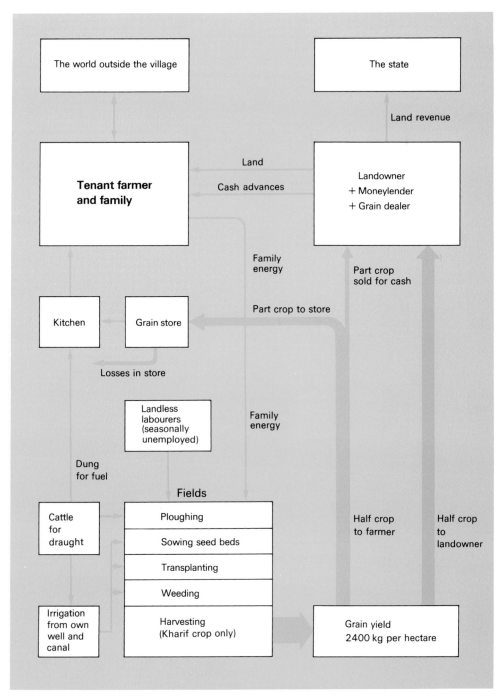

Fig. 4.33 Traditional economy of a subsistence rice farmer

The diagram contains the following labels:

- The world outside the village
- The state
- Land revenue
- Tenant farmer and family
- Land
- Cash advances
- Landowner + Moneylender + Grain dealer
- Family energy
- Part crop sold for cash
- Part crop to store
- Kitchen
- Grain store
- Losses in store
- Dung for fuel
- Landless labourers (seasonally unemployed)
- Family energy
- Fields
- Cattle for draught
- Ploughing
- Sowing seed beds
- Transplanting
- Weeding
- Irrigation from own well and canal
- Harvesting (Kharif crop only)
- Half crop to farmer
- Half crop to landowner
- Grain yield 2400 kg per hectare

Fig. 4.34 Harvesting rice by hand

his family he can sell the remainder at a profit. This is done through a co-operative of local farmers, which can negotiate better prices for the grain than an individual farmer would receive. The co-operative also acts as the distributor of high-yield varieties of seeds, fertilizers, and pesticides, which it obtains at special rates from government agencies. The farmer can borrow money from a rural bank organized by the co-operative to pay for labour and farm improvements.

By using high-yield varieties of rice with a shorter growing season the farmer can produce two crops each year. The first is grown during the kharif season and the second during the following cool, dry rabi season. Improved irrigation is essential to provide water for this second rice crop. With the correct application of fertilizers both crops will give a much higher yield than the traditional rice. Because they require more work the farmer can offer landless labourers a steady job all year round.

Greater efficiency is also evident in the home. A simple biogas plant uses cow dung to create heat for cooking and liquid manure for the fields. A properly constructed and insulated store prevents any losses from the family's grain supply. In all respects the farmer and his family are much better off as a result of investment in new techniques: the government's main task is to provide the credit that the farmer depends on.

17 a Make a copy of Fig. 4.36 (which is laid out in the same way as Fig. 4.33) and then insert each of the captions provided in the appropriate boxes.

b Label the arrows on the diagram to show what each one represents.

c Make lists of the advantages and disadvantages of this new system.

Fig. 4.35 Spraying young rice plants

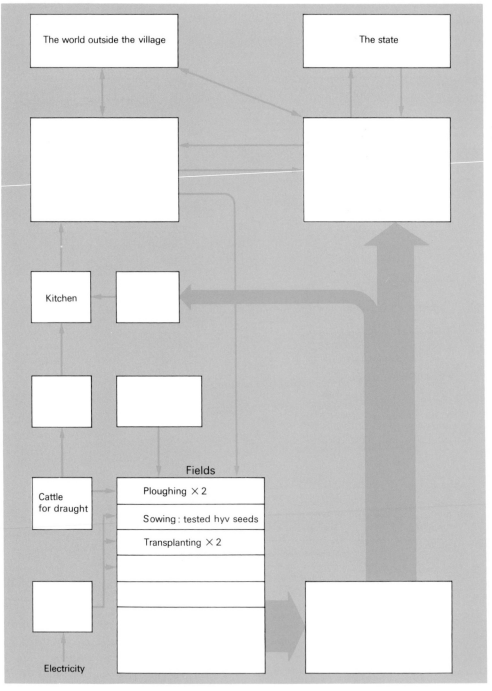

The world outside the village

The state

Kitchen

Fields

Ploughing × 2

Sowing : tested hyv seeds

Transplanting × 2

Cattle for draught

Electricity

1 Grain store (loss proofed)
2 Spraying to protect plants
3 Owner farmer and family
4 Improved irrigation by well
5 Permanent labour: less need for casual labour
6 Cow dung gas plant
7 Improved grain yield: 3800 kg per hectare
8 Applications of fertilizer
9 Farmers' co-operative for sales and marketing
10 Harvesting: kharif and rabi crops

Fig. 4.36 The economy of a modernized rice farmer

Land ownership and reform

Agricultural efficiency is greatly influenced by patterns of land ownership, which can be divided into three main types:

Owner occupation. This category includes all types of family farm where people work for their own good. A major problem in less developed countries is that the holdings are often too small to be worked profitably. In contrast, some farms may be too big. For example, in South America large estates, known as latifundia, are often left by their rich owners to be run by managers. A survey of seven South American countries showed that only one-sixth of the area occupied by latifundia had ever been cultivated. Yet the bulk of rural peasants have little or no land.

Another type of large estate is the plantation. This is also run by a manager, usually on behalf of a foreign company. Although plantations are very efficient, the benefits are rarely seen by the developing countries in which they are situated. Consequently many plantations have been nationalized or broken up in recent years.

Tenancy. This is where the farmer pays rent to a landowner, in the form of cash, produce, or labour. In less developed countries rents are often very high and the farmer has little security of tenure. This removes the farmer's incentive to improve the farm or increase his yield.

Communal ownership. This system means that the community in general benefits from the land that is worked by everyone together. It is found in many traditional societies based on tribes; it is also found in communist countries. The communist collective farms or communes have replaced small uneconomic land holdings and production has often improved. However, communal ownership can work against productivity since farmers feel that extra effort will not benefit them personally.

Clearly there is a need for programmes to reform the ownership of land so that it is distributed more evenly among the rural

Fig. 4.37 A team of tractors ploughing on a co-operative farm in Algeria

population. In most less developed countries land is the main source of wealth and it increases in value as rising populations create a greater demand for it.

Successful land reform programmes have been carried out in Egypt, Peru, Taiwan, Algeria, Chile, and Japan. For instance, before reform in Egypt about 150 000 landowners owned two-thirds of the farmland, while the remaining third was shared by $2\frac{1}{2}$ million peasants. When a socialist government came to power in 1952 the rich were stripped of their land and it was distributed to the peasants in one or two hectare plots. Other schemes have failed owing to the resistance of powerful landowners or the refusal of peasants to move to new lands.

The best examples of large-scale land reform are in two communist countries, the USSR and China (page 85). Both countries transferred the control of the farmlands to the peasants after major revolutions. These revolutions involved considerable suffering

and bloodshed but there is no doubt that the rural populations benefited greatly from the results.

However land reform is not much use on its own. It must be backed up by a full programme of agricultural development involving the introduction of new techniques and equipment. Often co-operatives are set up to help the farmer market his produce and to provide him with credit. One big advantage of land reform is that it can lead to an increase in rural employment, providing that the farmers use methods that rely on labour rather than capital investment.

FAO: What was life like for you before the redistribution of land?

Quispe: I began to work on the land at a very early age, because my father died and so did my mother. Our grandmother looked after us but life was hard for us four brothers. Those of us who worked on the haciendas (estates) had much to bear. They paid us almost nothing when we worked all day, from early dawn to dusk. With the years the daily wage rose but by then we had families. There were more mouths to feed, extreme poverty and insufficient clothing; our sons nearly died of cold and hunger. In fact we lost one child soon after birth. Because of this we always thought that things must change, that we would have to find a way of getting rid of the overbearing masters.

Several years ago one of my brothers went far away to work on a hacienda because owners came here recruiting people with promises of a good salary. But whatever their salary, which was apparently much more than in our region, they had to spend it in the hacienda shop, and everything there cost much more than its true value. Since my brother's earnings were not enough for him to buy food, they gave him credit; on purpose. Then, because he could not manage to pay back his debt, he had to remain there years and years, without even being able to marry, as though he were in an enormous open-air prison.

FAO: What does the agrarian reform mean to you?

Quispe: For me, for all of us, it means that at last we possess what is ours. But we are more than satisfied because we no longer even have to see the proprietors of the big profiteering haciendas. Now the peasant can educate his sons. It is a bit late for me because I didn't have the opportunity to educate mine. But I have to help my sons educate their sons. Now my grandchildren have enough to eat, they can be clothed and they can be sent to college, because what the earth produces is for our benefit and not for any master.

Fig. 4.38 An interview with Mariano Quispe

Fig. 4.39 Percentage of farm holdings in six size groups

Size (hectares)	Europe	North America	Central America	South America	Asia	Africa	Oceania
Under 1	21	2	33	13	46	37	1
1–4·9	39	6	40	32	42	46	5
5–9·9	19	7	8	13	8	9	6
10–49	18	36	12	27	44	6	22
50–99	2	24	3	6	–	–	16
100 and over	1	25	4	9	–	2	50

18 Read the interview with Mariano Quispe, a Peruvian peasant living in the valley of the Incas near Cuzco (Fig. 4.38). He was interviewed by the United Nations Food and Agriculture Organization. What does it tell you about the way the large landowners used to keep the peasants in poverty?

19 Using the information in Fig. 4.39, draw a bar graph for each region and then compare the patterns shown. Write a paragraph describing the variations and suggest reasons for them.

Another problem which land reform can solve is the fragmentation of farm holdings. In many less developed countries individual farmers may possess several small, widely scattered plots rather than one larger piece of land. This can give them a fair selection of good and poor soils but the increased travelling involved makes the system very inefficient. Also a considerable amount of valuable land is lost in the space taken up by field boundaries and tracks.

Fig. 4.42 shows an area of intensively cultivated farmland in the Kigezi district of Uganda. The pattern of land holdings is typical of a densely populated agricultural region, with a large number of tiny, irregularly shaped fields. The main reason for the maze of fields on the map is the way the local people pass their land on from one generation to the next. Fig. 4.40 shows this diagrammatically. In this case the sons (A,B,C,D) receive land from their father as soon as they are capable of working properly (A,B,C in diagram 1). It only becomes their own property, however, when they marry (A in diagram 2). At this time they also obtain an additional parcel of land for the maintenance of their family (A,B,C in diagram 3). When the father dies his remaining property is shared out among the sons (diagram 4).

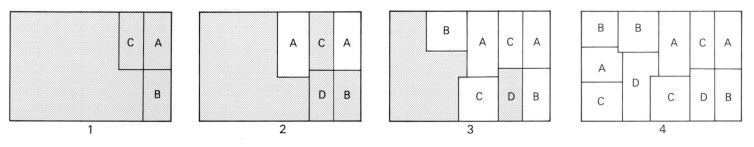

Fig. 4.40 The inheritance of land in Kigezi

Fig. 4.41 Terraced plots in Kigezi

20 The different types of shading on Fig. 4.42 represent the land holdings of five different farmers.

  a What is the total area covered by the map?

  b What is the approximate area of the largest and smallest fields on the map?

  c Imagine that each farmer wanted to visit all his fields in one day. Work out the shortest route for each farmer and then measure the direct distance he would have to cover, going from the centre of one field to the centre of the next. Why would the actual distance he would travel be much longer?

  d Which settlement would be the best one for each farmer in view of the position of his fields? Make a tracing of the shaded fields on the map and mark in the settlements you have chosen. Now measure the distance from the appropriate settlement to the centre of each of the farmer's fields and calculate the average distance he would have to travel. Which farmer is best situated?

Fig. 4.42 Land holdings in Kigezi, Uganda

Change on the Chinese communes

We will now look at the effect of land reform in China by studying developments that have taken place in agriculture there. In 1949 the communist revolution brought sweeping changes to China's predominantly agricultural population. The land, previously owned by a rich minority, was turned over to the mass of poor rural peasants. Various methods of dividing up the land were tried out and in 1958 the government set up people's agricultural communes. By the 1970s there were over 50 000 of these communal farming organizations, which formed the basic political, social and economic units of the countryside. Communes varied enormously in their size and physical characteristics but the pattern of organization was the same.

Following the death of Chairman Mao Tse-tung in 1976 there was a shift in political ideas. China's new leaders wanted to give the rural peasants more say in the way that they carried out their farming. They also aimed to increase agricultural production by letting families produce extra goods for their own use or for profit. This scheme, called the 'production responsibility system', was introduced in 1979 and has now spread throughout the country. Individual households make a contract with the state to produce a certain amount of crops each year. In return they receive a particular plot of land for fifteen years or longer. Each household is paid a fixed price for the goods it delivers to the state, but people can sell any surplus crops in the local 'free markets', where prices tend to be higher.

About 15 per cent of rural households have chosen to change to a specialized type of farming, such as livestock rearing or fruit growing, and this has led to considerable diversification of products. The overall planning of agriculture remains in the hands of communist party officials, who are also responsible for large-scale development schemes, but individual families are

Fig. 4.43 Threshing grain

now free to choose what crops they grow. Of course, the responsibility system has meant that harder working or more fortunate farmers have been able to earn substantially more than others. Some Chinese politicians think this is wrong: they feel that having wide differences in prosperity goes against the ideals of communism. But there is no doubt that the reforms have brought an impressive rise in production and rural incomes. Agricultural output has risen by 8 per cent a year since 1979.

The dominant crops are grains, especially rice and wheat, which now account for two-thirds of all home consumption. In 1979 80 per cent of all China's cultivated land was used to grow grain. This represented 80 million hectares, or 120 million hectares if multi-cropping is taken into account. Since then the area devoted to grains has fallen as some farmers have concentrated on raising poultry and pigs, marketing eggs and fish, and growing more fruit and vegetables. However, grain production has still increased, reaching a

Fig. 4.44 Harvest time

record total of over 400 million tonnes in 1984. In spite of the enormous home demand China has recently become a net exporter of grain, though it is still cheaper for China to import wheat from North America to supply cities on the coast.

The main problem for China is whether it will be able to feed itself in the future. By the year 2000 its population will have risen to at least 1200 million, which would require an annual grain production of 480 million tonnes. China hopes to achieve this by greater reliance on technology. Increased use of fertilizer, greater mechanization, high yielding crops, improved livestock and land reclamation will all play their part. Consequently, the need for human labour will be reduced and the agricultural workforce is planned to shrink to less than half its current size. The government intends to provide jobs for the surplus labour in new light industrial factories and services established in the countryside. The main consumers for these industries would be the rural peasants, spending the profits they have earned through the responsibility system.

21 This exercise involves you in a long-term planning programme for a Chinese commune. You have the job of organizing agricultural production on the commune for six five-year periods between 1960 and 1990. Fig. 4.47 is a plan of the commune (p. 88). It covers an area of 400 km², 200 of which are cultivated in 1960. The inhabitants live in three towns and a number of smaller villages.

To carry out the exercise you must work through the following steps, starting with the period 1960–5. Make a copy of Fig. 4.45 to fill in as you go through each stage.

1 The area under cultivation is entered for you in column C.

2 Throw a dice to find out the weather conditions:

    1 = very bad
    2 = bad
    3 = average
    4 = good
    5 = very good

Enter this in column D. If you throw a six, throw the dice again and follow the instructions on the chance card according to the number shown (Fig. 4.46). Throw the dice a third time to find out the weather (ignore sixes).

3 Find the number of people that can be fed by reading off the appropriate figure according to the weather from Fig. 4.48 (p. 89). Multiply this figure by the number of square kilometres under cultivation, in this case 200. Enter the result in column E and compare this with the commune population (column A). If the figure in column E is higher than the population total there will be a food surplus, but if it is lower then some people will go hungry. Enter the difference between A and E in column F (with a minus sign if E is lower than A).

4 The commune workforce is given in column B. 100 people are needed to farm 1 km² over a five-year period. Therefore 20 000 people are required to work the existing 200 km² of cultivated land (column G).

5 The remainder of the workforce (column H) is available to reclaim new land. The amount of labour required to bring each square kilometre into production is shown on Fig. 4.47. Decide how you are going to use the spare labour. On a tracing of Fig. 4.47 mark in the land that has been reclaimed by shading each square. You should use a different colour for each five-year period. Enter the appropriate number of square kilometres in column J.

6 Add the area of new land (column J) to the existing cultivated land (column C) and enter the total in column C for the next five-year period.

Fig. 4.45 Record card for commune planning exercise

Period	A Population (thousands)	B Workforce (thousands)	C Area under cultivation	D Weather	E Number of people fed	F Difference between A & E	G Workforce needed for cultivated land	H Spare labour	J New land added
1960–65	50·0	27·5	200 km²						
1965–70	56·5	31·5							
1970–75	64·0	36·5							
1975–80	70·5	40·5							
1980–85	76·0	45·0							
1985–90	82·0	49·0							

Fig. 4.46 Chance cards

1 Extremely good weather conditions. Each km² under cultivation supports 20 extra people for this period. Add 20 to figure in Fig. 4.48 for very good weather. Do not throw dice again.

2 Students brought in from nearby city to swell workforce. Add 1000 to columns A and B for this period only.

3 Some crops destroyed in storage. Foodstocks support 2000 fewer people for this period. Change figure in column E.

4 Severe floods. The 10 km² liable to flooding on Fig. 4.47 are now unsuitable for farming. If you want to return them to production, allocate 500 workers to each of the 10 km² for this period. If not, reduce figure in column C by 10.

5 Mechanization introduced on large scale. From now on workforce needed to farm existing land is 90 people per km². Therefore multiply figure in column C by 90 instead of 100 when filling in column G.

6 Drought. Each km² under cultivation supports 20 fewer people for this period. Subtract 20 from figure in Fig. 4.48 for very bad weather. Do not throw dice again.

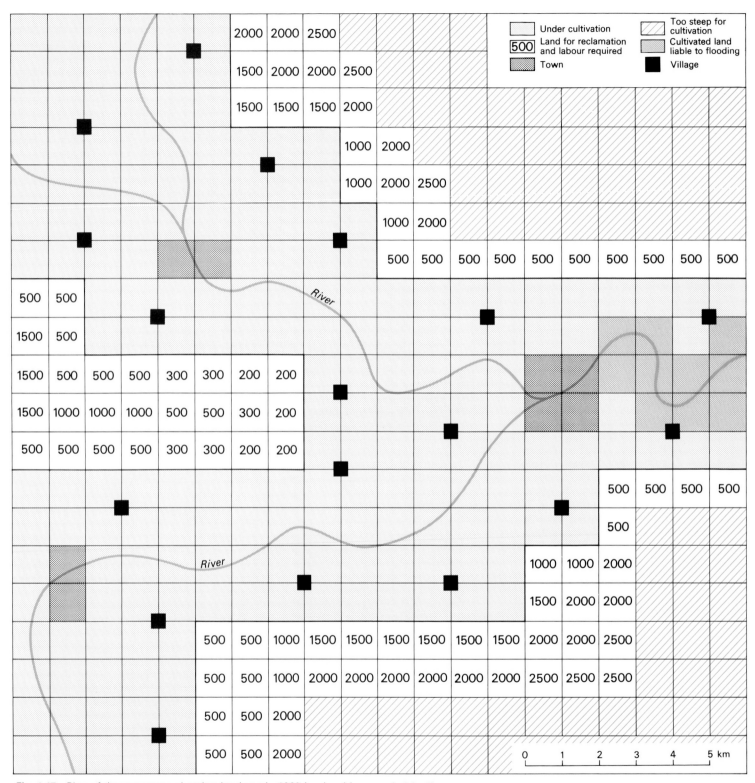

Fig. 4.47 Plan of the commune showing land use in 1960 (each grid square is 1 km²)

Fig. 4.48 The number of people supported by 1 km² of cultivated land

Period	Weather				
	Very bad	Bad	Average	Good	Very good
1960–65	230	240	250	260	270
1965–70	240	250	260	270	280
1970–75	250	260	270	280	290
1975–80	260	270	280	290	300
1980–85	270	280	290	300	310
1985–90	280	290	300	310	320

You are now ready to go on to the next five-year period, 1965–70, for which you should work through exactly the same steps as before. You can then carry on in the same fashion for each subsequent period up to 1990.

When you have completed the six time-periods you should have a traced map of the commune showing the full extent of the cultivated land. Since the overall population of the commune has increased between 1960 and 1990 you will need to mark in extra settlements on your map. These should take the form of an additional five km² of towns and eight more villages. Town squares can either be added on to existing towns or can be placed together to form new towns. The villages should be situated so that they serve the new areas of farmland. Draw in a system of main roads to serve the towns and villages.

Now consult your record card and commune map and answer the following questions:

a How much new land did you bring under cultivation?

b What effect would the expansion of the towns have had on this total?

c Why do you think the number of people which could be supported by each square kilometre increased with each time period?

d What was the total surplus or deficit in the number of people who could be fed during the thirty-year period? (Add the figures in column F). How did your total compare with other members of the class?

e How did the weather affect this total?

f How do you think the commune would have coped with a shortfall in its food supply?

g What did this exercise tell you about the relationship between population and resources?

h What other factors could have been included in this exercise to make it more realistic?

Summary

In this chapter we have seen how farming formed the basis for the development of man's civilizations. There are now many different types of farming throughout the world. Most agriculture in the Third World is carried out on a subsistence basis, with people growing crops for their own consumption. The demand for food is continually increasing as the population goes up. Third World farmers are held back by problems of poverty, poor health, pests, and unpredictable climates. Frequently patterns of land ownership lead to wasted effort or the exploitation of landless peasants. Some governments have implemented land reform programmes to redistribute land from a rich minority to the peasantry. The introduction of modern farming techniques has been a mixed blessing for developing countries. The green revolution has produced high-yielding crops but has increased the need for expensive fertilizers and machinery. Major agricultural developments, such as large-scale irrigation projects, have sometimes led to unexpected environmental problems.

Chapter 5 Health and hazards

Health and nutrition

People living in developed countries take good health and sanitation for granted, and it is easy to forget how much it costs to develop and maintain that security.

The requirements of a healthy life sound simple but they can be very difficult to achieve. A balanced diet is essential: this ensures healthy growth in children and provides resistance to infection. Pure water supplies are needed to avoid the dangers of water-borne disease. Good quality housing protects people from the harmful effects of climate and provides hygienic living conditions. A health service should be available for the treatment of illness and to educate people in hygiene and preventive medicine, while refuse disposal and sewage systems are necessary to remove waste safely and efficiently. Nowadays virtually everyone in developed countries enjoys living standards that meet these conditions. Yet the developed world has only been able to achieve this through massive investments of public money.

In comparison the developing countries are only just beginning to make progress towards a healthy society. They face many extra problems that make the task even harder. Economic difficulties mean that little money is available for improved medical services. Fig. 5.2 shows how poorly served the less developed countries are in comparison with the developed world. Rapid population growth undermines the effectiveness of whatever facilities are provided. The unreliable climate in the tropics makes food supplies less certain and the high temperatures encourage disease. Finally, the long distances and poor communications in many regions lead to severe difficulties in supplying medical help or spreading health education.

Diet is the key to a person's overall state of health. Food should provide the correct

Fig. 5.1 Indian mothers listen to a talk on nutrition in a village classroom

balance of carbohydrates, proteins, fats, vitamins, minerals, salts, and water. If one or more of these is lacking, then the person is likely to suffer from a deficiency disease.

Carbohydrates, proteins, and fats all provide the energy that is needed to keep someone alive. The energy supplied by food is usually measured in terms of calories. Different people have different energy requirements depending on their age, physique, and the sort of work they do. The average intake for healthy living is about 2500 calories per day but growing teenagers and people doing hard physical work may need as much as 4000 calories (Fig. 5.3).

1 **a** What types of food do you rely on to provide carbohydrates, fats, and proteins?
   b Find out what purpose vitamins serve in maintaining your health.

Fig. 5.2 Standards of health care

	Number of people per:	
	Doctor	Nurse
Low income countries	10300	9700
Middle income countries	4500	1900
Industrialized countries	630	210
Communist countries	400	240

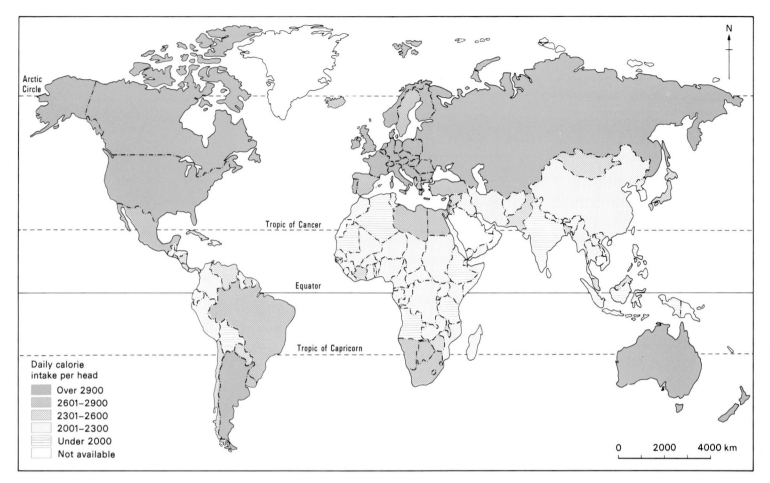

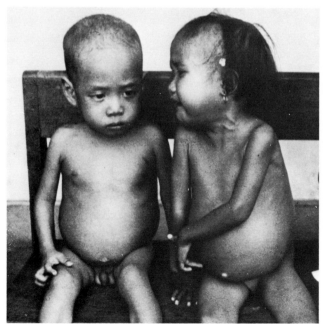

Fig. 5.3 World calorie intake

Fig. 5.4 Two children with kwashiorkor

It is important to understand the difference between undernourishment and malnutrition. Undernourishment refers to the lack of sufficient food, of any kind, to supply someone's energy requirements. Much more common though is malnutrition, when there is a lack of important proteins and vitamins in someone's diet, even though the total quantity of food may be adequate. In children malnutrition leads to a dreadful disease called kwashiorkor. Infants are especially liable to develop it when they are weaned from their mother's milk, which is full of protein, to the solid, starchy food commonly eaten by adults. The children in Fig. 5.4 are suffering from kwashiorkor: they have pot bellies swollen with fluid, puffy limbs, sores and thinning hair: they look weak and listless and their growth has slowed down. If they do not get protein-rich food they will eventually die.

Fig. 5.5 The development of a Tanzanian child between his first and third birthdays

Age in months	13	14	15	16	17	18	19	20	21	22	23	24	25	26	27	28	29	30	31	32	33	34	35	36
Weight in kg	8·6	8·6	9·1	9·5	8·6	8·2	8·6	9·1	9·5	10·0	10·5	10·5	10·5	10·9	11·4	11·8	10·9	10·5	10·5	10·9	11·4	11·8	12·3	12·3
Minimum weight*	8·0					8·9						10·0						10·9						11·6
Average weight†	10·2					11·1						12·3						13·2						14·1

Important events: 17 months – measles; 23 months – birth of sister; 29 months – malaria.

*The minimum weight is the lowest any child should register.   †The average weight is for a healthy and well-fed child.

Marasmus, a wasting disease caused by undernourishment, is common in the Third World today. It occurred in Britain in the nineteenth century, particularly among the poor children of the industrial cities. Another deficiency disease often found in Britain at that time was rickets: a bending of the bones caused by a lack of calcium.

Deficiency diseases, along with infectious diseases like measles and whooping cough, lead to high rates of infant mortality. Over 40 per cent of all deaths in less developed countries are among children under five, compared with only 3 per cent in the United Kingdom. Additionally, a poor diet in childhood can affect a person's potential for mental development. In general undernourished people are far more likely to catch diseases, especially during epidemics, because their body's natural resistance is much lower than that of someone with a healthy diet.

2 a Using Fig. 5.5, draw a line graph to show the changes in the child's weight in relation to the average and minimum levels. Put the child's age in months on the horizontal axis and the weight in kilograms on the vertical axis.

 b Mark in the important events at the appropriate ages. What effect did they have on the child's growth?

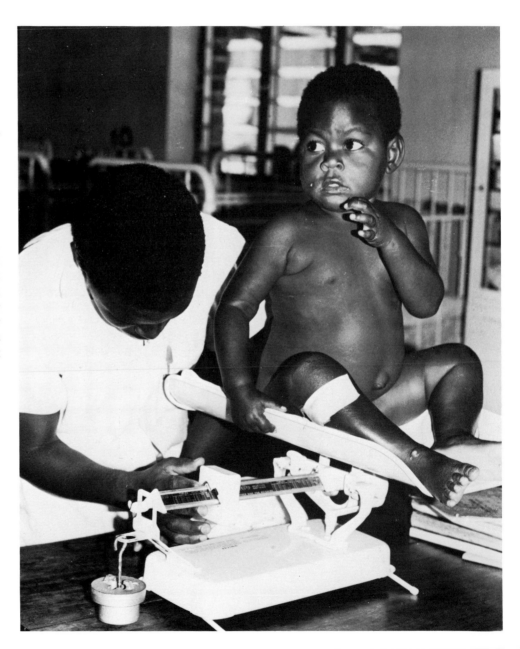

Fig. 5.6 Checking a child's weight at a clinic in Tanzania

3 Fig. 5.7 is a comparison of the average daily diet eaten by adults in India and Britain. Of course many people, especially in India, eat far less than this.

a Work out the total daily food consumption of the average Briton and Indian.

b What types of food form the main source of energy in each country?

c Which seems to be the better balanced diet? Why is this?

d What dangers to health might arise from each diet?

e Work out your diet for one day in the same way as the diagram. Is it well balanced?

f Find out roughly how many calories your diet represents. What is the average consumption for the class?

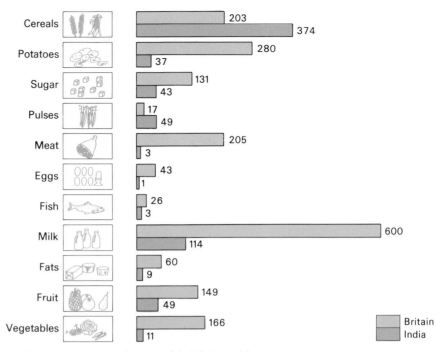

Fig. 5.7 Average daily diets (in grams) in Britain and India

In developed countries people observe simple rules of hygiene as a matter of course. This is easy to do thanks to the pure and plentiful water supplies, elaborate sewage systems, and wide range of cheap cleaning products. However, these facilities are very expensive to provide and are well beyond the reach of many people in less developed countries. Where no pure water supplies are available water should be boiled to make it safe, but the cost of fuel or firewood to do this could be prohibitive to a poor peasant. Education in simple hygiene is essential if the situation is to be improved in rural areas.

Fig. 5.8 Unhygienic conditions in the old part of an African city

Bringing health care to the countryside

One major failing of health services in developing countries is their uneven distribution. In particular trained doctors tend to be concentrated in the large cities, since these offer the best opportunities for work and the highest standard of living. Many doctors, having studied advanced medical techniques, go abroad to the developed countries where they can use them. Few are interested in tackling the relatively simple but tiring tasks of improving basic health and hygiene in the countryside. Investment in medical programmes is also frequently unbalanced. Large sums are spent constructing a sophisticated modern hospital in the city when the same money could have funded many basic rural health schemes.

In recent years some governments have recognized this problem and introduced health programmes based on medical auxiliaries. These are people from the countryside who are given short training programmes in the treatment of common diseases and in health education. They return to their local area, where they are known and trusted, and set up simple clinics and visiting services. The auxiliaries, who are far cheaper to train than doctors or nurses, also encourage birth control, vaccination, and improvements in family hygiene.

The use of medical auxiliaries was pioneered in China, where they are known as barefoot doctors. During the Cultural Revolution the structure of China's medical service was radically altered in favour of rural areas. The country's 1·3 million barefoot doctors, introduced at this time, now form the front line in community care, with a comprehensive support system as shown in Fig. 5.10. Medical students are selected and educated with community work very much in mind rather than academic knowledge. China has also incorporated elements of traditional medicine into its health service, such as acupuncture and herbal remedies.

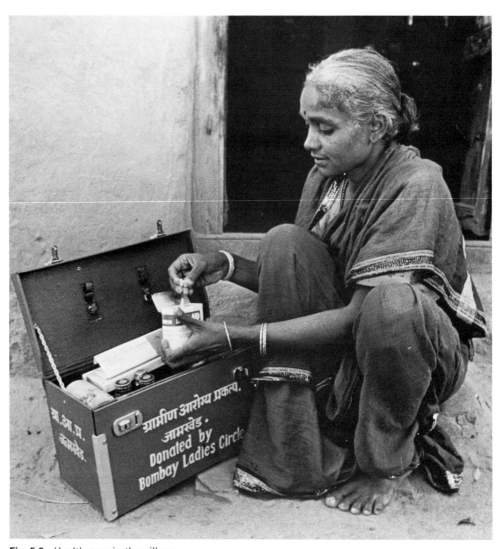

Fig. 5.9 Health care in the village

Where medical auxiliaries have been introduced, as for example in African states like Kenya, Malawi, Tanzania, and the Sudan, there is little doubt that rural people welcome the practical help and advice that the auxiliaries provide. Unfortunately in other countries the use of auxiliaries has been strongly opposed by established doctors who disapprove of their limited qualifications.

4 Look at Fig. 5.9.
  a What country is this?
  b Do you think the woman is a trained doctor or nurse? If not, what job might she be doing?
  c Is she likely to be from a city or the local area of the countryside?
  d What sort of medicines and equipment would you expect to be in the metal chest?
  e What types of disease or illness would she treat?
  f What do you think the Bombay Ladies Circle is? Why might it have paid for the medical chest?

Tanzania has a population of 16 million that is largely made up of poor subsistence farmers. Illiteracy is still widespread in rural areas and the size of the country makes communications very difficult. With conditions like this the radio represents a good way of reaching the population.

In 1973 a health education campaign was broadcast on the national radio network. Its aims were to provide information about specific diseases and encourage people to take positive action to prevent them. The campaign was named 'mtu ni afya', meaning 'man is health', and advance publicity had made it a household phrase by the time it started. Advertisements appeared in newspapers and on the radio, posters were displayed, and shirts and dresses were manufactured carrying the campaign symbol. Meanwhile district education officers were training 70 000 people to act as leaders for the radio study groups. Each group leader attended a two-day meeting and received a simple manual explaining the contents of the radio programmes. Twelve programmes were broadcast at the rate of one per week, to a total audience of 2 million, and the course proved very popular. The cost was extremely low because every group leader was an unpaid volunteer. The success of the campaign can be gauged by the construction of 700 000 new latrines throughout the country as a direct result of the course.

5 Fig. 5.11 is an illustration taken from the 'man is health' campaign manual. Redesign the illustrations so that they could be used as a series of flashcards without captions to accompany a talk to Tanzanian villagers.

Fig. 5.10 The structure of the Chinese health service

Barefoot doctor	Runs a clinic for 1000 people. Treats minor illnesses and promotes health and hygiene in the local area.
Mobile health teams	Train new barefoot doctors in their local area during the months of slack farming activity.
Street or commune hospital	Serves 25 000 people. Staffed by barefoot and fully trained doctors. Deals with simple medical and surgical problems.
District hospital	Serves 200 000 people. Has a fully trained medical staff. Offers a full medical and surgical service.
Major teaching hospital	Serves the entire population of a region. Trains doctors and surgeons. Offers a wide range of medical facilities including specialized treatment.

Fig. 5.11 Health education in Tanzania

1 Take water that comes from a good source.

2 Pour the water into a second jar. Let it settle.

3 Boil some of the water for drinking.

4 The boiled water should be kept in a good place and should be covered.

5 The remaining water can be used for washing utensils.

Cholera: an epidemic disease

Now we will look closely at three diseases which affect hundreds of millions of people in the Third World. Each is passed on in a different way.

Cholera is a highly infectious disease that can spread rapidly through the human population if favourable conditions exist. It thrives in conditions where sanitation is poor since the organisms find their way into the water supply. It is caught by swallowing food or water contaminated by the wastes of people suffering from the disease. These wastes, faeces or vomit, contain the infective comma-shaped bacillus. When the bacillus reaches the intestine it causes diarrhoea, violent vomiting, and painful cramp. The victim quickly loses large amounts of body fluid, including vital body

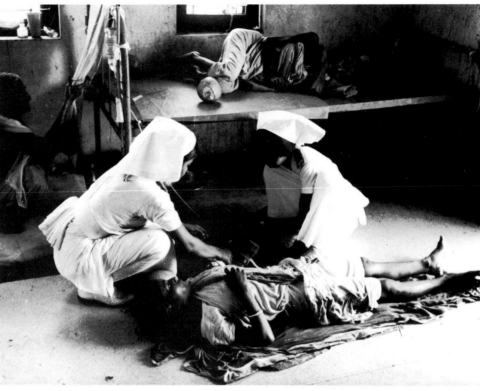

Fig. 5.13 Emergency treatment of cholera patients at a hospital in India

Fig. 5.12 Base map of West Africa

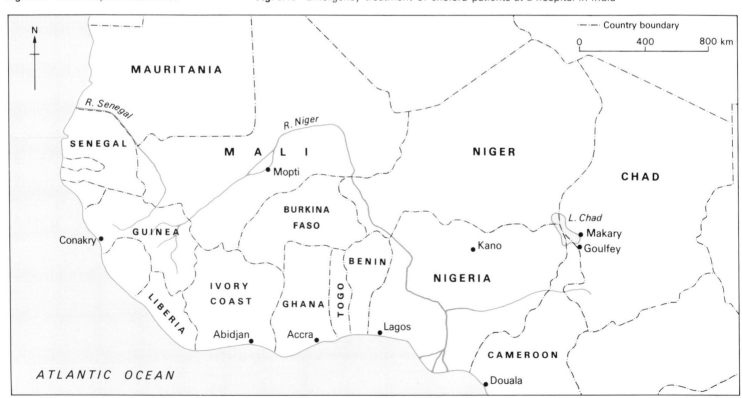

salts, which leads to severe dehydration. If left untreated cholera kills about 60 per cent of its victims within two to six days, though a person may die within a few hours. Nowadays prompt treatment using antibiotics and replacing the lost fluids can cure the disease completely.

In the nineteenth century ideal conditions for the spread of cholera existed in all large towns. The traditional home of cholera is in the hot, marshy lowlands of India, Bangladesh, Burma, and Thailand. Six times during the nineteenth century the disease advanced from this region to affect most of Asia, and on several occasions Europe and the USA as well. The occurrence of an epidemic on a continental scale is known as a pandemic. Britain was affected by four of the six pandemics, which killed millions of people worldwide.

In the twentieth century cholera gradually retreated back to India and by the 1950s it was thought that the disease was disappearing naturally. Then suddenly in 1961 a new pandemic flared up in Sulawesi and spread throughout South-East Asia with astonishing speed. The disease was a particularly vicious and deadly strain known as cholera El Tor. By 1970 cholera was present in South-East and Southern Asia, the Middle East, and North and West Africa.

6 a Make a copy of Fig. 5.12. On this base map plot the spread of cholera El Tor in West Africa from the information in Fig. 5.14. Use arrows to show the movement of infected people from one location to another and add a numbered key to explain who the carriers of the disease were.

 b Why were the outbreaks so difficult to control?

7 The small news item on the right appeared at the bottom of an inside page in a national newspaper in Britain in September 1979. Why do you think it received so little attention?

Fig. 5.14 The spread of cholera in West Africa

August 1970	Party of Guinean students fly home to Conakry from Moscow, where they are studying, after taking a holiday on the Black Sea. First cases of cholera El Tor diagnosed in Guinea soon afterwards: Black Sea resorts had already suffered from cholera.
September 1970	Infected cholera carrier flies from Conakry to Accra in Ghana.
October 1970	Fishermen of the Fanti tribe, originally from Ghana, leave Guinea and sail eastwards along the coast to Abidjan and Accra. They may have been following migrating fish, but some reports suggest that the Guinean government expelled them.
November 1970	The swampy, lagoon coasts provide ideal breeding grounds for the disease. Ghanaian fishermen move east, infecting the coast between Accra and Lagos in Nigeria. From Abidjan a fish trader takes the disease to the market town of Mopti, 1600 km north on the River Niger.
December 1970	The coastal spread of the disease continues east to Douala in Cameroon.
February 1971	Unknowing carriers take cholera from Lagos to Kano, where deaths reach 300 a day at the height of the epidemic.
April 1971	Cholera spreads from Kano throughout the towns of northern Nigeria. Smugglers carry the disease to the tiny town of Makary on Lake Chad.
May 1971	20 000 people assemble in Goulfey for a religious ceremony, having travelled from Cameroon, Chad and Nigeria. Cholera spreads rapidly through the visitors and the inhabitants of Goulfey. The infected travellers carry the disease back to their home districts.
August 1971	Following the infection of Mopti in November 1970 nomadic people who had visited the market there carried cholera into the surrounding countryside. Now mourners attending funerals in Mali contract the disease and carry it back to their homelands in Senegal. By the end of 1971 cholera is rife along the Senegal and Niger rivers.

Cholera deaths

The Zaire cholera epidemic has killed 3500 and affected 36000 people so far this year, according to reports reaching Kinshasa. Belgium, the former colonial power, has given aid along with Britain, West Germany, and America.

Malaria

Malaria is an infectious disease that affects over 200 million people today, mostly in the tropics (Fig. 5.15). The disease is caused by a tiny parasite carried by the female anopheles mosquito. If a mosquito bites someone infected with malaria it picks up the parasite as it feeds on that person's blood. In warm conditions the parasite matures inside the mosquito and passes back into the human bloodstream when the mosquito bites someone else. The parasite lodges in the person's liver and then produces thousands of offspring which invade and destroy the blood cells. In some cases malaria can kill but more often it brings on fever and robs the victim of his energy.

Malaria was common in Europe until the mid-nineteenth century when improved sanitary conditions and public health made it difficult for mosquitoes to breed. The widespread use of the drug quinine to treat malaria sufferers meant that the disease had been eliminated in Europe by 1900. However, it was not until the invention of the insecticide DDT in the 1940s that malaria could be tackled in the tropics. After 1950 the World Health Organization started a long-term programme of chemical warfare against malaria. Aerial spraying of mosquito-breeding grounds with DDT was carried out on a massive scale. The walls of houses were also sprayed with DDT since mosquitoes tended to rest there after biting people. Another technique was to spray oil on the stagnant pools and marshes where the mosquitoes laid their eggs. Then in the 1960s it was realized that DDT polluted the environment very badly and its use was strictly controlled. Now DDT is banned in Europe and North America.

Nevertheless, there were high hopes in the 1960s that malaria could be completely banished from large parts of the world. Unfortunately subsequent events have proved otherwise and the World Health Organization has been forced to admit defeat. Massive programmes in India and its neighbours were close to achieving eradication, but now the trend has been reversed. Malaria is

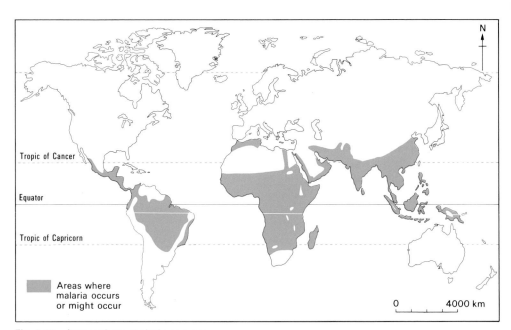

Tropic of Cancer

Equator

Tropic of Capricorn

Areas where malaria occurs or might occur

0   4000 km

Fig. 5.15   Areas where malaria can occur

Fig. 5.16   Taking blood tests as part of an anti-malaria campaign in Ghana

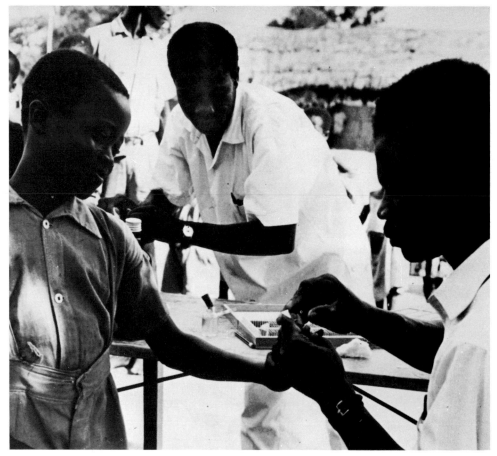

on the increase again throughout southern Asia and Central America. In Africa, where the situation has always been bad, the severe lack of medical facilities is making things worse. Virtually every child has caught malaria by the age of one, 10 per cent of them dying from the disease in infancy.

8 Study Fig. 5.17.

a Use the diagram to write an explanation of the way in which the malaria parasite (plasmodium) relies on both mosquito and man for its survival.

b Listed below are a number of ways in which the malaria cycle could be broken. Make a copy of Fig. 5.17 and mark in the points on the diagram where each line of attack would be made.

1 Destroy the mosquito larvae on the water surface (as they hatch from eggs) or as they are swimming in the water in search of food and oxygen.

2 Attack the adult mosquitoes, usually with insecticides, concentrating particularly on females resting after a blood meal.

3 Release large numbers of specially sterilized male mosquitoes which will swamp the natural, fertile males and therefore prevent breeding.

4 Protect susceptible people by the use of preventive drugs, which can now be administered on a large scale.

5 Treat infected people through the widespread application of drugs such as quinine and modern chemical compounds.

There are a variety of reasons for the resurgence of malaria. The most worrying is that some mosquitoes have developed resistance to the most common insecticides, while other breeds produce a strain of malaria that does not respond to the standard drug treatment. Fortunately so far these two characteristics have not occurred in the same breed of mosquito. Resistance is increased by the use of insecticides to

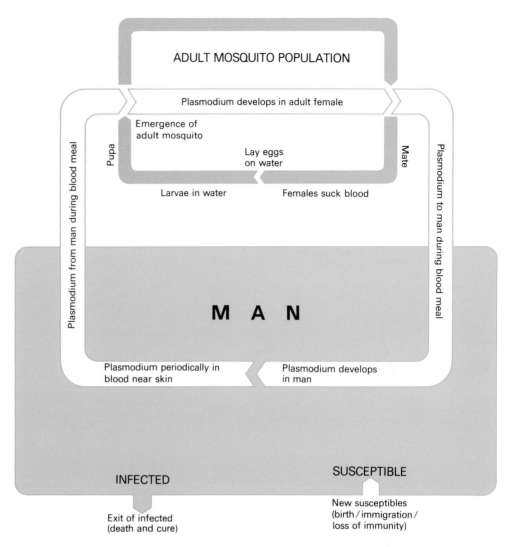

Fig. 5.17 The malaria cycle

protect crops. If insecticides were used purely to improve public health, then the build-up of mosquito resistance would be much slower. New insecticides have been developed to combat malaria but they are very dangerous, very costly, and can kill only certain mosquitoes. A further problem is that some mosquitoes have changed their breeding habits and are now much harder to reach.

A major setback to the eradication programmes has been the spiralling cost of the chemicals they use. Insecticides are oil-based, and the 1973 oil crisis led to a dramatic rise in costs which forced a reduction in the amounts of insecticides used. In

addition, the governments of several countries have switched money from malaria programmes to other projects as their budgets come under pressure.

The most practical solution now seems to lie in the control of environments where mosquitoes breed. This is very important in the rice-growing lands of South-East Asia where the abundance of standing water presents an enormous hazard. Malaria control also relies on developing a sense of responsibility in people, so that they take more precautions to protect their health. The Chinese have used propaganda in the rural communes to brand malaria as a social disease to be avoided at all costs.

Bilharzia

Bilharzia is a disease that is widespread in tropical countries, affecting over 200 million people, 10 per cent of whom die from the disease each year. It is common among poor farmers and fishermen who have to work frequently in polluted water. The disease saps their strength and can seriously affect their ability to produce the food they need. Fig. 5.18, which explains how the disease spreads, is an example of an educational programme for children in Brazil.

There are two main ways of tackling the eradication of bilharzia. The first is to educate people about the importance of sanitary conditions; getting them to use a latrine or bury waste. The second method is to kill the snails which harbour the larvae.

Although chemicals can be used for this they are not completely effective and require an expensive system of repeated treatments. The Chinese have waged a far more effective campaign by digging out and removing snail-infested mud from irrigation canals. Although there is a distant possibility that a simple vaccine against bilharzia may be developed the most practical way forward must be through education.

Fig. 5.18 How bilharzia spreads

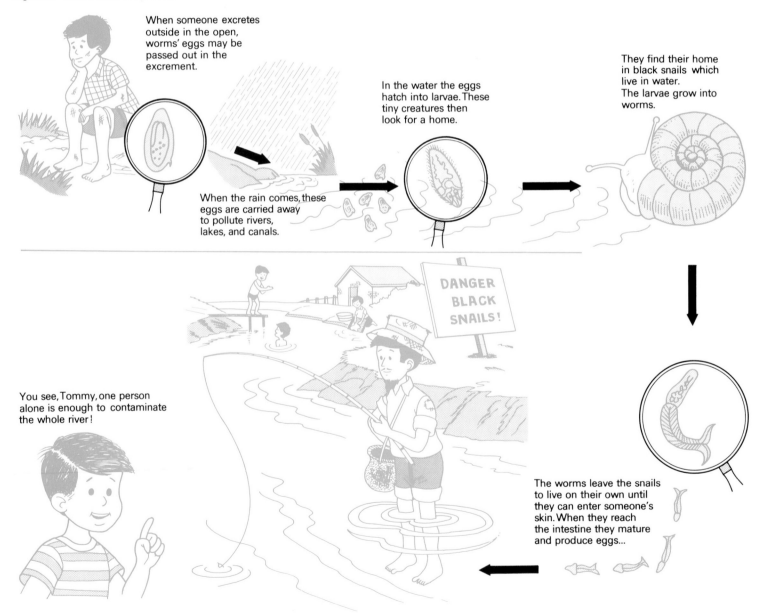

When someone excretes outside in the open, worms' eggs may be passed out in the excrement.

When the rain comes, these eggs are carried away to pollute rivers, lakes, and canals.

In the water the eggs hatch into larvae. These tiny creatures then look for a home.

They find their home in black snails which live in water. The larvae grow into worms.

DANGER BLACK SNAILS!

The worms leave the snails to live on their own until they can enter someone's skin. When they reach the intestine they mature and produce eggs...

You see, Tommy, one person alone is enough to contaminate the whole river!

Natural disasters

The term natural disaster is applied to the destructive effects of events such as droughts, floods, hurricanes, earthquakes, volcanic eruptions, and tidal waves. The severity of the disaster is usually judged by the toll of dead and injured, the destruction of property, and the overall number of people affected. It is not the natural event itself that is disastrous, but the impact it has on man. Some people think that the term natural disaster is misleading. It suggests that the disaster is unavoidable, an act of God, when in fact it is circumstances that lead to casualties and damage. It is argued that very often man is responsible for the circumstances that give rise to disaster. In recent years disasters have become more frequent and more destructive. A higher proportion of the people affected have died and the total number of people involved has increased. In 1973 alone there were twenty-five major disasters which killed 110 000 people, affected a further 215 million, and cost £500 million.

It is no coincidence that the people who suffer most from disasters are the world's poor as they cannot afford to protect themselves in the way that wealthier people can. If drought strikes they have fewer reserves to tide them over the hard times. Because they live in flimsy housing it is more likely to be destroyed when a hurricane or earthquake hits them. They have a lower resistance to disease and the after-effects of disaster because they are already weakened by an inadequate diet.

As landlessness and unemployment increase so the options open to the poor are narrowed. For example, it is only this century that hunger for land forced people to inhabit the flood-prone coastal lowlands of Bangladesh. Overpopulation is often quoted as a reason for the seriousness of disasters in poor countries. But people are only prepared to limit their families when they have achieved security. Until then having a large family is the easiest form of insurance, even if it increases the risk of loss.

Fig. 5.19   Devastation caused by a tropical cyclone in India

Fig. 5.20   Earthquake damage in Guatemala

Floods in Bangladesh and India

In 1970 a tropical cyclone moved northwards up the Bay of Bengal towards Bangladesh, at that time called East Pakistan. The cyclone, a violent storm with winds reaching 240 km per hour, built up before it a mass of water, known as a storm surge. As the surge swept towards the head of the bay the narrowing coastline forced it into a wall of water 7 metres high. In this area the coast consists of dozens of small, low-lying islands and the marshy flats of the Ganges delta. The water crashed across the islands, carrying away people in their thousands, and then poured over the delta flats to demolish hundreds of villages. Survivors clung desperately to trees as the water surged around them, filled with the floating bodies of men, women, children, and farm animals. Over 300 000 people died on what came to be called 'black Thursday', as well as 350 000 oxen and 150 000 cows.

The destruction of property was immense. Nine thousand fishing boats were wrecked and many ploughs, essential to agriculture, were lost. Eighty per cent of the rice crop was ruined and the land was badly affected by salt from the seawater. It could not be used again for farming until a long period of rains had soaked through the soil to remove the salt. But once the water had retreated there were far more pressing problems to be dealt with. The immediate need was for food, shelter, and medical supplies for the survivors. The Pakistan army was assigned to relief work and began by dropping food and supplies from the air. Much of this was wasted though when it smashed on impact or fell beyond reach of survivors. Effective relief operations could only begin after roads had been repaired or reconstructed.

In response to a United Nations appeal fifty countries sent a total of £25 million in aid. Most of this was used to provide short-term relief. To help rebuild the area's shattered economy the World Bank provided an interest-free loan of £11 million. This was to be used to re-establish settlements, the transport network, and the local fishing industry. But the following years gave little opportunity for recovery. In 1971 the country was engulfed by the short but destructive war that made it into the independent nation of Bangladesh. Two years later a serious drought slashed agricultural production at a time when world food prices were rocketing. In 1974 the farmers were hit again by disastrous floods. It is circumstances like this that have kept Bangladesh one of the poorest countries in the world.

9 In London a special barrier has been built across the River Thames at Woolwich (Fig. 5.22). It is designed to protect the capital from the effects of a storm surge.
   a Find out how the barrier works and how much it cost to build.
   b Why might London be in danger of suffering a storm surge?
   c What would be the consequences if a barrier had not been built?

Fig. 5.21 Animals drowned in a cyclone

Fig. 5.22 The Thames flood barrier under construction

The death toll in the floods in India's West Bengal state is at least 300 and the final figure undoubtedly will be much higher. Buses, trams, and cars in Calcutta stand in waist-deep water, having been stranded for more than five days. Shops have put up their shutters. The few offices open are thinly attended because public transport has broken down. The harried Chief Minister of the State, Mr Jyoti Basu, says: 'It's a real disaster'.

Mr Basu, who has taken personal charge of relief and rescue work, has just returned from persuading bakeries to step up production and pleading with wholesalers not to raise prices. Despite his unflagging efforts, Mr Basu has still to get the better of the worst floods ever to hit West Bengal. The rain, now in its fifth consecutive day, has flattened shanties, brought down houses, and silenced jute mills and factories. There is no drinking water, telephones do not work, trains limp into Howrah sta-tion days late, and naked children cry for food as drenched mothers stand helplessly outside collapsed huts pleading for help.

It will be days before Calcutta limps back to anything near normality. It will take weeks before damage from the flooded districts can be estimated and months to restore the shattered economy of the state, the most heavily industrialized in the country. Its two steel plants, most of the coal mines, and the two ports of Calcutta and Haldia are paralysed. Warehouses with jute manufactures and raw jute are under 3 metres of water and nearly all jute and padi fields have been washed away. Many power stations have ceased generating and officials say that few roads will survive.

The floods began with unrelenting and unseasonal rain on 27 September. About 750 mm fell in less than twenty-four hours before settling to a steady downpour that still continues. Then came reports of equally heavy rain in the catchment areas of the Damodar and other rivers which caused flash floods that created havoc in West Bengal's twenty-four districts.

The state estimates that crops on 1 million hectares have been destroyed for the third time this year. Part of the jute crop on 0·4 million hectares was harvested before the floods, but about half has probably been destroyed. Plans are being made to supply fertilizers and seed for wheat, potatoes, rice, and pulses but no one knows when distribution will begin and when farmers will be able to resume work. Tentative estimates are that damaged irrigation canals and river embankments will cost £12 million to repair.

The Chief Minister has asked for a relatively modest £180 million from the central government. This is probably intended for coping with immediate relief work, such as preventing the spread of disease.

Fig. 5.23 A report from the *Financial Times*, October 1978

The extract from a British newspaper (Fig. 5.23) describes the effects of flooding during heavy rainfall in West Bengal, the Indian state that lies next to Bangladesh. Before you read it make sure that you understand the difference between floods due to heavy rainfall and those due to a storm surge.

10 After you have read the newspaper report, locate the area in your atlas and find Calcutta (see p. 132).

a Why would you expect the city of Calcutta and its surroundings to suffer serious flooding in the event of heavy rainfall?

b How much rain fell in the first twenty-four hours? Compare this with the *annual* rainfall in your local area. What proportion of Calcutta's average annual rainfall of 1570 mm did this single day represent?

c Find the Damodar river, west of Calcutta. Why would heavy rain here add to Calcutta's problems?

Fig. 5.24 People drinking contaminated water during the West Bengal floods

d Make a list of all the problems that resulted from the floods. Divide them up into those that affected the city and those that affected the rural areas; did any affect both?

e Now divide the problems up into those that presented immediate difficulties and those that were likely to be long-term.

f How do you think international aid could be used best to tackle the after-effects of the floods?

Drought in the Sahel

Drought is one of nature's most common and persistent hazards, and is by no means limited to hot and dry countries. In 1976 Britain experienced a severe drought that put water supplies at risk throughout the country. But Britain normally receives rainfall all the year round and the wet winter that followed soon cured the shortage. Most tropical countries though experience distinct wet and dry seasons and consequently a failure of the annual rains can be disastrous. The most vulnerable areas are those with low total rainfall since even a small variation below the average can be critical.

The Sahel belt of West Africa is such an area. The word Sahel is Arabic for 'fringe' and refers to the belt of land that separates the southern edge of the Sahara desert from the much wetter area of the West African coast. It is a region about 300 to 500 km wide stretching from the Atlantic coast eastwards to the area of Lake Chad.

11 a Trace the outline of the West African coast from Fig. 5.25 and then draw a series of lines joining all the points with the same value. This will produce isohyets (lines of equal rainfall) for 100 mm, 300 mm, 650 mm, 900 mm, and 1200 mm.
  b What is the pattern of rainfall distribution in West Africa?

12 Transfer the information given in Fig. 5.26 to the appropriate areas of your map as follows:
  a Mark each region clearly with its name at the side of the map.
  b Shade in the different crop zones using appropriate colours: e.g. yellow for grain, light brown for groundnuts, dark green for roots, light green for rice, dark brown for cocoa, and red for oil palms.
  c Label the 300 mm isohyet as 'northern limit for crops' and shade blue the narrow strip of cultivated floodland along the River Niger in the Sahel (see also Fig. 5.12).
  d Also label the areas where cattle are raised along with crops and the grazing land used by the nomadic herders.
  e Write a paragraph describing the relationship between rainfall and land use in West Africa.

The Sahel receives all its rainfall during the summer months, with the bulk falling in July, August, and September. All crops must be grown during this short rainy season. Most rain arrives in the form of sudden downpours produced by tropical storms moving in from the Gulf of Guinea. This leads to wide local variations in rainfall and to a general unreliability from year to year. In marginal regions like the Sahel farmers are totally at the mercy of the weather.

Fig. 5.25 Average annual rainfall (millimetres) in West Africa

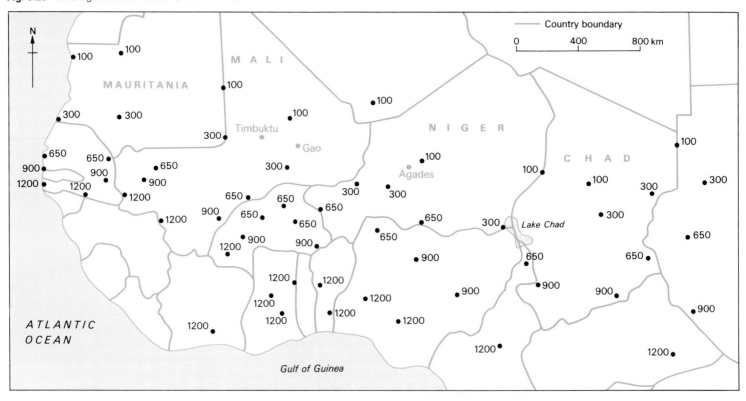

Fig. 5.26 Climatic and agricultural regions in West Africa

Region	Annual rainfall mm	Vegetation	Commercial agriculture	Subsistence agriculture
Coastal	Over 1200	Tropical forest	Cocoa in Ghana and SW Nigeria; oil palms in SE Nigeria	Rice on west coast; roots (cassava and yams) on south coast
Southern interior	900–1200	Savanna woodland	None	Mixed roots and grains
Sudan	650–900	Savanna grassland with trees	Groundnuts in N. Nigeria and Senegal; cattle in same areas	Grains (guinea corn and millet)
Sahel	300–650	Savanna grassland	Cattle grazing	Grains only along floodlands of R. Niger
Semi-desert	100–300	Scrubland	None	Nomadic herding
Desert	Under 100	None	None	Nomadic herding

Fig. 5.27 Rainfall in the Sahel as a percentage of the average rainfall

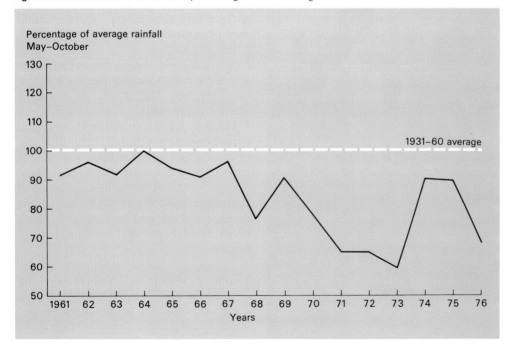

Between 1968 and 1973 the summer rains failed five times in the Sahel. Fig. 5.27 shows how the drought became progressively worse over the six-year period as rainfall dropped well below its normal level. By 1973 the drought was headline news throughout the world and foreign aid began to arrive in the stricken countries. The people worst hit by the drought were the nomadic herders, tribes like the Tuareg and the Fulani. As their traditional grazing areas dried up the nomads moved several hundred kilometres south in search of reliable water and better pastures. This brought them into conflict with the permanent farmers and put an even greater strain on the slim natural resources.

Inevitably the parched grassland and meagre water supplies could not support the added load and animals died in their thousands. Although the overall death-rate of the animals was about 35 per cent some nomads lost their entire herds and became destitute. During the previous major drought of 1914–18 the nomadic tribes survived through their traditional system of loans and obligations, which allowed them to build up new herds away from the worst areas of drought. Now their movement was limited by national boundaries and they could not rely on the old ways of coping with the crisis. The promise of free food drew them towards the relief camps at towns like Gao, Timbuktu, and Agades and many settled there permanently. However, the distribution of relief was highly unreliable due to poor transport facilities and much did not reach the worse-hit areas. Some food supplies fell into the hands of corrupt local officials, to be sold at inflated prices on the black market.

Weakened by malnutrition, the inhabitants of the relief camps were struck by epidemics of measles and influenza, causing many deaths. There is no way of knowing the true number of casualties since the Sahel stretches across several countries and the nomads had never been included in a census. It is possible that the influx of foreign aid that arrived in 1973 made the situation even worse by attracting nomads to the relief camps where it was distributed.

Fig. 5.28 A victim of the Sahel drought

Fig. 5.29 Tuareg nomads collect food at a relief camp in Niger

The aftermath of the drought left many problems. Large numbers of nomads were still living around the desert towns when the relief camps closed in 1975. Some had sold their herds with the intention of settling permanently. It has been suggested that governments saw this as an opportunity to solve their 'nomad problem' once and for all. One official said: 'We have to discipline these people, and to control their grazing and their movements. Their liberty is too expensive for us. This disaster is our opportunity.'

Yet the drought crisis and the loss of herds represented a severe economic setback for the Sahel countries of Mali, Niger, and Chad as they rely heavily on the income from meat sales to the West African market. In some cases their GNP was reduced by 50 per cent. This in turn led to a political crisis in several countries. Both Niger and Upper Volta had military coups in 1974. Since the drought the Sahel governments have been seeking aid from the United Nations to pay for ambitious agricultural programmes. The UN Food and Agriculture Organization has plans to replace the subsistence agriculture of the Sahel with commercial arable and livestock farming. These would involve the introduction of irrigated high-yielding grains as cash crops and the establishment of pasture management services. They would also spell the end for the nomads.

However, environmentalists believe that nomadic herding is the only reasonable way of exploiting the Sahel belt: any type of sedentary farming encourages desertification and will lead to the destruction of all vegetation. But the combined effects of the drought and the governments' action have undermined the nomads' traditional way of life.

13 Fig. 5.30 looks at the problems of the nomads from two viewpoints: the nomads' and the governments'. For each viewpoint there is a corresponding action; these are listed on the right of Fig. 5.30 and are not in the correct order. Decide which action goes with each view.

Governments' view

1 The nomads just wander aimlessly in a never-ending search for pasture.

2 We must limit this needless movement so we can collect taxes and use their labour.

3 We could encourage the nomads to raise herds for profit and benefit ourselves from trading with them.

 Nomads' view

1 We follow traditional routes that make the best use of a risky environment.

2 We must be able to move freely as our routes change according to climatic conditions.

3 We are not interested in selling our animals. They provide all our needs and are a sign of wealth.

A MAJOR DROUGHT OCCURS

4 The loss of human and animal life is shocking. We must solve the problem of drought.

5 We can use our superior technology to overcome the shortage of water.

6 The nomads' herds are very unhealthy and prone to disease. We can improve their quality.

4 Droughts and famines have always happened. We accept them as part of the risks we face.

5 The new water supplies are much more reliable and convenient. We must change our routes.

6 The new medicines will protect our animals. Now we can own more because fewer will die from disease.

OVERGRAZING AND CLIMATIC CHANGE LEAD TO INCREASING DESERTIFICATION

7 The nomads' herds are too large for the pastures available. We must reduce them.

7 The pastures are getting worse. We must keep as many animals as possible to allow for those that die.

MAJOR DROUGHT 1968–73

8 The nomads are to blame for the advancing desert. They must be settled permanently.

9 Now that the nomads are helpless we can make sure that they do not go back to their old ways.

8 Conditions in our traditional lands are hopeless. We must find better pastures.

9 Our herds have been destroyed. We have no option but to get food in the relief camps.

IN 1975 THE RELIEF CAMPS WERE CLOSED BUT THOUSANDS OF NOMADS WITHOUT ANIMALS STILL LIVE AROUND TOWNS

 Governments' action

A Large-scale vaccination programmes are carried out.

B Ways of improving the natural water supply are investigated.

C Nomads are persuaded to become settled farmers when crisis is over.

D Attempts are made to control nomads.

E Nomadic tribes are ignored by early colonists.

F Deep wells and storage tanks are dug.

G Attempts are made by colonists to set up livestock markets.

H Territorial frontiers established by colonists.

I Nomads are offered high prices to encourage them to sell animals.

 Nomads' action

A They fall back on traditional methods of surviving the drought.

B Their move to relief camps makes them dependent on food aid.

C The size of their herds increases, causing overgrazing.

D No changes are made in their traditional lifestyle.

E Even fewer animals than usual are sold.

F Herds are concentrated on new wells, causing overgrazing on surrounding land.

G Moving several hundred kilometres further south, they clash with permanent farmers.

H Only a few animals are sold, usually the worst.

I They become aggressive over loss of lands.

Fig. 5.30 How intervention altered the nomads' life in the Sahel

An earthquake in Nicaragua

In December 1972 an earthquake devastated Managua, the capital of the Central American republic of Nicaragua. The earthquake was not especially strong but it was centred right on the city and caused severe destruction. This was the fourth time within a hundred years that Managua had been hit by a significant earthquake. The previous time, in 1931, the city was almost totally destroyed. It was rebuilt then along traditional lines, with closely packed buildings and narrow streets. As an old Spanish colonial city, Managua's most important sections were clustered round the central square. The majority of houses were built of wooden slats filled with stone and mortar, though the poorest people made do with mud huts. Over the next forty years Managua's population swelled to half a million, representing 25 per cent of the national total. The layout of the city remained unaltered, leading to hopelessly overcrowded housing and congested streets.

When the 1972 earthquake struck the shocks lasted for two hours but 'the killer' came just after midnight. Buildings collapsed on people and rubble filled the streets. The traditional wooden houses were death traps with fires spreading rapidly through the crowded blocks. The few fire engines still operational could not get through the debris covering the roads. When the water supply failed the city was helpless. The death toll for the disaster was over 10 000, with a further 20 000 injured and 50 000 made homeless.

It was soon clear that the city centre had suffered the greatest damage while the surrounding areas were less affected. The government refused to send relief supplies into the city centre in the hope that this would force people to move out, so minimizing the risk of disease. Emergency food stocks, flown in from abroad, were left waiting at the airport. Inside the shattered city the food shortage led to rioting and looting as law and order broke down completely. Eventually the army was sent in to re-establish control.

14 What aspects of Managua's design and construction were responsible for the great loss of life in the earthquake? How might these dangers be reduced when rebuilding the city?

Once it was possible to assess the cost of the earthquake it was found to represent 40 per cent of Nicaragua's gross national product. The central business district of shops, offices, and government buildings was in ruins and 50 000 people had lost their jobs. Every hospital in the city had been destroyed and all the public utilities (sewage disposal, water mains, and electricity supplies) were totally disrupted.

Fig. 5.31 Survivors of the Managua earthquake leave the ruined city

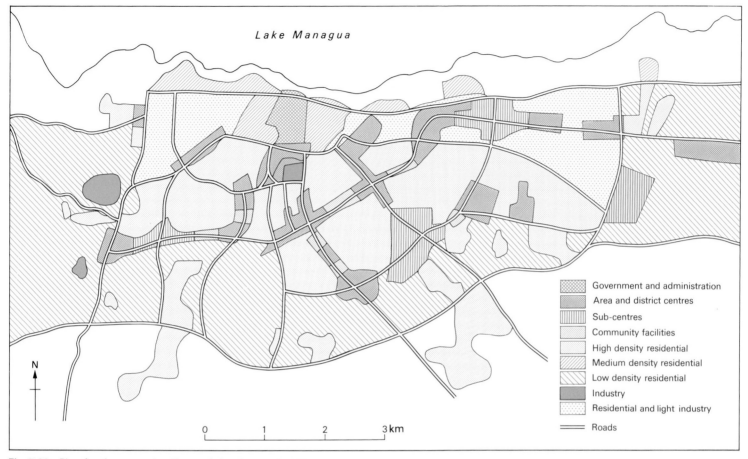

Lake Managua

Government and administration
Area and district centres
Sub-centres
Community facilities
High density residential
Medium density residential
Low density residential
Industry
Residential and light industry
Roads

N

0   1   2   3 km

Fig. 5.32 Plan for the reconstruction and development of Managua

The government set about the task of reconstruction very quickly. The possibility of moving the capital elsewhere was considered but rejected as uneconomic. In any case there was the danger of earthquakes throughout the entire region, so a new site would be no safer. A national emergency committee was set up to co-ordinate the relief programme and decide on a rebuilding plan. There were two key policies for the reconstruction of Managua: deconcentration and decentralization. The city was to be built at a lower density than before and would be constructed to much higher safety standards.

15 Look at Fig. 5.32. What features of the new layout for Managua reflect the principles of deconcentration and decentralization?

16 It will take up to fifteen years to rebuild Managua completely. If you were a member of the national emergency committee what order of priority would you put on each of the items in the following list: offices, shops, hospitals, water mains, low-cost housing, schools, electricity supplies, civic buildings, factories, sewers, medium-cost housing, telephone system, public parks, high-cost housing.

a Rearrange the list into the order of importance that you would support.

b Write a paragraph explaining your reasons.

Summary

Poor health is one of the greatest handicaps to development. Many people in the Third World have to survive on an unbalanced diet, making them weak and prone to disease. They cannot work so effectively and this reduces their ability to support themselves. The bulk of the suffering is in the countryside where there are few health facilities. Many diseases flourish in a tropical climate and their control or eradication is a long and costly process. The developing countries also tend to suffer more from natural disasters: hurricanes, earthquakes, floods, and drought are common and the poor are especially vulnerable to their destructive effects.

Chapter **6** People on the move

What is migration?

Migration, in terms of human movement, is usually concerned with a permanent change of home, but it can also apply to temporary movements such as those of nomads. Migrations are very difficult to classify because they differ so much. They can vary in their causes, the time taken, the distance travelled, the direction of movement, and the number and type of people involved. To study migrations properly they have to be measured: for this it is essential that people cross some sort of boundary where this movement can be counted. The most important of these are national frontiers and for this reason migration is often divided into two categories: internal and international. Internal migration covers movement within a country, international migration is the flow of people between different countries. The population of a country will fall or rise according to the number of people who leave it (emigration) and arrive (immigration).

Another broad classification is to distinguish between movements that are made voluntarily and those that are made due to force of circumstance. Voluntary or 'free' migrations are more common than forced movements and are generally prompted by a desire for better living standards or greater personal freedom. People who decide to migrate voluntarily will have been influenced by what are called 'push' and 'pull' factors. Push factors are aspects of their current life which encourage them to move away. Pull factors are the forces which attract the migrants to a particular destination.

Forced migrations can occur for a variety of reasons, both natural and man-made. Environmental disasters like floods or drought, leading to crop failure and famine, will always cause movement, though now international relief organizations help tackle such situations. The problems associated with overpopulation, especially in small poor countries, ensure substantial emigration, as in the case of the Caribbean islands. Sometimes migration is dictated by economic forces, the most notorious example being the trans-Atlantic slave trade which supplied cheap labour for American plantations. Finally, political pressure can cause large-scale migration: wars or persecution inevitably create refugees and there are many instances this century of people being displaced in their millions, as in Kampuchea during the 1970s.

1 a If you were able to live anywhere that you liked in the world, which country would you go to? Or would you choose to stay in Britain?
  b Make a list of the push and pull factors that you would take into account in making your decision.
  c On a world map plot the choices of everyone in the class. Which are the most popular countries? What are the pull factors that attracted people to different countries?

The size and structure of any country's population alters according to two factors: the natural change in the population (births against deaths) and the balance of migration into and out of the country. The difference between the number of people entering or leaving a country permanently is called net migration; the total number of immigrants and emigrants is called gross migration. Nowadays the developed coun-

Fig. 6.1 A boat load of Vietnamese refugees is taken in tow

Fig. 6.2 Migration into and out of the United Kingdom (thousands)

Year	Immigration	Emigration
1964	223	281
1965	210	286
1966	232	326
1967	241	286
1968	227	296
1969	224	306
1970	227	266
1971	196	240
1972	225	230
1973	183	255
1974	194	261
1975	197	220
1976	181	209
1977	162	198
1978	194	187
1979	205	209

tries operate strict controls on the number of immigrants who are allowed to settle permanently. This naturally affects the amount of emigration from the source countries.

2 **a** Using the information given in Fig. 6.2 draw a line graph to show the number of migrants into and out of the United Kingdom between 1964 and 1979. You should draw separate lines for immigrants and emigrants.

    b Shade the area between the two lines and label it net migration.

    c In which year was net migration i) highest, ii) lowest?

    d In which year was gross migration i) highest, ii) lowest?

Fig. 6.3 East African Asians expelled from Uganda arrive in Britain

Migration in the past

Migration started with the very earliest appearance of mankind on earth. Fig. 6.4 shows diagrammatically the way in which man's different racial groups developed and covered the continents of the world. These early humans, though few in number, needed to move continually to find food by hunting and gathering. As they became more effective in exploiting the land so larger areas were occupied. With the rise of town-based civilizations new patterns of migration occurred. The towns acted as magnets which attracted people from the neighbouring regions. However, it must be remembered that the total number of people involved in these early migrations was very small compared with the movements of the last five hundred years.

The chief movements since AD 1500 can be summarized as follows:

1 From all parts of Europe to the eastern United States and Canada.
2 From Spain and Portugal to South America, Central America, and Mexico.
3 From Britain to South Africa and Australia.
4 Slaves from West Africa to Brazil, the Caribbean, and the southern United States.
5 From India to South Africa, Sri Lanka, and Indonesia.
6 From China to Mongolia, Indonesia, and the Pacific.
7 From the eastern United States westwards to the Pacific coast.
8 From western Russia eastwards to Siberia and the Pacific coast.

3   a Using an atlas, mark the movements listed above on an outline map of the world. Use a different coloured arrow for each migration.
    b Find out the approximate period during which each of these migrations took place and add this information to an explanatory key for the map.

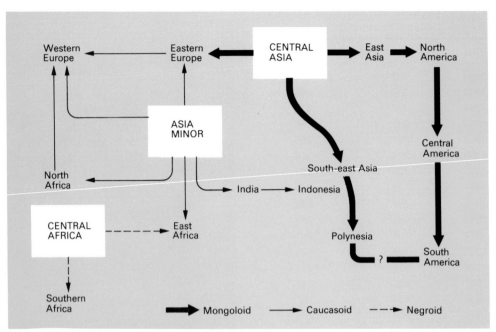

Fig. 6.4 Early migration of human groups

Fig. 6.5 European immigrants to the United States in the 1920s await clearance in New York

Colonization

Colonization is the term used to describe the control and exploitation of lands and their peoples by a foreign power. It is usually associated with the period between the sixteenth century and mid-twentieth century when European nations governed large parts of the world. Now, however, most countries have gained their political independence and been able to develop their national identity. The process of colonization began with the voyages of discovery by European navigators. Their explorations established worldwide sea routes which allowed the technically advanced European nations to amass wealth and resources. Eventually this helped to start the industrial revolution which gave Europe a long-lasting advantage over the rest of the world.

At first the Europeans were only interested in obtaining luxuries and precious metals from the lands they had discovered. Trading posts and fortified harbours were set up, but when these did not allow sufficient control over the native populations, the next step was to claim entire territories.

Fig. 6.6 Cape Coast castle, a seventeenth-century fort, built by Europeans in West Africa

Fig. 6.7 Europeans lunch inside a mosquito net in colonial Uganda

Fig. 6.8 Independence celebrations in the African republic of Rwanda

There were three types of territory that the colonists considered, the attractions of which varied greatly. The first type consisted of sparsely peopled tropical or subtropical areas which could be easily reached due to their coastal location. These areas were exploited straightaway to supply agricultural products that could not be grown in Europe. All along the warm coasts of North and South America and on the Caribbean islands Europeans grew rice, cotton, spices, sugar, tobacco, coffee, and bananas. Slaves were brought over in vast numbers from Africa to provide cheap labour for the plantations. When slavery was abolished the British and Dutch used contract labourers from India, China, and Indonesia to develop new zones of plantation agriculture in South-East Asia.

The second type of region included countries like India, China, Java, and Japan which were densely populated and usually tropical. Here the Europeans could not always gain direct control since large areas already had well developed civilizations. Where Europeans got control they set up large agricultural estates in less populated districts: otherwise they were forced to enter into trading agreements with local producers. Few Europeans migrated to these countries since there was little scope for employment, other than as managers and officials.

It was the third type of territory, temperate lands with small populations, that proved most attractive to European migrants. These lands were more like Europe in terms of climate and landscape and offered enormous potential for agriculture and settlement. Until the nineteenth century there was little migration to these colonies and their populations remained low. But after 1800, with the industrial revolution well under way, Europe's population grew rapidly and migration began to take off. Every year increasing numbers of people set sail for a new life in North America, Australia, southern Africa, or southern South America. The invention of the steamship and its use for ocean crossings after 1830 quickened the pace of migration. Between 1840 and 1930, the great period of voluntary overseas migration, over 50 million people emigrated from Europe to settle in these new lands.

Africa was the final continent to undergo full-scale colonization by the European powers. In what has been called 'the scramble for Africa' this vast land was divided up artificially between the colonial powers during the second half of the nineteenth century. By this time most parts of the Americas had gained their independence, as had Australia and New Zealand. The colonies in Africa, the Middle East, India, and South-East Asia had to wait until the years after the Second World War before independence was achieved.

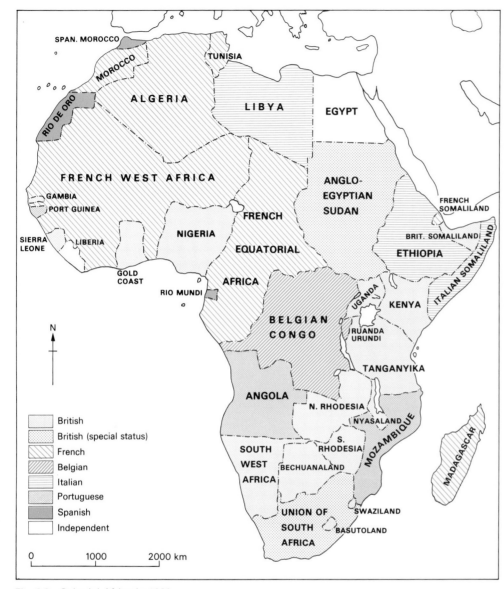

Fig. 6.9 Colonial Africa in 1939

Fig. 6.10 Nations of Africa in 1982

Country	Year of independence
Liberia	1847
Egypt	1922
South Africa	1931
Ethiopia	1941
Libya	1951
Sudan	1956
Tunisia	1956
Ghana	1957
Guinea	1958
Morocco	1958
Central African Republic	1960
Chad	1960
Congo	1960
Benin	1960
Gabon	1960
Ivory Coast	1960
Madagascar	1960
Mali	1960
Mauritania	1960
Niger	1960
Nigeria	1960
Senegal	1960
Somali Republic	1960
Togo	1960
Upper Volta	1960
Zaïre	1960
Cameroon	1961
Sierra Leone	1961
Algeria	1962
Burundi	1962
Rwanda	1962
Uganda	1962
Kenya	1963
Tanzania	1963
Malawi	1964
Zambia	1964
The Gambia	1965
Botswana	1966
Lesotho	1966
Swaziland	1967
Equatorial Guinea	1968
Guinea Bissau	1974
Angola	1975
Mozambique	1975
Zimbabwe	1980
Western Sahara	?
Namibia	?

4 Use an atlas to locate each country in Africa listed in Fig. 6.10 and then refer to Fig. 6.9 to find which European nation controlled that area in colonial times. Fill in this information on a copy of Fig. 6.10, using a third column headed 'colonial power'. When you have completed your table answer the following questions:

a Generally speaking, which regions of Africa became independent (i) before 1960, (ii) in 1960, (iii) between 1962 and 1967, (iv) in the 1970s?

b Why do you think so many countries became independent at the same time in 1960?

c Which European country held on longest to its African colonies?

d Find out why Liberia became independent so early (its name gives you a clue).

e Have any countries changed since this book was written?

The slave trade

The origins of slavery can be traced back to the town-based civilizations of the ancient world. The rapid development of these civilizations required enormous amounts of manpower which could not be supplied by the local population. Consequently the best means of obtaining labour was to capture foreigners through military campaigns and set these prisoners of war to work as slaves.

Slavery in modern times is associated with European colonization of the Americas. The plantations that produced tropical crops for Europe required huge inputs of labour. Europeans were too expensive to employ and were poorly adapted to hard physical work in a hot climate, while the original inhabitants were too few and usually unreliable. So to obtain the necessary cheap labour the European managers resorted to using slaves, transporting large numbers of black people from Africa against their will.

The slave trade across the Atlantic Ocean began as early as the fifteenth century, peaked between 1700 and 1810, and finally died out in the mid-nineteenth century. Estimates of the number of people moved vary considerably but it is probable that about 10 million Africans were imported into slave-using areas. It must be remembered though that many more died during

Fig. 6.11 Slaves cutting sugar cane on a plantation in the West Indies

Fig. 6.12 Loading plan of the lower deck of a slave ship

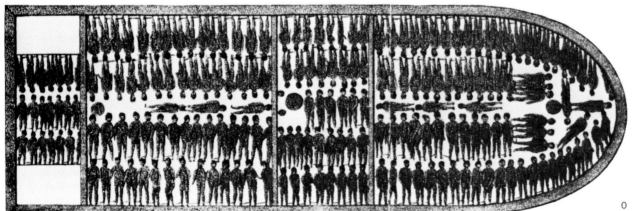

metres

0 1 2 3 4 5

the voyage (15 to 20 per cent on average) and on the walk to the African slave ports.

For Britain the movement of slaves formed part of a very profitable pattern of 'triangular' trade, as shown in Fig. 6.13. Ships left England carrying cargoes of rum, cloth, guns and metal goods, which were then exchanged for slaves in West Africa. From Africa the ships transported the slaves to the West Indies or the American mainland. Hundreds of slaves were packed into the ships' holds so that even if a large number died the traders would still make a good profit. In the West Indies the ships loaded up with plantation products like sugar, cotton, and tobacco and carried them across the Atlantic to Liverpool or Bristol. There the goods were sold as raw materials for British industry: sugar could be made into rum and cotton into cloth, which could then be sent back to Africa and traded for more slaves.

Slavery was abolished in the British Empire in 1833 but the trade continued illegally until the 1860s when the American Civil War finally put an end to slavery in the United States. The effect of the slave trade on Africa was disastrous. Over four centuries millions of men and women in the most active age groups were removed from their native lands. This represented a major population loss from which the continent has never really recovered. The impact on the New World was equally strong: slavery helped to create great economic wealth and introduced new racial groups and cultural variety to American life. This achievement was bought at the price of untold human misery, however, and political and racial strife is still a major problem today.

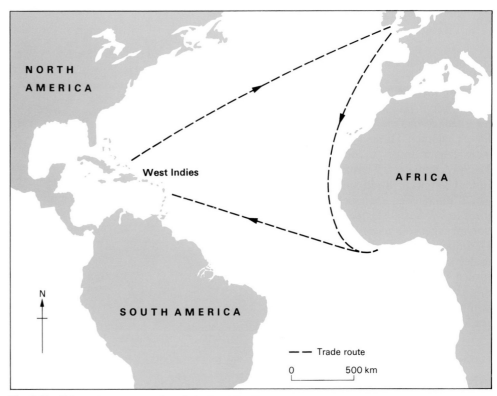

Fig. 6.13   Triangular pattern of trade in the Atlantic

Fig. 6.14   The Atlantic slave trade between 1700 and 1810

Departure point	Destination	Number of slaves (millions)
Angola	Brazil (Portuguese)	2·5
Nigeria	French Caribbean: Haiti, Guadeloupe	2·0
Gold Coast (Ghana)	British Caribbean: Jamaica, Trinidad, Barbados, Antigua	2·0
Gold Coast	Dutch Guianas (Surinam)	1·0
Cameroon	Spanish America: Nicaragua, Costa Rica, Southern Mexico	1·0
Gold Coast	British North America: Atlantic coast	0·5

5 **a** How many slaves are there in the plan in Fig. 6.12?

   b Use the scale to work out the surface area of the lower deck in square metres. Divide the area by the number of slaves to calculate the density of people in the hold.

   c The voyage from Africa to the Americas lasted about 100 days: what problems would the slaves have had to face during that time?

6 Make a tracing of the coastline in Fig. 6.13. By referring to the information given in Fig. 6.14, plot a series of arrows to show the main directions of the slave trade. Make the width of each arrow proportional to the number of slaves transported. A scale of 1 mm for every half million slaves is suitable. You will also need to use an atlas to locate the islands in the Caribbean.

Migration to work

One of the main causes of migration is the search for work. In the nineteenth century large numbers of poor, landless peasants from India, Java, and southern China travelled abroad to work in British and Dutch colonies. These coolies provided the main labour force in the plantations of Malaya, Sumatra, Burma, Ceylon, and Fiji. They were hired under a contract which guaranteed their return fare after three to five years' service. But the plantation managers often ignored this and of the 17 million Indians who left their country under contract over a quarter never returned. Although the period of coolie migration was relatively brief the total number of people involved probably exceeded the slave trade.

Fig. 6.15 Chinese workers help with a building project in the Sudan

Fig. 6.16 Turkish guestworkers

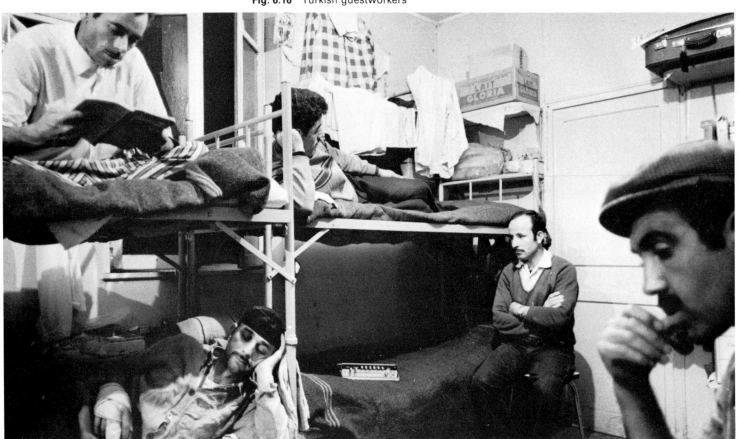

Fig. 6.17 Internal migration of population in Africa

This century many people have moved permanently to countries where jobs were freely available: West Indian migration to Britain in the 1950s is a good example of this. Nowadays though, developed countries are reluctant to accept permanent immigrants unless they can offer a special skill which is in short supply. Yet, when industry is booming, these countries want to draw on the pool of cheap labour which is available in less developed countries. They do this by encouraging temporary migration of workers, who are regarded as visitors even if they stay for a considerable time. West Germany and France rely heavily on workers from the poorer countries bordering the Mediterranean.

The case of Turkey demonstrates clearly the pitfalls of exporting men to work in the factories of Western Europe. In 1973 Turkey's 1·2 million migrant workers each sent back home about £500, which altogether was enough to pay for almost 50 per cent of Turkey's imports. Unfortunately the 1973 oil crisis affected European industry very badly and there was much less work available. Fewer foreign workers were needed so by 1976 the money earned by Turkish migrants covered only 17 per cent of the country's import bill. By 1977 20 per cent of Turkey's workforce was unemployed and the country was deeply in debt.

Similarly, a boom in employment in the oil-rich countries of the Middle East led states like Saudi Arabia, Libya, and Kuwait to import labourers from their poorer neighbours and also from as far away as India. Naturally this increased the earnings of the labourers' homelands, but overall it is doubtful that the countries benefited. It is thought that the loss of skilled manpower at home, and the bad effect this has on development, more than outweighs the advantage of the increased income.

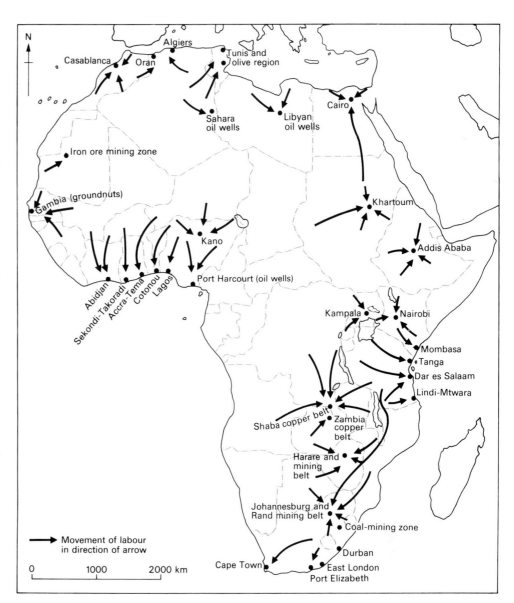

7 Study Fig. 6.17 together with a map of Africa in an atlas.
  a What types of economic activity attract migrant labour?
  b Which countries attract labour from other countries?
  c Which countries provide migrant labour for other nations?
  d Why do you think so many of the economically developed areas are on the coast?
  e What sorts of area are the migrants most likely to come from?

8 Look at Fig. 6.16.
  a Describe the guestworkers' living conditions.
  b What problems would be associated with this way of life?
  c What might each of the men be thinking?

Coloured immigration to Britain

Since 1950 there has been a rapid expansion of the numbers of coloured people living in Britain, though the immigration that has produced this increase has altered over the years. However, the current total of 2 million is still a very small proportion of the overall population, about 3·5 per cent.

9 a Use the data given in Fig. 6.18 to construct a line graph showing the number of coloured immigrants who have come to the United Kingdom. Put the years on the horizontal axis and the number of immigrants on the vertical axis.
   b Study the pattern shown by the graph and make a note of the years when there is a marked change in the trend of immigration.
   c As you work through the following section add labels to your graph to indicate the main events affecting immigration.

Small numbers of coloured people have been resident in Britain for several centuries. In 1750, for example, there were 20 000 black slaves in London, working mainly as domestic servants. The present coloured community developed originally when West Indians came over to work in

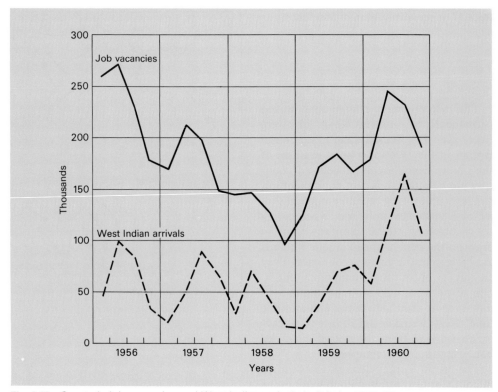

Fig. 6.19   Quarterly job vacancies and West Indian arrivals in Britain, 1956–60

Fig. 6.20   Many Asian immigrants run a family business, such as this newsagents

Fig. 6.18   Coloured immigration into the United Kingdom (thousands)

Year		Year	
1951	2	1966	44
1952	3	1967	54
1953	3	1968	51
1954	11	1969	46
1955	43	1970	40
1956	47	1971	46
1957	42	1972	69
1958	30	1973	32
1959	22	1974	43
1960	58	1975	53
1961	136	1976	55
1962	107	1977	44
1963	56	1978	43
1964	53	1979	37
1965	52	1980	36

Fig. 6.21 London Airport when the Commonwealth Immigrants Act was introduced

British factories during the two world wars. By the late 1940s the British economy was recovering from the Second World War and beginning to grow, causing a shortage of manpower for industries and services. News of this shortage and the resulting job opportunities spread quickly in the West Indies and from 1950 onwards an increasing number of migrants arrived in Britain.

It is often thought that this immigration was caused by the poor living conditions in the West Indies. While it is true that population pressure, poverty, and lack of opportunity encouraged migration, they did not cause it. The pull factor, the demand for labour in Britain, was the main reason as is indicated by Fig. 6.19. The majority of West Indians filled jobs that were not in demand by British workers.

10 a What relationship does Fig. 6.19 indicate between job vacancies in Britain and West Indian immigration? Is there any evidence of a time-lag between job vacancies and arrivals?

b The British economy was weak between 1956 and 1958: how is this reflected in the graph?

Between 1959 and 1962 immigration to Britain rose sharply as fear of government controls prompted people to 'beat the ban'.

A major part of the increase was from Asian immigration. There had been a low level of Asian immigration—chiefly of Sikhs from the Punjab, Hindus from Gujerati, and Muslims from the hill districts of Pakistan—since the division of Pakistan and India in 1947. However, after 1959 this accelerated and in spite of emigration restrictions at home, large numbers of Indians and Pakistanis entered Britain, nearly all of them unmarried young men.

Then in 1962 the Commonwealth Immigrants Act came into force. It established a system by which intending immigrants had to apply for one of three types of permit:

Category A: Those people who had been offered definite jobs.

Category B: Those people who had certain specific skills which were in short supply in Britain.

Category C: Those people who did not qualify under A or B.

A permit entitled the holder and his dependents to enter Britain, but the number of permits was strictly limited. In 1964 category C was discontinued and subsequent measures reduced the availability of permits still further. Since the mid 1960s the majority of coloured immigrants have been dependents, mainly women and children coming to join the head of the household already in Britain and mainly Asians since West Indian immigration had a higher proportion of women from the beginning.

After 1965 a quite separate group of Asian immigrants began to swell the number of arrivals in Britain. These were Asians who lived in East Africa and had chosen British citizenship when the African countries became independent. At first very few of these people planned to move to Britain since they had a prosperous and successful life in Africa. In time though political pressure forced them to leave and they moved to Britain in increasing numbers. The most significant year was 1972, when all British Asians were expelled from Uganda and about 25 000 refugees had to be resettled in Britain. By the end of the 1970s nearly all the 200 000 British Asians had made the move from East Africa.

Rural depopulation

The dominant pattern of migration within developing countries as shown in Exercise 7 is the continual drift of people from the countryside to the major cities. The main cause of this is the extreme poverty of life in rural areas, which reflects the many difficulties associated with subsistence farming. Wages for unskilled labourers are two or three times higher in urban areas, provided jobs are available. The seasonal nature of agricultural work ensures long periods of unemployment in the countryside so it is no surprise then that large numbers of young men and women leave their villages to seek a better life in the cities. Often they make their way to the shanty towns that have grown up in and around the cities. These act as a half-way house between rural and urban areas where the migrant is able to stay with relatives and friends. Some migrants are fortunate enough to find a job in the service industries that abound in the cities but for many the move leads only to continued unemployment and frustration. However, this unsatisfactory life is still preferable to the extreme poverty of the countryside.

11 Read the interview with a young African migrant from the countryside and then answer the questions.

When I first arrived in Mulago I looked for any person of my tribe I knew. I was lucky to find a friend and I stayed with him for three weeks before I found a place for myself. I had a little money when I arrived but after four days in Mulago almost half of it was stolen. My friend introduced me to his friends (not all of whom were of the same tribe) to ask for jobs. Eventually I found work as a sweeper in a big office.

I now live with a group of young men only one of whom is a member of my tribe but two others work in the same office as messengers. When a member of my tribe goes home I give him messages for my wife and if I have any money I will give him some of that too. I am now trying to get better work where I can get more money. So I went to see a Ganda friend of mine. He likes me because I can speak his language. But I do not really like the Ganda people because they treat us all with contempt.

On Sunday I play football. There are people from many different tribes in my club but we get on well together. I sometimes get tired of living here and having to buy all my food. If I get tired of work I go home but I always come back.

Fig. 6.22 The destination of many Peruvian migrants: a shanty town in Lima

a In what way do tribal links work for the migrant?

b Why do you think he left his home and wife?

c What kind of work would he have done at home?

d What kind of jobs are migrants likely to get in the city?

e Do you think the migrant will be able to improve his situation?

f Why do rural areas suffer because of this type of migration?

g How could this migration be halted?

12 Look carefully at Fig. 6.22.

a What suggests that this is a migrants' community?

b How recently do you think this settlement was built?

c How many different types of building material can you identify?

d Where might these materials have been obtained?

e Make a simple outline sketch of the scene and add labels to indicate the main features.

13 Make a copy of the outline of Fig. 6.23. Shade each region according to the number of migrants as follows:

0–25 000	light colour
26 000–50 000	medium colour
51 000–75 000	dark colour
Over 75 000	darkest colour

a Refer to an atlas map of Peru showing the main physical features. Does the pattern of migration on your map reflect the physical geography of the country?

b Does the distance from Lima affect the number of migrants?

c Does the size of a region bear any relationship to the number of migrants it sends to Lima?

d What role is the difficulty of transport likely to play in affecting the number of migrants?

e What does the migration pattern tell you about the distribution of population in Peru?

Fig. 6.23 The birthplace of migrants to Lima

123

Transmigration in Indonesia

Occasionally migration is a planned process, organized by governments for a specific purpose. In this example and the following section migration has been implemented for very different reasons. In Indonesia people have been moved to agricultural settlement schemes in virgin forest land, while in Tanzania the scattered rural population has been concentrated into new villages.

Indonesia consists of over 13 000 islands which stretch in an arc between Malaysia and Australia. Less than a quarter of the islands are occupied but they hold a population of 140 million (Fig. 6.24). By the year 2000 this is expected to rise by a further 100 million people.

14 Use an atlas to identify the main islands that make up Indonesia.

    a Referring to Fig. 6.24 write a few sentences describing the pattern of population density in Indonesia.

    b What pattern of migration between the islands might arise because of this distribution?

The traditional centre of Indonesia is Java which has long attracted migrants from throughout the other islands. Although Java has only 7 per cent of the country's land area it supports 65 per cent of the population, with an average density of 660 persons per km². In comparison the outer islands are very sparsely populated: for example, the average density in Sumatra is only 38 per km². The reasons for this are found in the physical geography of the islands. Java's soils are extremely fertile, being composed of rich volcanic ash that has been carried down to the plains as alluvium. Rainfall is lower than on the outer islands and the land was more easily cleared for rice-growing in irrigated padi fields. The outer islands are covered with tropical rain forest and suffer from very heavy rainfall. The native peoples had to adopt a system of shifting cultivation since clearance of the forest inevitably led to a rapid loss of soil fertility.

In spite of the disadvantages there have been several attempts to establish permanent farming settlements on the outer islands. The main aim has been to create employment for Java's expanding population and at the same time develop the natural resources of the thinly inhabited islands. After 1949, when Indonesia was united as an independent state, its leader General Sukarno pushed the idea of 'transmigration' to the outer islands and his successor has continued the policy.

Originally the government only sought farmers for the transmigration projects but a shortfall of volunteers led to other people being recruited. Now migrants are also drawn from retired servicemen, the homeless and unemployed of the cities, and young people seeking their first job. Each migrant undergoes training in agriculture or a specialist skill before he and his family depart. Meanwhile land in the project area has been selected and cleared. Each family receives between 2 and 6 hectares of land, depending on the nature and fertility of the soil. New villages house between 200 and 500 families, therefore each one requires the clearance of several thousand hectares of forest.

For their first year the provincial government gives each family a living allowance made up of cash, food, materials, and basic farming equipment. Funds are also available for the construction of temporary housing and community buildings such as

Fig. 6.24 Population density in Indonesia

clinics and schools. A committee of village leaders supervises the day-to-day running of the settlement, though in the early years a project officer is present to advise them. After five years the village is officially recognized by the government.

So far the transmigration projects have had mixed results. Certainly a substantial number of villages has been established but agricultural production has remained disappointingly low. Many migrants, particularly those from Jakarta, find it hard to come to terms with the hardships and isolation of their new existence. Some have become so discouraged that they have migrated back to Java. The farmers tend to be the best migrants since they are used to agricultural work and have a more optimistic attitude. Recently the government has encouraged the mixing of migrants with local people to create a more stable community. The success of the projects really depends on the quality of the support which the government gives to the new villages.

15 From what you have read in previous chapters can you suggest some problems that the farmers are likely to face in cultivating land cleared of tropical rain forest?

16 **a** Why do you think the government chose the settlement layout shown in Fig. 6.26? What are its advantages and disadvantages?

b Draw an alternative plan incorporating the same features and explain the reasoning behind it.

Fig. 6.25 Farmer's house on a transmigration project in Sumatra

Fig. 6.26 Layout of a planned transmigration settlement

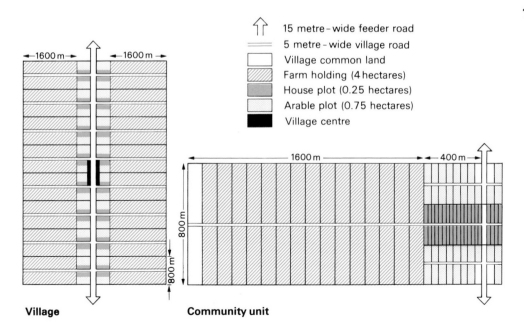

↑ 15 metre-wide feeder road
═ 5 metre-wide village road
☐ Village common land
▨ Farm holding (4 hectares)
▨ House plot (0.25 hectares)
☐ Arable plot (0.75 hectares)
■ Village centre

Village

Community unit

Ujamaa villages in Tanzania

At the time of independence in 1961 most Tanzanians lived in scattered homesteads as subsistence farmers and herdsmen. Less than 10 per cent of the rural population lived in villages, most of which were traditional and unplanned.

In 1967 President Nyerere's Arusha Declaration stressed the importance of self-reliance, equality, and co-operation in improving life in Tanzania. His government introduced an urgent programme to regroup people in villages, based on the idea of 'ujamaa' or 'family' villages. Ujamaa villages operate on the old African family system of shared work and wealth. President Nyerere calls this 'African socialism' and believes it is the fairest means of distributing Tanzania's small income from agricultural products. Establishing the new villages has involved the movement of large numbers of people over relatively short distances. Most resettlement has taken place within regional boundaries but the change in population distribution has been quite dramatic. In the less developed, sparsely populated areas there has been a marked concentration of people along certain chosen transport routes.

17 Study Fig. 6.27. Between which years did the fastest increase in the number of villages take place? How does the table indicate that some amalgamation of villages has occurred since 1973?

18 a Make three copies of Fig. 6.28. Using one map for each year given in Fig. 6.27, plot the number of villages. You should do this by shading in each region according to the following colour key:

Less than 200   light colour
200–399   medium colour
400–599   dark colour
Over 600   darkest colour

b Compare the patterns that your

Fig. 6.27   Number of villages in Tanzania

Region	1970	1973	1976
1 Arusha	25	95	209
2 Dar es Salaam	—	—	10
3 Dodoma	75	336	331
4 Iringa	350	659	464
5 Kigoma	34	129	145
6 Kilimanjaro	9	24	284
7 Lindi	285	589	257
8 Mara	174	271	270
9 Mbeya	91	715	501
10 Morogoro	19	118	341
11 Mtwara	465	1103	466
12 Mwanza	28	284	535
13 Pwani	56	188	256
14 Rukwa*	—	—	155
15 Ruvuma	120	242	269
16 Shinyanga	98	108	425
17 Singida	16	263	256
18 Tabora	52	174	283
19 Tanga	37	245	299
20 Ziwa Magharibi	22	85	491
Total	1956	5628	6247

* Previously part of Mbeya and Tabora regions

Fig. 6.28   The regions of Tanzania (numbered as in Fig. 6.27)

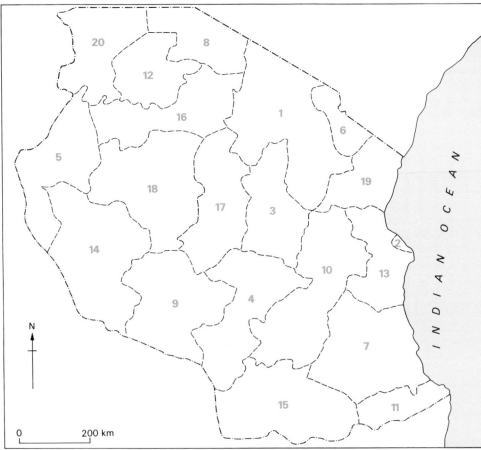

maps show with an atlas map of Tanzania. Which parts have the most new villages? Where are they in relation to the coast, the highlands, and the main cities?

c Write a paragraph summarizing the pattern of change over the six-year period: refer to specific regions by name wherever you can.

How successful has the village programme been? Since it has a very wide range of long-term objectives, covering many aspects of social, economic, and political development, it would be wrong to judge them at this early stage. Nevertheless, there are several problems arising from the way the plan has been put into action. There was considerable resistance from some farmers to the relocation programme and eventually a substantial number had to be moved by force. Naturally this has led to anger and resentment which can undermine community spirit in the villages. Also forced resettlement can destroy the farmers' initiative and make them dependent on government direction and support. Because they were not consulted in the planning stages of the scheme some villagers lack a personal commitment to its success. Others have become discouraged when the government was unable to provide the resources necessary to support their villages at the start. Time will tell whether the ujamaa villages can overcome these difficulties and achieve the progress that President Nyerere hoped for when he started the programme.

19 Consider the points listed below and for each one explain whether it would be an advantage or a disadvantage to have the rural population concentrated in villages:
   a the provision of medical facilities;
   b the introduction of compulsory primary schools;
   c the spread of an infectious disease;
   d the improvement of crop and livestock production;
   e the allocation of land to farmers;
   f the danger of casualties from natural disasters.

Fig. 6.29 Building huts in an ujamaa village

Summary

Migration takes many different forms and occurs at every level from local to world-wide. During colonial times Europeans travelled abroad to control and exploit large parts of the tropics, sometimes settling there permanently. Nowadays air travel has made international movement easier than ever, but migration is closely controlled by governments. Coloured people have come to live in Britain from its former colonies, though now the number of immigrants is strictly limited by law. The commonest type of migration within the Third World is from the countryside to the city. Rural peasants, mostly male, are flocking to the cities in search of work and higher wages. A few governments have tried to counter this by planned migration to settlement schemes in thinly populated areas.

Chapter **7** The exploding cities

Urbanization

It is estimated that the number of urban dwellers in the Third World will increase by four times between 1950 and the year 2000. This chapter looks at the causes and effects of this startling growth.

The last 150 years have seen a dramatic change in the proportion of the world's population living in cities and the proportion living in countryside. The percentage of the population living in cities has been increasing steadily and now the rate of change is accelerating. This process is known as urbanization. In the nineteenth century the development of industry in Europe, and later North America, led to the urbanization of these countries. By 1900 80 per cent of Britain's population lived in urban areas. Now it is the Third World countries that are undergoing urbanization, while the growth of cities in the developed world has slowed down. There are two main reasons why the cities in the developing countries are growing so fast. The first is that they have high population growth rates (as do most of the rural areas) and the second is that they are swelled by migrants from the countryside.

1 a Using Fig. 7.1 draw up a table to show the population of each city in 1960, 1980, and the estimate for 2000.

   b By measuring the angle of each line on Fig. 7.1 draw up a rank order for the rate of growth of the cities
   i) between 1960 and 1980,
   ii) between 1980 and 2000.
   (Rank 1 will be the fastest growing city over each period.)

   c Which two cities on the graph are not in the Third World?

   d How does their rate of growth compare with that of the other eight cities?

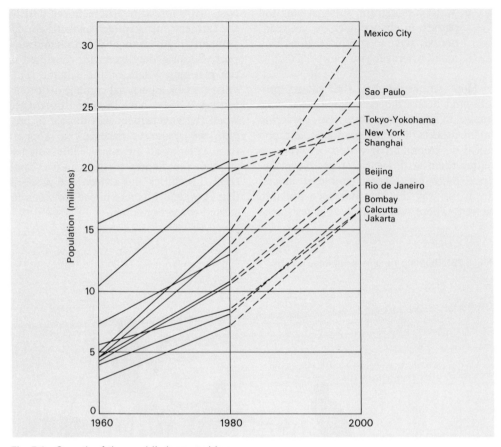

Fig. 7.1 Growth of the world's largest cities

Fig. 7.2 The growth in the number of million cities

Latitude	1–3	3–5	5+	1–3	3–5	5+	1–3	3–5	5+	Size of city (millions)
60°										
50°	8	2	1	9	3	1	19	2	2	
40°	9	2	1	15	5	1	34	3	4	
30°	8	2	1	19	3	2	36	3	6	
20°	3	–	–	8	3	–	13	3	2	
10°	2	–	–	6	2	–	9	1	2	
0°	–	–	–	2	1	–	9	1	–	
	Early 1930s			**Early 1950s**			**Early 1970s**			

Another way of looking at the changing pattern of growth of the world's cities is to study the number and position of million cities, i.e. those with over 1 million people.

2 **a** Some of the information given in Fig. 7.2 has been used to draw the bar graph shown in Fig. 7.4. Using exactly the same axes draw two other bar graphs to show the number and location of million cities in the early 1950s and the early 1970s.
  b For each period make a note of the latitude belts in which the number of cities grew most noticeably and in which size categories the growth took place. If necessary use an atlas to remind yourself of the position of the latitude belts on a world map.
  c Bearing in mind that most developing countries are located within or close to the tropics, does the pattern shown by the graphs confirm what has been said so far about the way urbanization has occurred?

The rapid development of Third World cities has led to many problems. Because many city dwellers are squatters it has been impossible to plan the growth of the built-up areas. Large sections of the cities are without basic public services such as a clean water supply, mains drainage, electricity, or refuse collection. Unlike Europe or America urbanization in the developing countries has been accompanied by only a small amount of industrial expansion. Consequently there is little chance of factory employment in the cities and many people have to turn to odd jobs to scrape a living. A high proportion of people are employed in services as domestic servants, bootblacks, cleaners, nightwatchmen, repairmen, and guards. Jobs are frequently broken down into very small portions so that a larger number of people can be employed. The main problem continues to be the gulf between the rich minority who dominate the wealth in developing countries and the vast majority who have little or nothing.

Fig. 7.3 Sao Paulo, Brazil: one of the fastest growing cities in the Third World

Fig. 7.4 Million cities of the world in the early 1930s

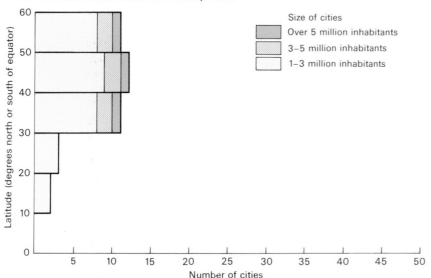

Size of cities
- Over 5 million inhabitants
- 3–5 million inhabitants
- 1–3 million inhabitants

Primate cities

One puzzling feature of some developing countries is that the population of the largest city in the country is many times higher than that of the second largest city. Where this is the case the primary, or first city, is known as a primate city. This situation is shown best by studying the pattern of city sizes in Latin American countries.

3   Using the information in Fig. 7.6 construct a series of graphs, one for each country listed, with city population on the vertical axis and rank order of city size on the horizontal axis. Plot a point for each city and join the points up with a straight line. Then compare the patterns shown on the graphs and answer the following questions:
   a Which four countries have the most clearly marked primate cities?
   b What is special about the Brazil graph?
   c How is Colombia's graph different from the others?

Fig. 7.5 Skyscrapers in central Buenos Aires, the capital city of Argentina

Fig. 7.6 Population of the ten largest cities in selected Latin American countries (millions; cities under 0·1 million omitted)

City rank	Mexico	Argentina	Brazil	Chile	Peru	Colombia	Venezuela	Bolivia	Ecuador
1	11·3	8·4	8·0	3·2	3·3	2·9	2·2	0·7	0·8
2	2·0	0·8	7·0	0·2	0·3	1·4	0·7	0·2	0·6
3	1·6	0·8	1·6	0·2	0·3	0·9	0·4	0·1	0·1
4	0·5	0·5	1·0	0·2	0·2	0·7	0·3	0·1	—
5	0·5	0·5	1·0	0·2	0·2	0·3	0·3	0·1	—
6	0·5	0·4	0·9	0·2	0·2	0·3	0·2	—	—
7	0·5	0·3	0·6	0·1	0·1	0·2	0·1	—	—
8	0·4	0·2	0·5	0·1	0·1	0·2	0·1	—	—
9	0·4	0·2	0·5	0·1	0·1	0·2	0·1	—	—
10	0·3	0·2	0·4	0·1	0·1	0·2	0·1	—	—

Fig. 7.7 Population of the largest city as a percentage of total urban population for selected Latin American countries

There has been a lot of argument over the reasons for the development of primate cities. This is not made any easier by the varied characteristics of the countries which possess primate cities. Nevertheless it seems clear that a city is likely to become much larger if it dominates the political and economic life of the country. In particular, a city's control over the nation's import and export trade will allow it to grow out of all proportion. Some geographers say that primate cities are a good thing because their size enables business and industry to operate more efficiently there, so improving a country's economy as a whole. Other people claim that the primate cities have grown too large and have become inefficient because of their size. Developing countries cannot afford to solve the problems of traffic congestion, overcrowding, water shortage, and pollution that are common in their largest cities. It is also suggested that the primate cities have grown at the expense of the rest of the country. Money is poured into the main centre while outlying cities and rural regions remain undeveloped through lack of funds. From a social point of view it seems that primate cities encourage a system which favours a small, wealthy minority. Obviously the case of each country is different but a more even spread of investment would probably help the bulk of the population that still lives in poverty.

4 **a** Use an atlas to find the position of each country listed on Fig. 7.7. On a copy of the map of Latin America fill in the pie diagrams to show the appropriate percentage for each country using the figures in the list. To find the correct angle you must multiply each percentage by 3.6.
  b Does the pattern shown by the pie diagrams match up to the graphs you drew for Exercise 3? Write a short explanation of the pattern shown on your map.

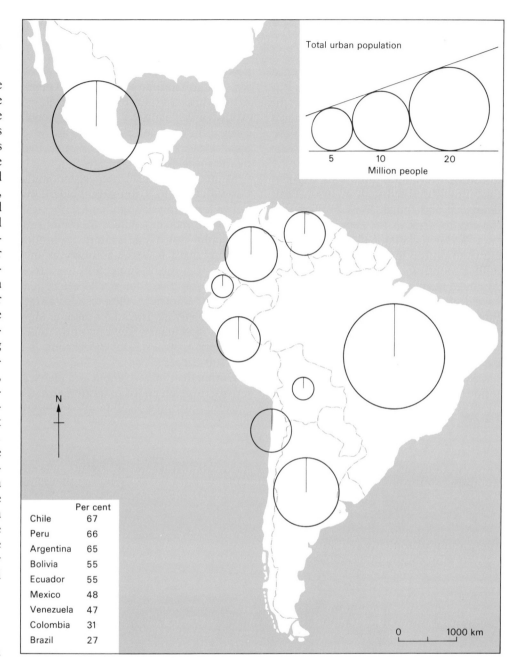

Total urban population

Million people

	Per cent
Chile	67
Peru	66
Argentina	65
Bolivia	55
Ecuador	55
Mexico	48
Venezuela	47
Colombia	31
Brazil	27

0   1000 km

5 By the mid 1980s cities of 5 million to 15 million people will be common throughout the Third World. The largest cities will have more than twice London's population. Imagine that your town or city doubled its population over the next five years. What problems would this cause? What would life there be like?

131

Calcutta

Calcutta, India's largest city, has seemed full to bursting point for many years. It is built on flat, swampy land alongside the River Hooghly, one of the largest channels in the Ganges delta (Fig. 7.9). Temperatures are high and the summer monsoon brings heavy rainfall.

Calcutta developed from a trading-post established by the British in 1690. Trade flourished and Indian workers flocked to the city to work in the expanding industries. Today Calcutta is the focus of a vast region of eastern India containing over 150 million people, most of whom are peasants. Although many of its traditional industries have declined Calcutta is still a vital centre for the Indian economy and migrants from the surrounding area continue to move there in search of work and a better standard of living.

Calcutta faces many problems, the most serious of which is a severe housing short-age. About one-third of the city's 9 million inhabitants live in bustees; these are slums of dried-mud shacks that are frequently flooded and fall apart during the rainy season. Large families often live in a single room, while others have no home at all. It is estimated that a quarter of a million people sleep in the open and many more are pavement dwellers living in temporary shelters by the roadside.

Sanitation is virtually non-existent in the bustees. Calcutta's drainage system was built a hundred years ago: now sewers leak constantly and contaminate the water supply. In the bustees one lavatory, an earthen pit, may have to serve as many as fifty people. Rubbish is dumped in the streets and can stay there for weeks before it is collected. Naturally, these conditions are an ideal breeding-ground for disease. Most bustee inhabitants have worms, while dysentery is widespread and cholera is a constant danger.

During the 1960s a complicated plan was drawn up which aimed to tackle Calcutta's

Fig. 7.9 The situation of Calcutta

Fig. 7.8 Living conditions in a bustee

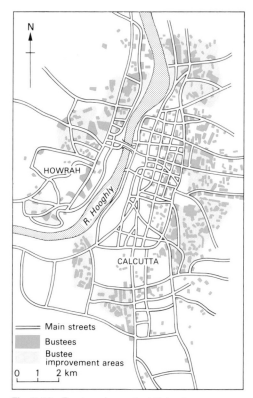

Fig. 7.10 Bustees in central Calcutta

desperate situation. It was put into action in 1970 by a specially created city department called the Metropolitan Development Authority. However, it soon became clear that there was neither the money nor the resources to carry out the plan in full. For example, the sheer size of the housing problem forced the authority to accept the bustees as part of the city's housing and try to make them habitable. This is being done by paving alleyways, digging storm drains to carry away rainwater, providing more water taps, and installing concrete lavatory blocks. During the 1970s more than half Calcutta's bustees were improved in this way. One major benefit of this approach is that it preserves the close community spirit of the bustees and does not destroy the system of small industries and services which employ many of the inhabitants.

Transport is another major headache for Calcutta's planners. The appalling congestion that grips Calcutta during the rush hours is mainly due to shortage of land:

Fig. 7.11 Vegetable traders line the pavement of a street in Calcutta

only 6 per cent of its area is taken up by streets, compared to 20 per cent in most Western cities. Buses and trams are hopelessly overloaded and it is common to find up to fifteen people clinging to the outside of the vehicles. At present there is only one bridge across the Hooghly river (Fig. 7.10). Half a million people cross daily on their way to work in Howrah,

causing enormous traffic jams. A second bridge is under construction as is an underground railway but both projects are a long way from completion.

6 Look at the photographs on pages 132–4. Make a list of all the things in them that indicate the problems Calcutta faces as a city.

Fig. 7.12   The makeshift shelter built by a family of street-dwellers

Fig. 7.13   A regular occurrence during Calcutta's rainy season

Fig. 7.14   Migrants into Calcutta

Age	Percentage female	Percentage male
60+	1·0	1·0
55–59	1·0	1·0
50–54	1·0	2·0
45–49	1·5	3·0
40–44	2·0	6·0
35–39	2·5	11·0
30–34	3·0	14·0
25–29	4·0	13·5
20–24	4·5	12·0
15–19	3·5	7·0
10–14	3·0	4·5
5–9	1·0	1·5
0–4	0·5	0·5

7 **a** Using Fig. 7.14 draw a population pyramid for migrants into Calcutta using the same technique as for Exercise 10 on page 33.

 b Describe the pattern of the pyramid. Why do you think it is so unbalanced and what effect would this have on life and work i) in Calcutta, ii) in the rural villages that the migrants left?

8 Read the following quotation from a recent newspaper report about Calcutta:

> One of the most fascinating sights in Calcutta is the excavation of the tube tunnel. The building of the pyramids must have looked like this: several thousand coolies, wearing only loincloths and headscarves, digging out the clay subsoil by hand and carrying it away in straw baskets. Instead of a pneumatic pile driver, a gang of fifteen men haul a huge stone up on ropes over a pulley supported by a bamboo frame, and drop it: haul and drop, haul and drop.

 a What are the advantages and disadvantages of this approach to large-scale construction work?

 b Why would the Development Authority be keen to use these kinds of methods?

Squatter settlements

Squatting is the most widespread and serious problem that affects Third World cities. Squatters are people who occupy land for which they do not pay. Most of them are forced to do this since they cannot afford any kind of legal housing in the city and usually there is a severe shortage of housing in any case. Living conditions can vary enormously even within the same city. Many squatters' homes are no more than makeshift shelters, built out of any waste material that can be found, such as flattened oil-cans or old packing cases. In some cities though, squatters have built proper houses which are often as good as government housing and considerably less expensive to construct.

We have already seen how the Development Authority in Calcutta has set about improving the bustees by providing basic public services. Now other governments have acknowledged the advantage of improving squatter settlements rather than pulling them down. Few could afford to rehouse the squatters anyway. The size of the problem is too great.

9 Use an atlas to find the location of the cities listed in Fig. 7.16. On a world map mark in each city as a column proportional to its total population; divide the column to show the number of people living in slums and squatter settlements in each city. Shade the two sections of each column in different colours to emphasize the proportion living as squatters.

10 Read the description of a real squatter's life, his family, and his living conditions which is given in Fig. 7.15. Then write an account of what you imagine a day in Vicos's life would be like. If you like you could write it in the first person, as if you were Vicos.

Fig. 7.15 Profile of a squatter

Name: Vicos.
Age: Twenty.
Sex: Male.
Place of birth: Sitio.
Home: A squatter settlement in Salvador, north-east Brazil.
Family: Vicos lives with two aunts, Betty and Sheila. Betty is separated from her husband and has one daughter. Sheila is married to Romano, a bricklayer, and they have nine children, between two and fourteen years old. Vicos followed his aunts to Salvador when he was fourteen.
Employment: Vicos earns £12 a month doing odd jobs in a local cafe. He is the only member of the family in regular employment: Betty and Romano are too ill to work.
Living accommodation: The family lives in two small shacks, known as barracas. Each barraca has two rooms which are low and dark under the thatch roof. There are no windows and only the front door lets in any air or light. On the muddy earthen floor stand a table and some chairs: the remaining furniture consists of wooden platforms used by the adults as beds. The children sleep on the floor. After dark light is provided by a single kerosene lamp.

Food: Meals are cooked on a brick hearth. The main food is manioc meal and beans, with occasional oddments of meat, fish, or cheese that Vicos brings back from the cafe. Fruit, either pawpaws or bananas, is a rare luxury. The family owns some dishes but has no cutlery so everyone eats with their fingers.
Water: This has to be collected from streams or public taps a long distance from the barracas and carried home in oil cans. Since water is so hard to get it is used just for cooking and drinking. Baths are taken in streams or the sea which is also used as a lavatory along with the nearby sand dunes. The small children relieve themselves in the street.
Personal possessions: Vicos owns three white cotton shirts and two pairs of cotton trousers as well as a zippered cotton jacket. He and Romano are the only two who wear shoes. They also both possess a transistor radio, like nearly every other adult male, so that they can hear the daily news and follow their favourite sport, football.

Fig. 7.16 Slum and squatter populations for selected Third World cities (millions)

City	Total population	Squatter and slum population
Manila	4·4	1·5
Jakarta	4·6	1·2
Seoul	5·5	1·2
Karachi	3·4	0·8
Bombay	6·0	2·5
Calcutta	9·0	5·3
Lima	2·9	1·2
Caracas	2·4	1·0
Rio de Janeiro	4·9	1·5
Bogota	2·3	1·4
Kinshasa	2·0	1·1
Ibadan	0·8	0·6

Fig. 7.17   Squatopoly board

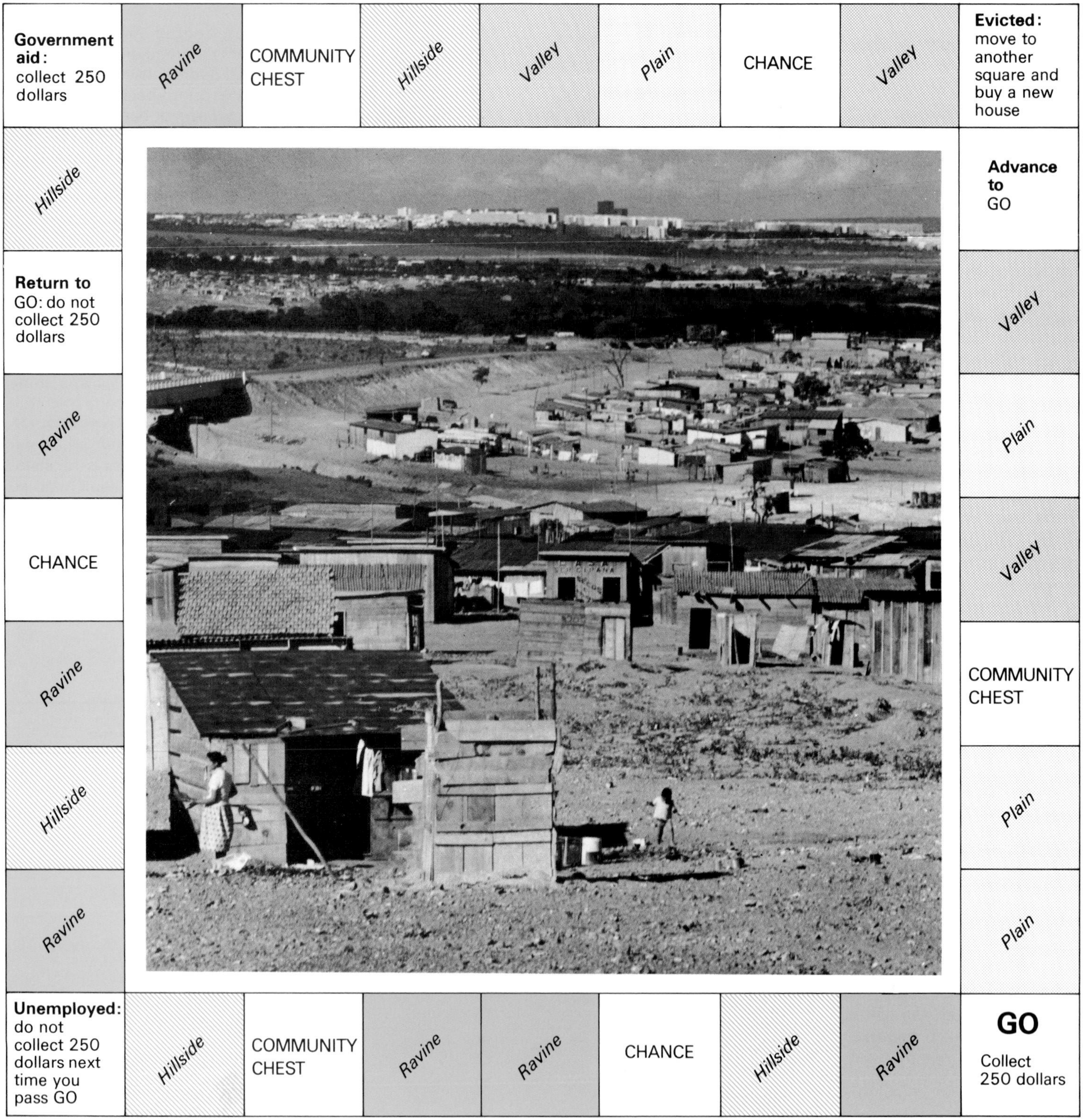

Government aid: collect 250 dollars	Ravine	COMMUNITY CHEST	Hillside	Valley	Plain	CHANCE	Valley	Evicted: move to another square and buy a new house
Hillside								Advance to GO
Return to GO: do not collect 250 dollars								Valley
Ravine								Plain
CHANCE								Valley
Ravine								COMMUNITY CHEST
Hillside								Plain
Ravine								Plain
Unemployed: do not collect 250 dollars next time you pass GO	Hillside	COMMUNITY CHEST	Ravine	Ravine	CHANCE	Hillside	Ravine	**GO** Collect 250 dollars

11 This exercise is a game called Squatopoly based on the development of squatter settlements in South America. It shows how squatters are able to improve their living conditions by work, outside help, and good luck. As you play it you will also become aware of the pitfalls and uncertainties of their way of life.

Type of house	Events	Money held in dollars		
		Income	Outgoings	Balance
None	Arrived in city			100

Fig. 7.18 Scorecard for squatopoly

Fig. 7.19 Types of land and houses

Type of land	Type of house	Cost of house (dollars)	Rent (dollars)
1 Ravine	Cardboard shelter	Nil	10
2 Hillside	Wooden shack	250	15
3 Valley	Earthen-brick	300	20
4 Plain	Concrete block	500	25

1 Squatopoly works best with groups of four players. Each player needs a dice, a counter, and a copy of the scorecard (Fig. 7.18).

2 At the beginning of the game each player is a migrant to the city who has just arrived from the countryside. Each migrant has few personal possessions but has managed to save 100 dollars: this is the amount of money that you start the game with. The aim of the game is to work your way up to the best type of house that is available to a squatter.

3 There are four different types of land that can be occupied and each of these allows you to build a different kind of home (Fig. 7.19). You can only move from one type of land to the next when you have sufficient money to build a house on the land you are moving to; you must also follow the sequence shown in Fig. 7.19, without missing any out.

4 a All players start on the GO square (Fig. 7.17) and take it in turns to throw the dice. You move your counter the number of squares shown on the dice in a clockwise direction. If you throw a six you can move to the square of your choice within the next six squares.
b At the beginning of the game all players are looking for an unoccupied ravine square where they can put up a makeshift shelter. Two or more players cannot occupy the same square.
c To occupy a particular type of land you must land directly on a vacant square and pay the house purchase price immediately.
d If you land on a *Chance* or *Community chest* square you must throw the dice again and follow the instructions given for the number on the dice shown in Figs. 7.20 or 7.21 on p. 138.
e Every time you pass GO you collect 250 dollars, which represents your annual wages.
f If you land on a square occupied by another player you must pay rent according to the figures given in Fig. 7.19.
g If at any time you have to pay more money than you hold in cash then you must sell your house for its purchase price and move to one that you can afford after you have settled your debt.

5 While you are playing the game make a note on the scorecard of how much money you hold after each throw: also write down details of anything that happens to you, e.g. moving house, losing your job, being evicted, etc.

6 There are no real winners in this game but you could stop when the first player owns a concrete house on the plain and holds 500 dollars in cash.

1 Your parents come to live with you and you have to support them. In future collect only 200 dollars each time you pass GO.

2 Violent rainstorm hits city. If you live in a ravine, miss your turn while you rebuild your shelter. If you live elsewhere, pay 100 dollars to repair your home.

3 Free bricks available from nearby building site. Use them to improve your home. You can charge an extra 10 dollars rent as long as you occupy that square.

4 Your daughter gets job as domestic servant. Her pay added to family income so in future collect an extra 50 dollars each time you pass GO.

5 Government builds highway through valley and plain. If you live there, throw the dice again. An odd number means your house is destroyed; you must move, paying the price of a new home.

6 There is a water shortage, but the standpipe by your home is still working and you charge other people to use it. Collect 20 dollars from each player.

Fig. 7.20 Chance cards for squatopoly

Fig. 7.21 Community chest cards for squatopoly

1 You and your neighbours install drainage pipes. Unless you live in a shelter collect 100 dollars, which represents the increase in the value of your house.

2 Temporary jobs provided working on government-sponsored improvement schemes. From now on you can land on the UNEMPLOYED square without penalty.

3 Price of building materials increases. Pay an extra 150 dollars when you move to your next house.

4 Government guarantees you will not be evicted from your present home. As long as you occupy it you may land on the EVICTED square without penalty.

5 If you live on the plain an electricity supply is to be introduced. Pay 50 dollars for its installation and in future charge 30 dollars rent to anyone who lands on your square.

6 Red Cross team arrives and distributes clothes and medical supplies. Advance five squares.

Singapore: a city state

Singapore's position at the southern tip of the Malay peninsula, commanding the sea routes between India and China, made it a very valuable possession for Britain which acquired the island in 1819 and developed it as a port and naval base. In 1963 Singapore became part of the newly created Federation of Malaysia but was forced to withdraw two years later. Since then it has followed its own course as an independent state.

During colonial times Singapore became the focus of immigration from other parts of Asia, especially China. This is reflected in the racial mixture of its present population: 76 per cent Chinese, 15 per cent Malays, and 7 per cent Indians. However, since 1965 Singapore's democratic government has attempted to forge a strong national identity among the island's 2·2 million inhabitants. At first sight Singapore does not seem to be in a strong position to survive on its own. The island is only 585 km^2 in area which means that there is intense competition for land, with population densities reaching 375 000 people per km^2. In addition the city cannot even supply all its water needs and relies heavily on the Malaysian mainland to make up the balance. Nevertheless, the last fifteen years have seen the city state make remarkable leaps forward.

A combination of vigorous private enterprise and co-operative trade unions has achieved an impressive economic expansion. Singapore has seven large oil refineries, making it the third largest refining centre in the world after Houston and Rotterdam. The repair and servicing of bulk tankers is carried on at Jurong, Keppel, and in the former naval yards of Singapore harbour (Fig. 7.22). The discovery of oil beneath the South-East Asian seas has led to a booming industry in the manufacture and servicing of undersea drilling rigs. A large number of international oil companies operating in the area have made Singapore their local headquarters. The state's other major source of income is electronics and associated precision industries such as watches, cameras, and optical goods. Singapore can supply the financial investment and highly skilled labour force that these industries require. A massive industrial estate has been developed at Jurong to provide space for the expanding factories. At the same time a smart western-style business district has sprung up in the city centre to house Singapore's growing commercial and banking activities.

The government's biggest task has been

Fig. 7.22 Singapore island: land use

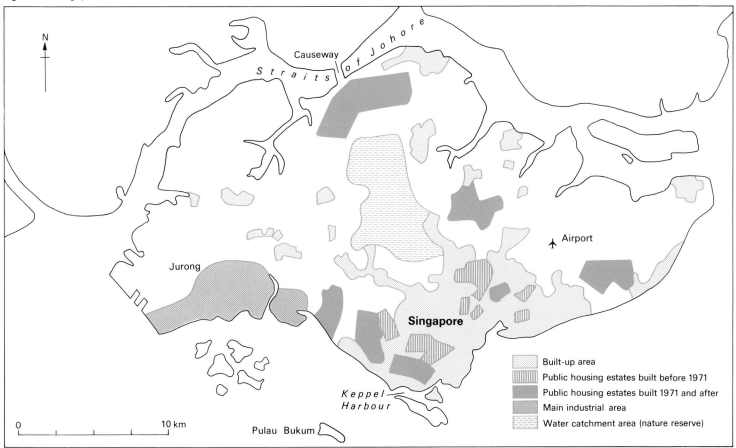

Built-up area
Public housing estates built before 1971
Public housing estates built 1971 and after
Main industrial area
Water catchment area (nature reserve)

0   10 km

the provision of adequate housing for Singapore's overcrowded population. At the time of independence there were 100 000 squatters living in shanty towns around the city. There was a chronic housing shortage and people were packed like sardines into the crowded shophouses of the old city. The shophouses are three- or four-storey nineteenth-century buildings, originally designed to house a single family with a shop or small workshop on the ground floor. They are now divided into a maze of small cubicles separated by makeshift partitions (Fig. 7.23), whole families often occupying a single cubicle. Details of some of the families, their jobs, and living conditions are given in Fig. 7.25.

The government set out to solve the problems of the overcrowded city by establishing a massive public housing programme. By 1980 about 70 per cent of the population had been rehoused, mostly in flats in multi-storey blocks. However, such progress has led to problems that are more usually associated with developed countries: the social disadvantages of high-rise living; the need to restrict family sizes; the pressure on land for industry and recreation. Only time will tell how successfully the government can tackle these difficulties but on its past record Singapore will meet the challenge with energy and skill.

12 Refer to Fig. 7.22 to answer the following questions:

a Why would you have expected the main built-up area to develop on the south coast of the island?

b Describe the position of the public housing estates built i) before 1971, ii) in 1971 and after. What is the main difference and why do you think this is?

c Where would you expect Singapore's main water reservoirs to be sited?

d Why do you think Jurong was chosen for the industrial estate?

e Why would the airport be so important to Singapore?

f One of the large oil refineries is situated on Pulau Bukum. Why is this an excellent place for it?

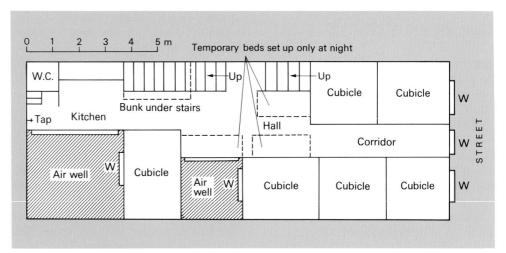

Fig. 7.23 First-floor plan of a shophouse

Fig. 7.24 Shophouses in an old part of Singapore

Fig. 7.25 Some residents of Upper Nankin Street, Singapore

Name	Age Husb.	Wife	Number of children (living with them)	Place of birth Husband	Wife	Husband's job	Size and position of cubicle	Furniture
The Wong family	38	37	Two, aged 5 and 4 years	Indonesia	Singapore	Casual labourer	3·6 × 3·2 m in an attic	Double bed, sideboard, 2 chairs
The Lee family	31	26	Five, aged between 6 years and 2 months	Guangdong (Kwangtung), China	Singapore	Odd job man in factories	2·1 × 3·0 m on first floor	Double bed (1·5 × 1·8 m), 2 sideboards
The Lam family	47	43	Seven, aged between 16 years and 18 months	Guangdong, China	Guangdong, China	Bricklayer	2·4 × 2·1 m on second floor	Double bed, sideboard
The Leong family	49	45	Three, aged between 14 and 4 years	Guangdong, China	Guangdong, China	Carpenter; unemployed due to illness	2·7 × 2·4 m on first floor	Double bed, sideboard, shelf
Wong Kwok Tong	66	—	Two, aged 26 and 24 years	Guangdong, China	—	Retired	2·7 × 2·1 m on first floor	Double bed, sideboard, table
Yip Sam Mui	—	62	One, aged 32 years. Her other six children died, most in infancy	—	Guangdong, China	Her son works as a smelter in an engineering shop	No cubicle: two bunks in a first-floor corridor	None

13 Look at the information about some of the residents of Upper Nankin Street given in Fig. 7.25.

a Find Guangdong (Kwangtung) Province on a map of China. Which other British colonial island is situated nearby? Why would the presence of this island have made emigration to Singapore easy?

b Why would you expect people from the same area of China to live close to each other, as in Upper Nankin Street?

c What kind of jobs do the men have? What disadvantages are associated with this type of job?

d Choose one of the families and draw a scale plan of their cubicle. Then to the same scale draw in a rectangle to represent each person who sleeps in the cubicle. Adults should be represented by a rectangle 1·7 × 0·5 metres and children by a rectangle 1 × 0·25 metres. Compare your plan with those drawn of other cubicles. This should give you an idea how crowded the shophouses of Singapore are.

Fig. 7.26 High-rise flats in one of Singapore's public housing estates

Kinshasa: a colonial city

Kinshasa is the capital city of Zaïre, formerly a colony of Belgium. In colonial times the city was called Leopoldville, after the Belgian king. Situated 400 km inland on the banks of the Congo river, it was founded in 1881 by the explorer Sir Henry Stanley who established a small river station there. The city grew slowly up to the 1920s when, due to improved river transport and good rail links to the sea, its trade began to flourish. The Second World War encouraged the development of industry and from then on the city expanded rapidly. Since the country gained its independence in 1960 American trade and investment has transformed Kinshasa into a bustling city of 2 million people, over 50 per cent of whom are squatters.

14 The two paragraphs below describe the sequence of development of Leopoldville between 1880 and 1960. The figures in brackets refer to the hexagons marked on the simplified plan of the city (Fig. 7.28).

  a Make a copy of Fig. 7.28 numbering each hexagon lightly in pencil.

  b Devise a colour scheme to represent the six types of land use listed in the key.

  c Read through the following passage and shade in each hexagon according to its correct land use.

  d When you have completed your plan write a paragraph describing the pattern of land use in Leopoldville in 1960.

Although there was no master plan for Leopoldville it is possible to identify the main stages of its development. One important factor was that the Belgian authorities were always careful to separate the European housing areas from those of the Africans, known as *cités*. The first development took place around the Stanley station and consisted of commercial and industrial areas (1), with adjoining European (2) and African (3) housing. About 8 km to the east

Fig. 7.27 Central Kinshasa with the Congo river in the background

is a larger, more recent area of development which is centred on the port and the original African town of Kinshasa. This too is divided into areas of business and industry (4–7) and African housing (8, 9). The area in between, called Kalina, remained empty for a long time before the Second World War and a large military camp was situated there in the post-war years (10, 11). It was also used as a neutral zone which separated the European housing along the river banks (12–14) from the African housing to the south-east.

After 1950 the pattern of the city changed dramatically. African migrants flooded into the city and were housed in a series of *cités* around the old town (15–18) and stretching off to the south-east (19–24). A belt of new industry was also established in this area (25–27). Meanwhile the European population too was growing and these newcomers were housed in isolated areas to the extreme west, well away from the African developments (28–30).

15 a On the land-use map you produced for Exercise 14 shade in another twenty hexagons to show the development of Kinshasa after 1960 as follows:

  10 hexagons of squatter settlements

   6 hexagons of business and industry

   2 hexagons of government-built housing (for Africans)

   2 hexagons of high-class residential suburbs (mainly European)

You have to decide where you think this building will have taken place. Remember to introduce a new category of shading for the squatter settlements and include this in the key.

  b Write a paragraph explaining the reasoning behind your distribution of these new areas of development.

Fig. 7.28 Simplified map of Leopoldville in 1960

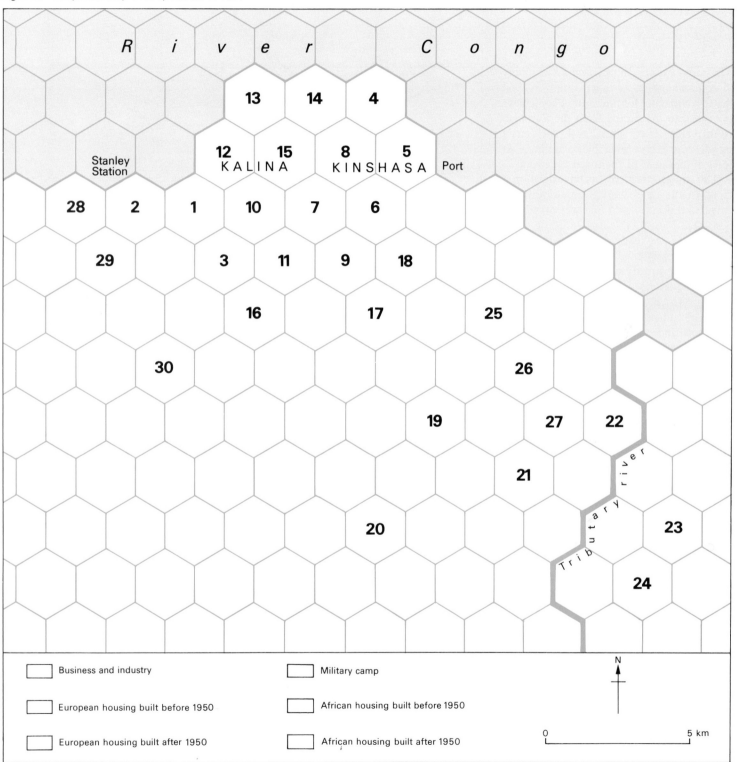

- Business and industry
- Military camp
- European housing built before 1950
- African housing built before 1950
- European housing built after 1950
- African housing built after 1950

0 _____ 5 km

Self-help squatters in Lusaka

The rapid expansion of Lusaka's economy after Zambia became independent in 1964 made it a magnet for migrants. People have poured into the capital from the Zambian countryside ever since and the city's population is now over half a million. At least 40 per cent of them are squatters.

The squatter settlements have developed close to the chief workplaces for ease of travel and occupy land that was previously considered unsuitable for building (Fig. 7.29). It is not really accurate to describe these settlements as shanty towns since they consist mostly of proper houses built by the squatters out of cheap, sun-dried bricks which are then plastered and painted. The houses are rarely over-crowded since the squatters can build on extra rooms when they like. However, in spite of their neat appearance, the settlements still face many problems. The water from their wells is often polluted by the pits that serve as lavatories. The unpaved roads are passable in the dry season, but they turn into quagmires when the rains arrive. There are no schools or clinics. Because their settlements are illegal the squatters have had to govern themselves and try to develop their own public facilities through community improvement schemes.

Recently the city council has attempted to accelerate this process of upgrading the squatter settlements by launching a major programme to help the four main ones. The chief difficulty was finding a way to provide resources without removing the self-help spirit of the squatters. Before any improvements could be made the government had to agree that the squatters would be allowed to stay on the land they had occupied. So it issued the squatters with licences that gave them ownership of the land under and im-mediately surrounding their houses for thirty years. All the remaining land is re-garded as common property.

The city council has helped improve the settlements by installing standpipes to pro-

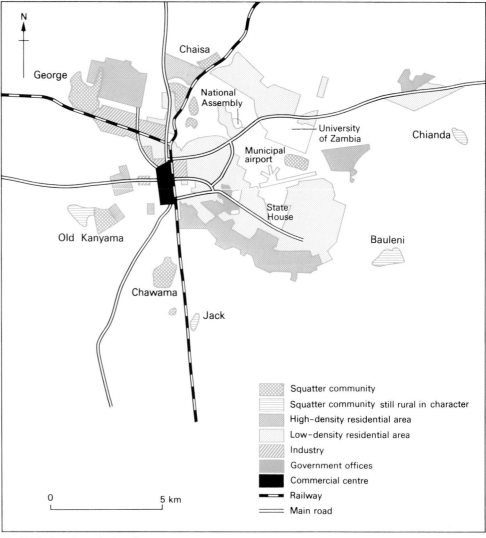

Fig. 7.29 Land use in Lusaka

Legend:
- Squatter community
- Squatter community still rural in character
- High-density residential area
- Low-density residential area
- Industry
- Government offices
- Commercial centre
- Railway
- Main road

vide a fresh water supply. Local people do the construction work, such as digging ditches for the water pipes, and are paid for this by the council. Every family pays so much a month in water rates: this money is collected as a lump sum from all those using a particular standpipe. If anyone's payment is late then the water supply to the stand-pipe is cut off. Consequently the neigh-bours soon make sure that everyone is fully paid up.

As improvements proceed some squat-ters build better houses in newly developed areas. All the planning for these new settle-ments is done by the local people with tech-nical help from a special team set up by the city council. So far this approach has been very successful because the squatters are given a sense of pride in their achievements and everyone has a personal stake in the success of the community.

16 A slogan used by the Lusaka city council's housing project unit is 'We are co-operators. Let us work together.' Using this idea design a poster that encourages squatters to improve their homes with the unit's help.

Fig. 7.30 Squatter housing that is very similar to a country village

Fig. 7.31 New housing built with the aid of the city council

17 Figs. 7.30 and 7.31 show two squatter settlements in Lusaka. Make a list of all the differences you can see between the two neighbourhoods.

18 Comment on the size and position of the following land uses in Lusaka (Fig. 7.29):
a Commercial centre.
b Industry.
c Squatter communities.
d Rural squatter communities.
What things on the map suggest that Lusaka is Zambia's capital?

Summary

The growth of the Third World's urban population is a major feature of the twentieth century, resulting from natural population increase and migration from the countryside. Many migrants become squatters, building makeshift homes on wasteland in and around the city. These illegal settlements vary in quality from place to place, though many lack basic amenities. Cities are also the most prosperous parts of Third World countries because they are the centres of industry, commerce, and government. There is usually a modern, western-style central business district where foreign firms have their offices as well as a high-class residential area occupied by the privileged wealthy minority.

Chapter **8** Transport: the essential link

Types of transport

It is easy to forget how much we rely on transport in the developed world. Unless you live close to your school you will have to use some form of transport to get there each day. You may travel by bus, by train, by car, or perhaps by bicycle. There is frequently a choice between two or more different methods. Many families own a car and can use it for a wide variety of purposes. There is a dense network of local and major roads which makes it easy to reach other towns and cities. The railway system provides fast long-distance travel and takes millions of commuters to their jobs every day. If you are travelling abroad on holiday or on business then jet aircraft can carry you to most countries in a matter of hours. The ports handle the massive amount of ocean-going trade on which Britain's economy depends.

1 Fig. 8.1 lists twelve factors which can be used to judge the efficiency and suitability of the four main types of transport.

  a Make a copy of the table and then give each type of transport a score out of four for each factor depending on how good you think the type of transport is. Use the following guide for scoring: very good 4, good 3, fair 2, and poor 1.

  b Add up the total score for each type of transport and compare these with other members of the class. Which types were considered best? Why might it be misleading to consider one type of transport to be 'better' than another?

Fig. 8.2 Simplified diagram to show the importance of transport to commercial agriculture

Fig. 8.1 A comparison of the four main types of transport

		Road	Rail	Water	Air
1	Speed				
2	Directness				
3	Cheapness over long distances				
4	Cheapness over short distances				
5	Cost of construction				
6	Movement of heavy, bulky goods				
7	Movement of large number of passengers				
8	Ease of access along routes				
9	Reliability				
10	Safety				
11	Adaptability to change				
12	Effect on environment				
	Total				

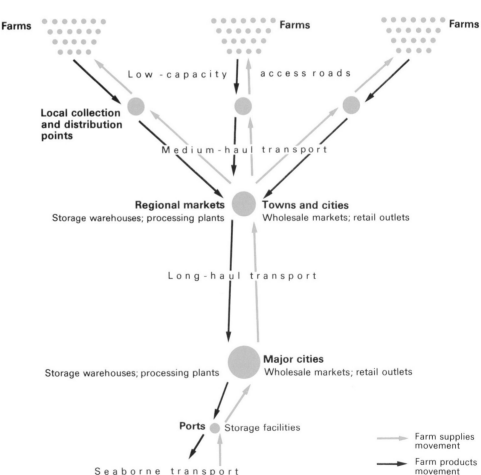

146

2 **a** In what ways would the transport requirements of less developed countries be different from our own?

b Which factors listed in Fig. 8.1 would be most important in a less developed country?

c What other forms of transport would be common in the less developed countries?

Transport systems in the less developed countries are usually very poor. The bulk of the population cannot afford to travel far and normally has little reason to do so. Long-distance transport is chiefly concerned with the movement of goods, raw materials, and agricultural produce. Many less developed countries get a large proportion of their income from the export of these primary products. An inefficient or poorly developed transport network can harm this trade severely. These countries also depend on the import of manufactured goods, chemicals, and fuel from the wealthier nations. If port facilities are inadequate then such vital supplies can be delayed for months.

3 **a** Write a paragraph explaining the main features of Fig. 8.2.

b What type of transport would you expect to be used for each stage of movement i) in a developed country, ii) in a less developed country?

c In how many different ways might the system be inefficient? At what points could the flow of goods be held up?

d Using Fig. 8.2 as a guide draw a similar diagram to show the way in which transport serves industry.

Fig. 8.3 The four main types of transport

Measuring efficiency

Since transport networks vary so much it is useful to have methods for comparing them. Naturally it is not possible to make direct comparisons between different types of transport, for instance between air routes and roads, because the means of travel and the routes covered differ so much. However it is possible to compare two networks of the same type. We might want to see how a network has changed over time, by comparing its layout in different years (Fig. 8.4). Alternatively we could compare the networks of two or more regions to find out how their efficiency varies.

The efficiency of a transport network depends on a large number of factors. Networks can be judged in terms of their length, the number of settlements they link, speed of travel, their capacity to transport goods and people, and the reliability of the service they offer. If we simply consider the routes themselves we can divide any network into two elements: the lines of transport (links) and the points they join (nodes). A node may be a type of settlement or it might be a junction where two or more links meet.

Dividing a network into links and nodes allows us to measure its efficiency. This is normally done by assessing the connectivity and accessibility of the network. Connectivity is the degree to which the nodes of a network are connected to each other. It is expressed in terms of an index which can be calculated by dividing the number of links

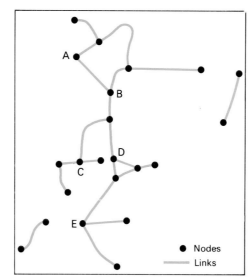

Fig. 8.5 A simplified diagram of Angola's road network in 1968

by the number of nodes. For example, Fig. 8.5 shows the number of links and nodes that the road network in Angola contained in 1968. Note that all junctions and the ends of any links represent nodes. In this case the network consists of 21 links and 22 nodes. Therefore its connectivity index is $\frac{21}{22}$ which equals 0·95. The higher the value the better connected the network is.

4 **a** Draw simplified diagrams like Fig. 8.5 of the networks for 1961 and 1974 shown in Fig. 8.4.

b Calculate the connectivity index for each of those two years. Do the indices suggest that the connectivity has improved between 1961 and 1974?

Fig. 8.6 Shortest path matrix and accessibility index for five points on Angola's road network in 1968

	A	B	C	D	E	Index
A	0	1	3	3	5	12
B	1	0	2	2	4	9
C	3	2	0	2	4	11
D	3	2	2	0	2	9
E	5	4	4	2	0	15

Accessibility measures the ease with which you can travel between the nodes of a network. On Fig. 8.5 five nodes have been identified by the letters A to E. A matrix has been drawn up on which is entered the number of links that have to be used to travel between each pair of nodes (Fig. 8.6). It is called a shortest path matrix because the number of links entered represents the smallest number of links that separates each pair of nodes. By adding up the totals for each row on the matrix we can find the accessibility index for each node. The node with the lowest index represents the most accessible place. The greater the index for a node the less accessible that place is.

5 **a** On the simplified diagram of the 1974 network which you drew for Exercise 4, mark in the five nodes lettered A to E from Fig. 8.5.

b Construct a shortest path matrix like that in Fig. 8.6 and fill it in for the situation in 1974. Calculate the new accessibility index for each node.

c Has the pattern of accessibility changed between 1968 and 1974 for the five points?

Fig. 8.4 The development of the road network in Angola

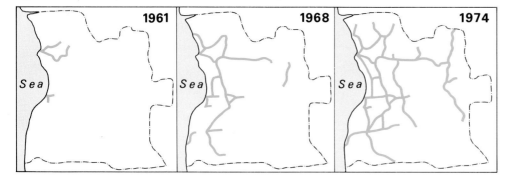

The growth of transport networks

Although every country is different, some generalizations can be made about the growth of transport networks in developing countries. It is simplest to think in terms of a series of stages represented by the six diagrams in Fig. 8.7.

Stage A. The country in this example is a tropical region with an accessible coastline. At first there is little economic development of the country's resources. The coast is dotted with scattered native fishing villages and a few trading posts established by foreign powers. Routes from the coast extend only a short way inland.

Stage B. Links are established between the coast and two inland settlements (I_1 and I_2). These might be mining centres or market towns for the collection of agricultural produce. The two ports with the best access inland (P_1 and P_2) expand and develop local feeder routes.

Stage C. Smaller settlements grow up on the main routes inland and each settlement develops feeder routes from its local area. The two ports continue to expand at the expense of the smaller ports.

Stage D. Economic development of the country is proceeding, probably under colonial control. Increased trade requires a better connected transport network. Routes are established linking the two ports and the two inland towns. Two of the intermediate towns (N_1 and N_2) begin to grow.

Stage E. There has been a dramatic improvement in the connection of the main settlements. Virtually every one has a direct link with every other. The increased movement of trade and people between these places has led to further development along the routes.

Stage F. By this stage economic activity has reached a peak and the transport system is fully developed. High-priority major routes have been built to join the two ports and the most important inland settlement,

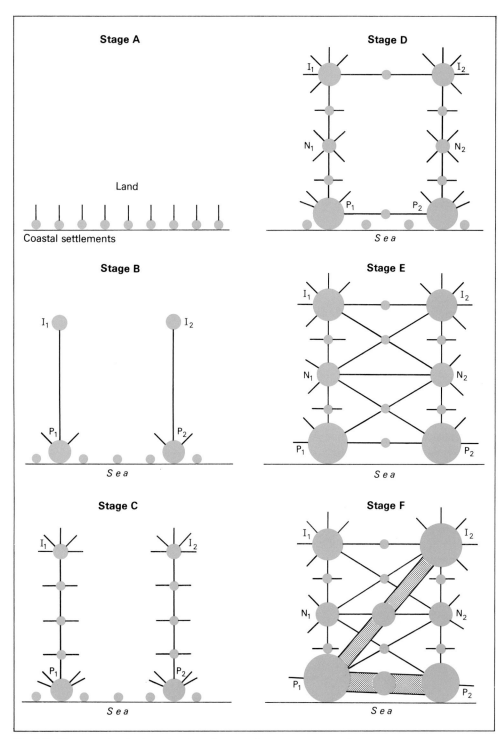

Fig. 8.7 The growth of a less developed country's transport network

which may well be the national capital.

One important point to note about this simplified model is that there is no attempt to describe the type of transport in use, as this will vary over time and from country to country.

Port development in Ghana

Most developing countries rely heavily on the international shipping network. Seaborne trade is essential for the export of their primary products and the import of food and manufactured goods. The efficiency of the network depends largely on the size and quality of the port facilities. It is easiest to develop ports along coasts that offer a number of sheltered deepwater sites in bays or estuaries.

6 Study an atlas map of Africa and locate each of the following major ports: Accra, Alexandria, Algiers, Cape Town, Casablanca, Dakar, Dar es Salaam, Durban, Lagos, Luanda, Maputo, and Mombasa. Mark them on a traced outline of the African coast.
  a Which countries does each port serve?
  b Suggest reasons for the growth of ports at each of these points.

In Ghana, as along the whole West African coast, there is a complete lack of natural harbour sites. The smooth, gently sloping shoreline has no clear inlets and even the largest rivers have very shallow mouths. As a result of these drawbacks Ghana's port system has grown up in an unusual fashion. It does not represent the logical sequence of development that can be found in more favoured parts of the world (Fig. 8.8).

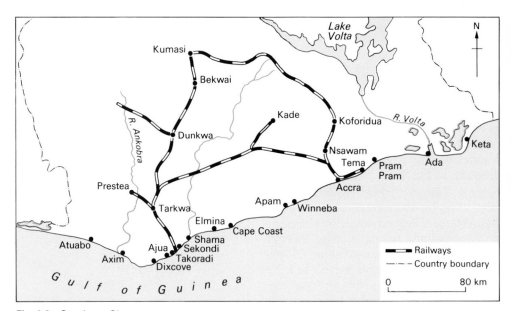

Fig. 8.8 Southern Ghana

Stage 1. Before the arrival of Europeans small fishing villages were the only coastal settlements. Then from the late fifteenth century Europeans began to establish forts on the coast to control trade and for storage of cargoes to be shipped abroad. They also provided victuals and water for visiting ships. Ships anchored offshore, beyond the surf zone, and goods were transferred to the beach in the ships' boats or by local canoemen. Competition between the European powers led to a continually changing pattern as forts were destroyed and rebuilt. The main cargo throughout this period was slaves being transported across the Atlantic to the Americas.

Stage 2. After 1800 trade became increasingly dominated by the British and the Dutch and in 1872 the British gained complete control of the coast. It was only after this time that routes were pushed inland to colonize the interior of the country. The routes ran from the coast to Kumasi, the major inland market town and focus of routes from the north. The abolition of the slave trade meant that exports now consisted chiefly of agricultural and mineral products from the interior. These were moved from Kumasi by the easiest routes to the ports of Cape Coast, Axim, and Accra. Consequently these three surf ports became the main centres of trade in the late nineteenth century.

Stage 3. As trade expanded the colonists wanted to build railways from the coast to Kumasi to provide a more efficient transport network. However, the most important ports at this stage (Cape Coast, Axim, and Accra) were unsuitable for further development. Instead a pier was built at Sekondi in 1898 and a railway line constructed linking the new port with Kumasi. Since Accra was the territory's capital it was chosen as the terminus for a second railway line to Kumasi and a pier was built in 1907. However the port suffered from silting,

Fig. 8.9 A surf boat off Cape Coast

Fig. 8.10 Cargo ships at anchor in Takoradi harbour

emphasizing its unsuitability. During this stage the surf ports of Atuabo, Dixcove, Ajua, Shama, Elmina, Apam, and Pram Pram were closed. They were unable to compete with the improved facilities at Sekondi and Accra, which now handled a much higher proportion of the total trade.

Stage 4. Starting in the 1920s, with the completion of the coast road between Sekondi and Accra and the railway to Kade, settlements on the main transport routes began to expand. Nsawam, Koforidua, Tarkwa, Dunkwa, and Bekwai all grew rapidly during this period. Before long it became clear that Ghana required a proper deepwater port and that neither Sekondi nor Accra was appropriate. A new artificial harbour with a large protective breakwater was constructed at Takoradi and opened in 1928, causing the closure of nearby Sekondi. The new port monopolized the handling of traditional exports such as rubber, timber, and palm oil, as well as the new imports of coal and petroleum products. The remaining surf ports of Cape Coast, Winneba, Ada and Keta also declined in importance.

Stage 5. In 1962 Accra's congested and outmoded port was superseded by the modern deepwater harbour of Tema. Following the

opening of Tema the surviving surf ports were closed and all trade now passes through the two deepwater harbours. Takoradi handles the high tonnage export traffic in timber, manganese, and bauxite while Tema's trade is based on the export of cocoa and aluminium ingots. Tema is also far more important for the import of dry cargoes and crude oil. The transport network now consists of a triangle of major routes (road, rail, and air) which link Ghana's three largest concentrations of population and economic activity: Accra-Tema, Takoradi-Sekondi, and Kumasi.

7 **a** Match each diagram in Fig. 8.11 to the appropriate stage described in the text above. Then make a copy of the diagrams in their correct sequence, numbering each stage. By referring to Fig. 8.8, identify the main ports at each stage and label them on your diagrams.
   b Now write an account of the main changes that took place from one stage to another.
   c How closely does the sequence of development match the model described on page 149? Make a list of the main differences and similarities.

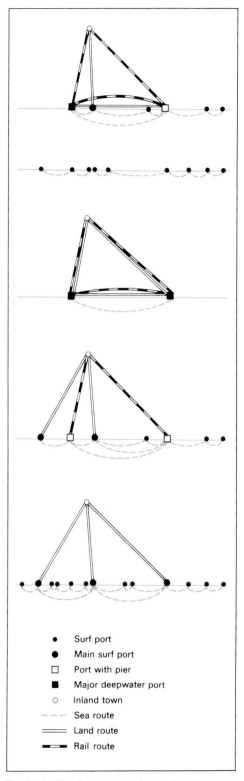

- ●   Surf port
- ⬤   Main surf port
- □   Port with pier
- ■   Major deepwater port
- ○   Inland town
- ---   Sea route
- ═   Land route
- ▬   Rail route

Fig. 8.11 The five stages of port development in Ghana

Inland transport on Lake Volta

Until recently water transport in Ghana was not very popular. The country's largest river, the Volta, was quite unsuitable for long distance travel. Bars at the river's mouth prevented large ships entering, rapids interrupted its course, and the water level dropped dangerously low during the dry season.

Then in 1966 a large dam across the Volta at Akosombo was completed. Its main aim was to generate electricity for the city of Accra and a new aluminium smelter at Tema. A huge lake, 8500 km² in area, collected in the valleys behind the dam (Fig. 8.12). This lake, stretching 400 km through the heart of Ghana, provided a valuable new means of access to the interior. In 1969 the Volta Lake Transport Company was formed, owned jointly by the Ghanaian government and a British shipping company. Transport operations started the following year and in 1975 the government took over the company completely. Now regular passenger and freight services are well established over the full length of the lake. There is one passenger vessel with room for fifty passengers in cabins and many more on deck.

8 Refer to Fig. 8.13 to answer the following questions:
   a Which stretches of the lake were busiest?
   b In which direction did most movement take place?
   c Which times of the year provided the most traffic?
   d How did the total number of passengers change between 1973 and 1975?

During these early years economic problems tended to reduce passenger traffic, since many people preferred the cheaper alternative of canoe travel. A valuable addition to the passenger trade is the use of the boat for tourist cruises, especially to visit

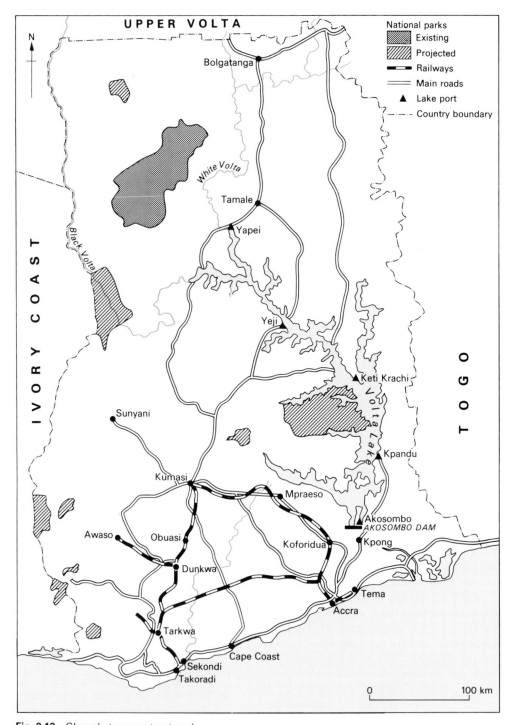

Fig. 8.12   Ghana's transport networks

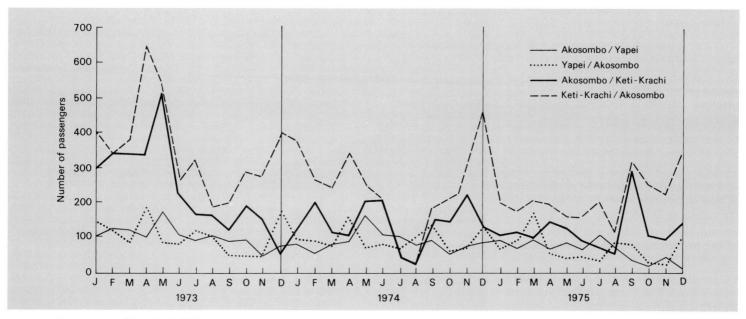

Fig. 8.13 Passenger traffic on Lake Volta

Fig. 8.14 The Yeji ferry crossing Lake Volta

the new national parks near the lake. The transport company also operates two freight vessels. Northbound traffic consists mainly of agricultural supplies and equipment, whereas southbound traffic is predominantly farm produce, notably rice and cotton.

Transport on Lake Volta still has several problems to contend with. Vessels have been plagued by mechanical problems, leading to breakdowns and interrupted services. Port facilities require urgent improvement with the provision of proper piers and ramps at all terminals. In comparison with the north-south road route the lake journey is relatively slow. However, this time difference is reduced by the delay that road traffic faces at the Yeji ferry crossing. The big advantage which water transport has to offer is that it is far cheaper for moving heavy goods. For a country like Ghana, which imports all its fuel, this can mean valuable long-term savings.

9 If Ghana could afford to extend its main road network by 500 km, where do you think the new roads should be built? Mark your proposals on a copy of Fig. 8.12 and write a paragraph explaining the reasons for your plan.

Air transport

Many parts of the less developed world are so remote that overland transport is out of the question. If the population is spread over great distances or the environment is hazardous, then air travel is the most practical means of access. This is particularly true of mountain areas like the Andes or Himalayas, of extensive deserts or forests, and of long island chains such as Indonesia. Where these regions are being opened up for economic development, as in the Amazon Basin, the aeroplane is an essential part of the pioneer process. Landlocked countries often have to rely on aircraft for moving freight: Chad, in Africa, has to export all its frozen meat to the coastal markets in this way.

Fig. 8.15 This transport brings supplies to a mining camp in a forested area of eastern Bolivia

Fig. 8.16 Less important air routes in India

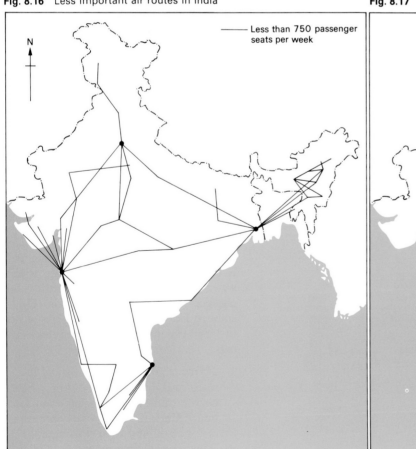

Less than 750 passenger seats per week

Fig. 8.17 Base map for Exercise 11

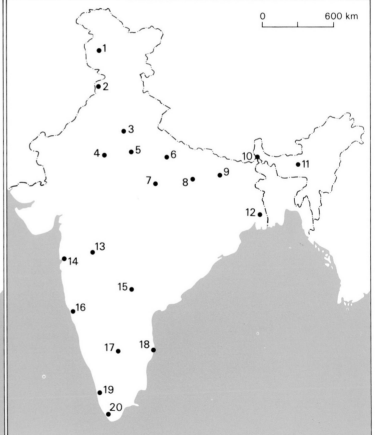

0   600 km

International air passenger traffic is also important to the less developed countries. It provides a vital link with the economies of the developed world and brings in large numbers of businessmen and tourists. In times of crisis aircraft are used to fly in urgently needed relief supplies, such as food, medicine, and clothing.

10 Study Fig. 8.16.
  a What is the pattern shown by the less important services?
  b Which four cities do these routes converge on?
  c What purposes do you think these routes serve?
  d Where would you expect the more important services to operate?

11 a Make a tracing of Fig. 8.17. Use an atlas if necessary to find out the names of the numbered cities.
  b Using the information in the route matrix (Fig. 8.18), mark on your map each service by drawing a line between the appropriate cities. The width of the line should indicate the importance of the route, as follows:
  A (750–1500 seats): 1 mm wide
  B (1500–3000 seats): 2 mm wide
  C (3000–6000 seats): 3 mm wide
  D (over 6000 seats): 4 mm wide
  c How does this map compare with the pattern you predicted in Exercise 10?
  d Which cities are served by the busiest routes?
  e Which parts of the country are not served by main routes?
  f Suggest some reasons for the pattern of routes shown on your map. A map of India's physical geography will help you with this.

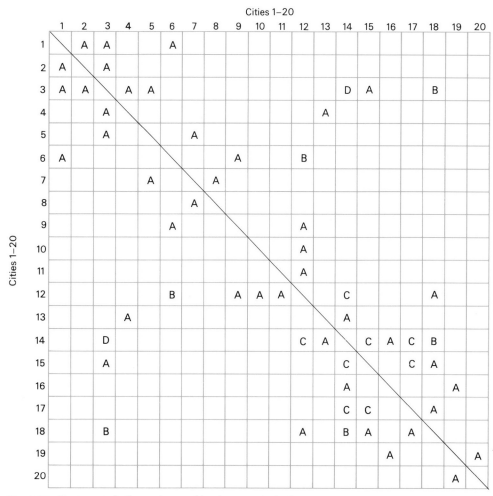

Cities 1–20

Cities 1–20

	1	2	3	4	5	6	7	8	9	10	11	12	13	14	15	16	17	18	19	20
1		A	A			A														
2	A		A																	
3	A	A		A	A								D	A			B			
4			A									A								
5			A				A													
6	A								A			B								
7				A			A													
8							A													
9						A						A								
10												A								
11												A								
12						B		A	A	A			C			A				
13			A										A							
14		D										C	A		C	A	C	B		
15		A											C				C	A		
16													A					A		
17													C	C			A			
18		B										A		B	A		A			
19															A					A
20																		A		

Fig. 8.18 Route matrix for major weekly air routes in India

Fig. 8.19 Landing strip in the rain forest of Ecuador

Zambia and the freedom railway

Railways are the lifeline by which Zambia survives, as it is a landlocked state, sharing its borders with eight other central African countries. It relies on rail links through these neighbours to reach the ports which handle its imports and exports. Over 90 per cent of Zambia's earnings come from the export of copper, a bulky product that is moved most cheaply by rail.

When Zambia became independent in 1964 its transport system was geared towards the south, with most trade passing through Rhodesia (now Zimbabwe) to Beira in Mozambique. But Rhodesia's unilateral declaration of independence in 1965 revealed the vulnerability of this route, and in 1973 the rail link was cut when Rhodesia closed its border with Zambia due to political conflict.

However, even before Rhodesia's UDI, President Kaunda of Zambia and President Nyerere of Tanzania had considered the construction of an alternative rail route. This would run from Zambia's copper belt to the port of Dar es Salaam in Tanzania. The cost of such a project was well beyond the means of the two African countries. They tried without success to borrow money from the World Bank, several western states, and the USSR. Then early in 1965, when President Nyerere visited Bei-

Fig. 8.20 Base map for the Tazara railway route

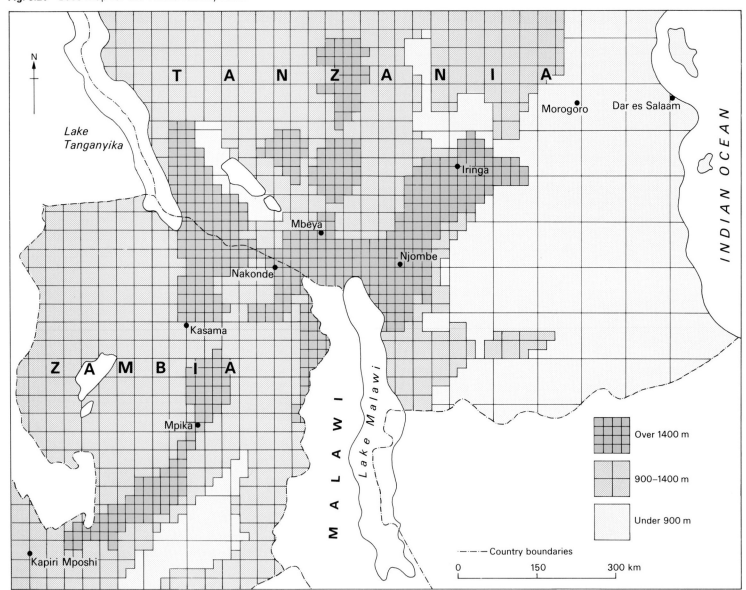

jing (Peking), the Chinese offered to finance the line and give help in its construction. It was called the Tanzam or Tazara railway (Tanzania-Zambia Railway Authority).

Any large-scale construction project, such as a major railway line, needs very careful planning. A well-chosen route will cut costs substantially. Although costs go up as the length of track increases, the shortest route is unlikely to be the cheapest. This is because the shortest route, a straight line between two places, takes no account of the nature of the land between them. It is usually less expensive to go round physical obstacles, such as mountains or lakes, than to find some means of crossing them. Changes of route for this reason are known as negative deviations.

In some cases routes will be lengthened deliberately so that they can be used to link up places along the line of travel. These may be towns or cities, agricultural areas, or perhaps mining locations. For the deviation to be worthwhile the benefit that comes from the increased trade must outweigh the extra construction costs. Such alterations to the route are called positive deviations.

12 Look at Fig. 8.20 and locate the two terminals for the railway: Dar es Salaam on the Tanzanian coast and Kapiri Mposhi in the Zambian copper belt. The land which separates them varies a great deal in its height and steepness.

Assume that the cost of railway construction in the map area is as follows:

under 900 m	£1 million per square crossed
900–1400 m	£2 million per square crossed
over 1400 m	£3 million per square crossed

a Lay a piece of tracing paper over Fig. 8.20 and mark on the following routes (you have to stay inside the borders of the two countries):
i) the shortest route between Dar es Salaam and Kapiri Mposhi.

Fig. 8.21 Track-laying ceremony at the Tanzania-Zambia border

ii) the cheapest route linking the two terminals, without necessarily passing through any intermediate towns.
iii) the cheapest route linking the two terminals *and* passing through at least five of the intermediate towns.
b Compare your routes and their costs with those of other members of the class. Go back over your planned routes for (ii) and (iii) and mark in two separate colours those sections of the routes that you consider to be positive or negative deviations.

Plans for the Tazara railway were agreed with China in 1968 and two years later construction began. About 35 000 workers, including 15 000 Chinese, were involved in the project. The railway was built westwards from Dar es Salaam so that it could be used to transport materials and equip-

ment from the port as it progressed inland. The 1900-km route required the construction of 300 bridges and 21 tunnels. One-third of all these major engineering works are found in the 160-km section between Mlimba and Makumbaku, where the line makes the steep climb up to the Southern highlands (Fig. 8.22). Additional problems were presented by areas of soft soils and seepage, particularly during the rainy season.

The line crossed the Zambian border in mid 1973 and reached the terminal town of Kapiri Mposhi in early 1975. It took some time before the railway became fully operational since 8000 personnel—engineers, shunters, signalmen, station staff, etc.—had to be recruited and trained. The total cost of the scheme was £170 million, which China provided as an interest-free loan to be paid back over thirty years. This represented a considerable sacrifice on the part of China, which is itself desperately in need of better railways.

13 Look at the actual route of the Tazara railway on Fig. 8.22.
  a Which of the routes you chose is it closest to?
  b What does it tell you about the way the route was planned in real life?

When it was opened the Tazara line was called the great Uhuru (meaning freedom) railway. It was seen as a symbol of independence from the white dominance of South Africa and Rhodesia. But between its planning in the 1960s and its completion ten years later the political situation had changed enormously and new competition had emerged.

When the route to Beira was closed in 1973 Zambia was forced to take emergency measures to keep its trade flowing. A state-owned transportation company was set up with Tanzania to run fleets of lorries along the highway to Dar es Salaam, while there was increasing use of the Benguela railway leading to the Angolan port of Lobito. In fact, by the time the Tazara line was opened, the Benguela railway was carrying a large proportion of Zambia's trade. Then in mid 1975 the Benguela line was closed by a civil war in Angola and Zambia became completely dependent on its road and rail routes to Dar es Salaam.

The limitations of the Tazara railway now became apparent. In addition to the inadequate rolling stock, problems arose from the congestion and inefficiency of Dar es Salaam as a port. In spite of recent expansion Dar es Salaam simply could not handle all the trade that was being funnelled into it. With the added load of all Zambia's shipments, especially its bulky copper exports, Dar es Salaam was beset by chronic delays. By late 1978 the situation was so bad that President Kaunda was forced to re-open the rail link through Rhodesia, in spite of the political implications at the time. Tazara is now squeezed by road transport to Dar es Salaam and by rail transport south. If the railway is to avoid losses it needs to carry 80 per cent of Zambia's copper production.

Although Tanzania stood to gain less than Zambia from the Tazara railway, it

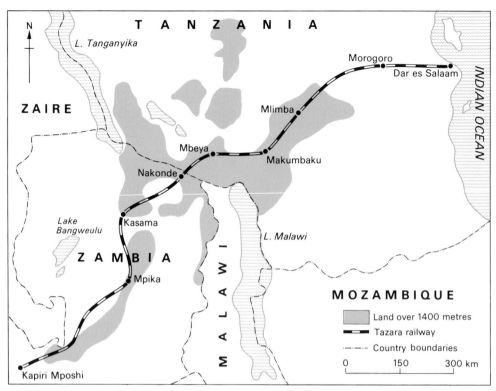

Fig. 8.22 The route of the Tazara railway

Fig. 8.23 The line's first passenger service arrives in Dar es Salaam

was still seen as a crucial part of national development. It will help to open up the previously neglected south-western region for farming and to encourage the exploitation of known coal and iron ore deposits in the same area.

14 Refer to an atlas to find another ten developing countries which share Zambia's problem of being land-locked. Mark them on a world map and draw in the routes you think each country would rely on to reach the sea.

Coltrania

The final set of exercises in this chapter is concerned with the overall development of an imaginary country's transport network. Consequently you will need to consider all aspects of the work you have done so far on transport. It would also be useful to refer back to the section on tropical forests in Chapter 3.

Coltrania is situated in the tropics; it has a population of 100 million and the total area is 8 million km². The Coltranian population is made up of a range of racial mixtures, incorporating European, native Indian, and Negro elements. The only surviving pure natives of the country live as scattered tribes in the rain forest of the North. They are thought to number approximately 100 000 but some tribes are virtually untouched by civilization and are potentially hostile to intruders.

There is an acute shortage of agricultural land and of jobs for the growing population of the South West, resulting in a continuous flow of migrants to the provinces of the South and South East. Coltrania's population is growing at the rate of 2½ per cent each year.

Basic information about the country is provided in Figs. 8.24, 8.25, and 8.26. Study the maps and table carefully before you answer the following questions.

15 Write a brief description of Coltrania, indicating the main characteristics of its population distribution, economic activities, and urban development.

Fig. 8.24 Coltrania: settlement and economic activity

Fig. 8.25 Basic data for the regions of Coltrania

Region	Population %	Area %	Value manufactured goods %	Minimum monthly wages
North	4	42	0·5	173
South West	30	18	6·5	151
South	43	11	79·0	225
South East	18	7	13·0	208
Centre East	5	22	1·0	173

16 Comment on the state of development of the country's transport network. What factors are likely to have led to the present pattern?

17 a Trace the railway network from Fig. 8.26. Then make a simplified diagram in order to calculate the connectivity index. All towns marked on the map should be regarded as nodes, as should the junctions between two links and the end of a link, whether a town is situated there or not.

   b Compare your result with the connectivity index for the road network, which is 1·16. What does this tell you about the relative efficiency of each system?

The Coltranian government wants to integrate the North region (Fig. 8.27) with the rest of the country. Ten years ago the capital of Coltrania was moved from Rollins in the south to Braxtonia. The move was part of the policy of the government to draw attention to the interior and north of the country and to encourage settlement and economic development there. Currently the main transport network for the North is the system of navigable waterways.

18 Look at Fig. 8.27 in order to study the accessibility of the area.
   a Draw a simplified diagram of the waterway network.
   b Construct a shortest path matrix (see p. 148) for the following towns: Hemphill, Sheppville, Burrello, Zoller, Dolphyaba, Burtonia, Zawinul, Samrivers, Mingus, Barbieri.
   c Calculate the accessibility index for each town.
   d Write a paragraph describing the general pattern of accessibility in the North region.

A serious drought in the South West has put pressure on the Coltranian government to provide new areas of farming land for migrants in cleared areas of the North's

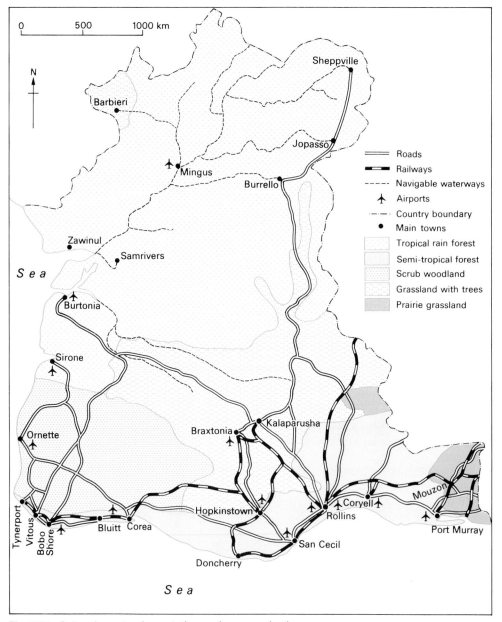

Fig. 8.26 Coltrania: natural vegetation and communications

tropical rain forest. Also the government is eager to exploit the valuable mineral deposits of the North for both home use and for export. Information about these resources is given in Fig. 8.27. To make these projects possible the government intends to construct a system of 10 000 km of unpaved roads.

19 a Using a copy of Fig. 8.27 mark in the road system that you would recommend the government to construct in order to open up the North region.

   b Describe the reasoning behind your plan. What further information would be useful in drawing up the final plan?

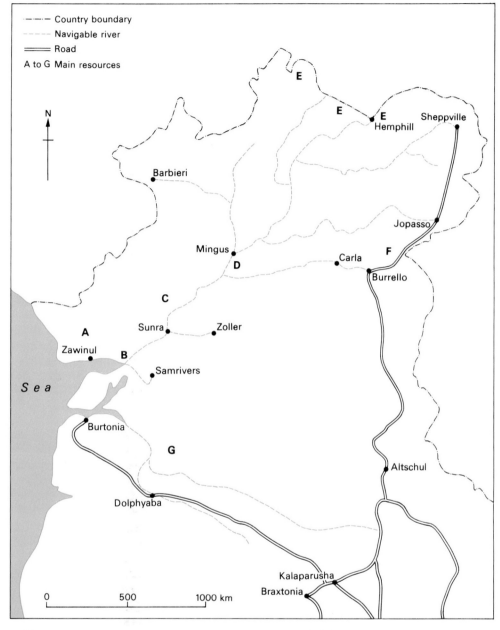

Summary

Efficient transport systems are an essential part of development. We have seen how various techniques can be used to assess the efficiency of transport networks. Generally speaking, networks in developing countries tend to be relatively simple and are often outdated or overused. Governments do not have the funds to build elaborate systems like those found in developed nations. Only a minority of roads are surfaced and few people can afford to own cars. Railways were usually constructed by colonial powers and reflect their requirements for moving goods rather than people. Developing countries rely heavily on the export and import of goods by sea, but suffer from inadequate port facilities that hold up shipments. Air transport is useful in opening up remote areas, but some governments have invested in expensive airports and airlines when there is no real justification for them. The lack of a proper transport system makes it very difficult to unify and administer a country due to the isolation of some regions.

A: Manganese mines—the ore is transported by train to a port near Zawinul.

B: Forestry projects based on plantations of a few commercial species.

C: Bauxite deposits.

D: Oil and manganese deposits.

E: Large oil deposits discovered in two neighbouring countries adjacent to this area.

F: Tin deposits, possibly among the largest in the world.

G: Enormous deposits of high-grade iron ore. These would require a new rail link to the sea for export.

Fig. 8.27 North region of Coltrania and its resources

Chapter 9 Industry and trade

The demand for jobs

In this chapter we shall look at the difficulty of developing industry in the Third World and the changes in employment that this will involve. The first major hurdle which the less developed countries must face is simply providing enough jobs for their growing populations.

In recent years developed countries have faced a mounting unemployment problem; there are at least 15 million people out of work in the western world. So far governments have cushioned the effects of this by providing unemployment pay and free health and education facilities, but in the less developed countries there are no such benefits. The unemployed, who number over 300 million, have nothing to fall back on, since most developing nations cannot afford to supply unemployment pay, family allowances, and free social services. They have no retraining schemes or job creation programmes to improve the situation, and the problem is becoming more serious all the time. It is estimated that 1000 million new jobs will have to be created by the end of the century.

The great majority of people in less developed countries work in agriculture, and because farming operations are so seasonal, there are usually several months of the year when little work is available. This represents a form of hidden unemployment. The introduction of machines has also reduced the demand for labour, making many landless peasants redundant. However, the adoption of high-yield varieties and improved irrigation can increase labour requirements because of multiple cropping. The main problem is that the rural population has a much lower standard of living than most town dwellers. Nearly all the jobs in industry are found in urban areas and those people lucky enough to get one earn far better wages than their rural counterparts. Even without a proper job there are far more opportunities to get money in a big city.

To help to solve the employment problem worthwhile jobs need to be created in rural areas as an alternative to agriculture. It has been suggested that income must be spread more evenly so that the persistent migration to the cities is halted.

Fig. 9.1 It is increasingly difficult to find jobs in Britain

Fig. 9.2 Waiting for work outside the docks in Freetown, Sierra Leone

The structure of industry

When looking at the structure of industry it is usual to divide it into three categories: primary, secondary, and tertiary.

Primary industry is concerned with the exploitation of natural resources and raw materials. It includes agriculture, forestry, fishing, and mining.

Secondary industry deals with the manufacturing of products. These may be made directly from raw materials or they may be assembled from components produced by other secondary industries.

Tertiary industry consists of jobs that provide a service but do not actually produce any goods. These cover a wide range of businesses and professions including health services, education, police forces, armed forces, government offices, and management in private industry. Tertiary industry also includes people involved in transport and the retail trades.

Fig. 9.3 The structure of employment in selected countries

Country	Percentage of workforce employed in:		
	Primary industry	Secondary industry	Tertiary industry
Tanzania	83	6	11
India	74	11	15
Indonesia	60	11	29
Nigeria	56	17	27
Brazil	41	22	37
Jamaica	28	17	55
USSR	17	47	36
Japan	13	39	48
UK	2	43	55
USA	2	33	65

1 Copy out the definitions of each type of industry and make a list of five jobs for each category as examples.

2 Use the data given in Fig. 9.3 to draw a divided bar graph that shows the employment structure of each country.

a How does the employment structure of developing countries differ from that of the developed world?

b What reasons can you suggest for this pattern?

c Why do you think Jamaica has a relatively high percentage employed in tertiary industry?

Fig. 9.4 Primary, secondary, and tertiary stages in the cotton industry

The development of industry

The less developed countries account for only 7 per cent of the world's industrial production and their industries provide jobs for only 13 per cent of their workforce. Many developing countries are eager to expand their industrial capacity, but this presents many difficulties. One major drawback is their lack of technical knowledge. Only 2 per cent of the world's research and development is carried on in developing countries. Consequently they have to rely on technology supplied by the developed world. This is very costly to buy and is frequently inappropriate to the developing countries' needs. Big multinational firms have developed these techniques for their home operations where a large amount of machinery is used. The less developed countries cannot afford this equipment: they want industries that will take advantage of their abundant cheap labour and ease the unemployment problem.

In the past Third World governments have too often financed large-scale prestige projects such as steelworks, oil refineries, and highly mechanized factories. Because these plants are so expensive they are usually developed in co-operation with the multinational firm that supplies the equipment and expertise. These multinational firms rarely make use of local industries and bring in all the components they need from abroad. Similarly, they prefer to employ their own businessmen as managers rather than training new people. Labour requirements for these plants are deliberately low, though the basic workforce is normally recruited from the developing country.

3   Mahatma Gandhi, the famous Indian political leader, said: ' . . . . men go on saving labour until thousands are without work and thrown on the open streets to die of starvation. Today machinery helps a few to ride on the backs of millions.'
How is Gandhi suggesting that inappropriate industrial development can encourage social inequality within a developing country?

Fig. 9.5   A high-technology factory: the Volkswagen assembly plant in Lagos, Nigeria

Appropriate technology

Appropriate technology is seen as a way of avoiding the disadvantages of high technology industries. It refers to the development of smaller-scale industries that suit the resources of the less developed countries. Appropriate technology avoids high expenditure on capital equipment and energy and instead it aims to make maximum use of the labour available. By offering employment to a larger number of people it spreads the profit of industry more widely and because it places emphasis on skilled labour, it provides more job satisfaction. It does not set out to replace traditional industries but rather to develop them so that they are more competitive. Appropriate technology makes maximum use of locally available resources, preferably renewable ones, and aims to make effective use of waste products through recycling. This helps to preserve the environment.

For appropriate technology to work properly it must serve the needs of the people at a price they can afford. For this reason it has been most successful in providing simple, cheap machines that fulfil existing requirements. Examples of these are man-powered water pumps, machines for grinding and threshing grain, basic windmills, and simple agricultural equipment. Fig. 9.7 is an example of a very cheap biogas installation that has been developed in Tanzania. Dung is put into the well at the far right with an equal amount of water and goes into a large pit under the gas tanks. As it ferments a slimy mixture floats to the surface and is taken off at the opening in the middle to be used for fertilizer. The gas rises from the pit and is trapped in seven oil drums, held in place by a wooden framework. A tube links the gas holder directly to a simple cooker, made by punching holes in a can which fits inside an ordinary charcoal stove.

Fig. 9.6 Trying out a simple reflective solar cooker. Experiments using heat from the sun are going on all over the world

Fig. 9.7 Another example of appropriate technology

Encouraging small industries

Small industries are a vital factor in the economy of less developed countries. They consist of local enterprises operated by families or individuals in the city or countryside. Frequently they are based on traditional skills such as weaving, pottery making, wood and leather working, food processing, and simple metal forging. City industries also deal in more advanced work connected with things like electrical goods, plastics, glass, paper, and light engineering. The main feature of all these concerns is that they are quite separate from the large industrial organizations. They usually operate outside the government regulations laid down for industry. Because of this they are referred to as the 'informal' or 'unorganized' industrial sector. The informal sector also includes a multitude of street traders and odd job men.

It is estimated that the informal sector employs 30 per cent of the industrial workforce in South East Asia and Latin America and as much as 80 per cent in India and Africa. Yet so far very few governments of developing countries have tried to help these industries. If they were given assistance in the form of loans and advice, there is great potential for growth. Since they are often considered illegal, they find it hard to get official credit and this denies them the money they need to expand. City-based industries are usually located in slums or squatter communities where transport facilities and public services are very poor. As a result of these disadvantages small industries are very vulnerable to competition.

Industries in rural areas face more problems than those in urban centres. They tend to be smaller and more traditional, while their scattered distribution limits the market they can serve. Sometimes they are plagued by middlemen who supply raw materials at high prices and then buy back finished goods at a much lower rate, giving themselves a handsome profit. The rural industries are being badly hit by the migration of people to the cities and by the flood of cheap mass-produced articles that are replacing traditional goods. But small industries offer a vital means of keeping people in the countryside. They provide valuable employment during slack periods in the farming year and represent an important source of income for many families. One country which has given wholehearted support to its small industries is India.

India is not merely a country of small industries. It is the ninth largest industrial producer in the world and has a wide range of advanced, modern manufacturing organizations which employ 5 million people. But the informal industrial sector accounts for about four times that number. (Remember that the country's total workforce is nearly 300 million, the vast majority of whom are employed in agriculture.) Every year India has to create 6 million new jobs and small industries represent an important source of work. As long ago as 1954 India set up a small industries development organization (SIDO) which offers training, advice, and specialized services to small firms. More recently the government has established a network of district industry centres which provide a full range of technical, managerial, and financial facilities under one roof. Laws have been made to limit the manufacture of over 600 products to small industries: these include quite elaborate electronic and light engineering goods. Naturally, this protects small firms from competition from larger organizations.

The Indian government subsidizes the traditional rural industries of handloom weaving and spinning, even though they are becoming increasingly uneconomic. The management of these industries is in the hands of workers' co-operatives, while the state acts as middleman. Inevitably their products cost more than factory-made goods, but the Indian government is obliged to support and protect them for social reasons. Unemployment is already very high in rural areas and everything possible must be done to prevent a further decline in opportunities for work.

Fig. 9.8 Traditional pottery-making in India

Fig. 9.9 Finishing jeans in Hong Kong

Trade

Trade is an essential part of every country's economic system. This is partly because no country can hope to provide all its requirements from its own resources. It is also because trade is a major way of increasing national wealth. At present world trade is dominated by the developed countries. The less developed nations, apart from oil-exporting countries, have little control over the amount of goods that they can sell abroad or the prices that they are paid for them. This is due to the structure of their trade, that is the types of good that they import and export.

4 Look at Fig. 9.10.
  a What is the major difference between the types of product that Nigeria imported and exported in the two years? What reasons can you suggest to explain this difference?
  b How did the nature of Nigeria's trade alter between 1966 and 1980? Do you think the country was better or worse off in 1980? Why?
  c Can you suggest any disadvantages arising from the new pattern of exports?

Most developing countries rely on the export of primary products (raw materials and agricultural goods) for the bulk of their earnings. To some extent this is the result of the geographical distribution of valuable minerals and the fact that some crops can only be grown in tropical conditions. However, it also reflects the pattern of trade that developed during the eighteenth and nineteenth centuries. The European powers had a ready-made market in their colonies where they could sell industrial goods in exchange for food and raw materials. In some cases the European countries actually restricted industries in their colonies if they competed with their own factories. Britain deliberately limited the production of cotton textiles in India to protect its own textile industry in Lancashire.

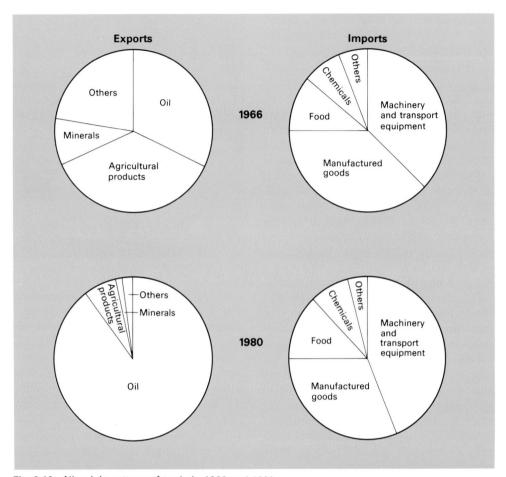

Fig. 9.10 Nigeria's pattern of trade in 1966 and 1980

By 1970 most developing countries had gained political independence from their colonial masters, but this did not make them economically independent. They were still forced to rely on the same pattern of trade that existed before. For example, in Africa the railways consist mainly of single lines running to ports which are of no use for trade between African countries.

In the last few years the Third World has pressed for a better deal in international trade. So far the developed countries have refused to make any agreements that would achieve a substantial redistribution of wealth in favour of the developing countries. However, in 1973 the Western world was rocked by an oil crisis that had widespread effects on the international economy. The Organization of Petroleum Exporting Countries (OPEC), composed of Third World countries, withheld the supply of oil to force up the price. In the space of a few months the cost of oil increased fourfold. This made people in developed countries aware of the extent to which they relied on raw materials from the less developed world (Fig. 9.11).

The following year saw a special session at the United Nations where all nations acknowledged the right of the poor countries to a fairer share of the wealth created by trade. But the developed countries have not taken any positive action. At the end of the 1970s the developing countries were even worse off. They had suffered particularly from the increasing price of oil, more so than the developed countries.

The demands of the Third World for a fairer trade system centre on six main issues which have been discussed at a number of international conferences under the banner of UNCTAD (United Nations Conference on Trade and Development).

1 *A better deal for raw commodities.* Three-quarters of the developing countries' export earnings come from the sale of raw materials, the prices of which can vary enormously depending on the demand that exists for them. For example, Fig. 9.12 shows the changes in the world price of copper between 1966 and 1978. The effects on a country like Zambia, where copper accounts for 95 per cent of the export trade, are very serious. Zambia finds it virtually impossible to plan ahead because it has no idea what its income might be from one year to the next.

By comparison, the price of manufactured goods, which developed countries chiefly produce, has risen steadily over the past twenty years. The developing countries are finding that there is an increasing gap between their export earnings and the cost of their manufactured imports. They want to protect the purchasing power of their exports by stabilizing prices. One way of doing this is for producers of a particular commodity to build up stocks when the price is low and gradually release them when the price has risen, but this requires considerable financial backing and can be impractical with agricultural products. Alternatively the developing countries would like the prices of raw materials to be linked to the cost of manufactured goods, so that when the cost of their imports goes up, their income from exports would also increase. This is known as indexation.

2 *Improved access to western markets.* Less developed countries do not rely totally on raw commodities. In 1977 the Third World produced 10 per cent of the world trade in manufactured goods. Because their home markets are limited by low purchasing power they naturally turn to foreign sales, especially in the developed countries. However, because the developed countries want to protect their own products, they set quotas and impose tariffs that raise the price of Third World manufactures. The developing countries want to see these quotas and tariffs removed.

Fig. 9.11 British motorists queue for petrol during the 1973 oil crisis

3 *The control of multinational corporations.* The Third World would like to see more control of the giant multinational firms that handle 60 per cent of the Third World's trade. The largest firms, which have annual turnovers that are higher than the gross national product of each of the eighty poorest countries in the world, have become the new colonial powers.

4 *Changes in the international monetary system.* Under the present system the values of national currencies alter according to international exchange rates. These are determined by the state of major currencies like the dollar, sterling, and deutschmark.

Since currency values control earnings from trade these rise and fall as well. The Third World wants a more stable system and a say in how it is organized.

5 *Debt relief.* Debts on past aid have threatened to stem the flow of new aid from rich to poor countries. Today aid is either given or loaned interest free or at low rates of interest, but in the 1950s and 1960s high rates of interest on aid were common.

6 *Aid.* Developing countries want rich countries to keep to a commitment, made in 1975, to give 0·7 per cent of their national income to the poor countries.

Fig. 9.12 The changing price of copper

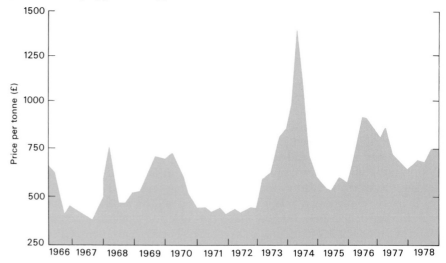

Mexico: the new oil power

Mexico is a developing country that has struck riches. It has huge oil reserves which could, if carefully exploited, transform the lives of its people. Already its proven oil wealth places it in the top league, well ahead of the USA and the UK. Optimistic forecasts suggest that its total reserves could even exceed those of Saudi Arabia.

Small-scale drilling started as early as 1901, but when in 1938 Mexico nationalized its oil industry, the foreign firms were forced out. Little further development took place until 1972 when a new oilfield was discovered at Reforma in south-east Mexico. The state-owned oil firm, Petroleos Mexicanos (Pemex), soon realized that these deposits were very valuable. More discoveries were made throughout the states of Chiapas and Tabasco and oil production began to take off. Further exploration revealed extensive deposits in the Gulf of Mexico, offshore from the state of Campeche. It now seems likely that the rocks underlying the Yucatan peninsula could contain a giant series of oil and gas deposits, but so far only 10 per cent of the area has been properly surveyed (Fig. 9.13).

The development of production and processing operations had to face various problems. The Mexicans are determined to maintain complete control over their oil and have refused to seek help from the multinational oil companies. Because of this progress has been relatively slow as Pemex builds up its expertise and trains new staff. Production has also been held back by a lack of oil refineries and deep-water port facilities. Throughout the 1970s virtually all the natural gas that occurs with the oil was simply burnt off as it was separated from the oil. Now a gas pipeline has been constructed, running 1290 km along the Gulf coast to the Texas border. This allows surplus gas to be sold to the Americans, who also buy 90 per cent of Mexico's exported crude oil.

The new industry is already making its mark on the landscape. Large areas of tropical forest have been cleared to provide

Fig. 9.13 Mexico and its oil development areas

Fig. 9.14 New installations to process Mexico's oil wealth

sites for refineries, ports, and petrochemical plants. Local rivers have become heavily polluted and offshore fisheries have been affected. In June 1979 an offshore exploration well blew up and created an enormous oil slick that polluted hundreds of square kilometres in the Gulf of Mexico for several months (Fig. 9.16).

The effect on the quiet coastal states of south-east Mexico has been dramatic. Thousands of farm labourers have left the land to work in the oil industry, which offers wages four times higher than those in agriculture. Reforma has become a colossal shanty town, while Villahermosa's population tripled in size to 300 000. Land values have soared and food is 30 per cent more expensive than in Mexico City. Pemex has built large areas of new housing in Villahermosa for its workers and a new airport has been constructed. Tabasco's road network has suffered greatly from the heavy oil traffic and the government has had to invest in a new transport system.

The income from oil is having a significant effect on Mexico's economy. Between 1980 and 1982 Mexico intended to spend 68 per cent of its earnings from oil, or £12 000 million, on a comprehensive programme of public investment. This would concentrate on the neglected areas of agriculture, education, health, housing, and transport. The scale of Mexico's problems demands action of this kind.

Mexico's population is currently over 70 million and is growing by about 3 per cent a year. About 40 per cent of its population is under fifteen years of age, which means that the demand for jobs will increase rapidly in the 1980s. Already 20 per cent of the population is unemployed and a similar proportion is seriously underemployed. At least 800 000 jobs need to be created each year just to prevent unemployment increasing. A safety valve for population pressure has been illegal immigration into the south-western United States, where there are over 10 million Mexicans. Migration is also swelling Mexico City, which has a population in excess of 12 million and all the problems of congestion that go with it.

Mexico will also have difficulty in fitting

Fig. 9.15 The states of Mexico (numbered as in Fig. 9.17)

its large peasant workforce into its planned industrial society. Two-fifths of the labour force work on the land and farming is notoriously inefficient. Food production cannot keep pace with population growth and Mexico is having to import increasing amounts of grain. The government is attempting to link the state-owned smallholdings together as co-operative farms to increase their efficiency. In some areas though the quality of the land is so poor that no amount of re-organization could make them more productive. The government is also introducing schemes to establish village industries to help the rural economy.

5 For this exercise you need to organize yourselves into groups of five. The group represents a team of Mexican government officials whose job it is to plan the spending of Mexico's oil income over the next three years. This is expected to be about £18 000 million. One-third of this total will be invested in Pemex, leaving

£12 000 million to be spent on other development priorities. Each official is responsible for the allocation of funds to one particular aspect of development. First of all you should decide which member of the group will represent each of the following departments:

Agriculture and rural development
Social services—education, health, and housing
Industry (excluding oil)
Transport
Government administration of states and cities.

Now work through the stages given below:

a Hold a meeting to decide what percentage of the £12 000 million should be devoted to each department. It is each official's responsibility to present the argument for his department as strongly as possible.

Fig. 9.16 The Ixtoc well is finally capped after losing oil for nine months

Fig. 9.17 Information about the states of Mexico

State	A	B	C	D	E
1 Aguascalientes	37	74	16	0·8	80
2 Baja California	22	77	18	1·2	96
3 Baja California (T)	35	67	8	1·0	68
4 Campeche	46	50	14	0·8	84
5 Coahuila	30	71	18	1·1	87
6 Colima	44	46	9	0·8	86
7 Chiapas	73	39	5	1·0	63
8 Chihuahua	36	70	13	1·1	79
9 Mexico City	2	71	31	—	100
10 Durango	55	69	9	1·0	72
11 Guanajuato	49	64	17	1·1	76
12 Guerrero	52	39	8	0·9	73
13 Hidalgo	61	54	10	0·9	70
14 Jalisco	34	72	21	1·2	83
15 Mexico	30	62	25	1·1	91
16 Michoacan	59	55	10	1·2	76
17 Morelos	43	55	13	1·3	94
18 Nayarit	59	48	8	0·9	83
19 Nuevo Leon	17	64	30	1·4	87
20 Oaxaca	72	41	9	0·9	78
21 Puebla	56	53	14	1·0	86
22 Queretaro	48	54	13	0·8	69
23 Quintana Roo	53	41	6	0·8	68
24 San Luis Potosi	53	57	11	1·0	69
25 Sinaloa	51	53	9	1·0	75
26 Sonora	38	74	10	1·0	81
27 Tabasco	59	46	6	0·9	76
28 Tamaulipas	33	60	12	1·2	80
29 Tlaxcala	55	56	17	0·9	90
30 Veracruz	53	53	9	1·2	79
31 Yucatan	55	50	11	1·1	87
32 Zacatecas	64	68	7	0·9	66

A: Percentage of total labour force employed in agriculture.
B: Percentage of population living in a dwelling with more than one room.
C: Percentage of total labour force employed in manufacturing.
D: Connectivity index of the state main road network.
E: Percentage of total population living in settlements of 500 inhabitants or over.

b Having decided on the percentage to be given to each department, multiply this figure by 120 to show the funds available in millions of pounds. For example, if 10 per cent is to be spent on transport then its total funding will be £1200 million.

c Each official should make a copy of Fig. 9.15 and then, using the information given in Fig. 9.17, construct a choropleth map for the aspect of development for which he is responsible, as indicated below:
Agriculture and rural development: column A
Social services: column B
Industry: column C
Transport: column D
Government administration: column E.
Every choropleth map should have four categories of values, though it is up to the person drawing the map to choose the most appropriate categories.

d When the choropleth maps are complete study them carefully, along with Fig. 9.18, which shows the pattern of population density in Mexico. Use them to decide how much of your departmental budget you should allocate to each state. This should not be divided into amounts smaller than £10 million. Write a paragraph explaining the reasoning behind your distribution of funds.

e Add up the total amount of money allocated to each state by the five departments and show this information on another choropleth map.

f Now answer the following questions:
  i) How did your team's allocation of funds compare with the choice made by the Mexican government, shown in Fig. 9.19?
  ii) Which parts of Mexico received the most and the least investment according to your team's distribution of funds?
  iii) Can you suggest reasons for this?
  iv) How did this pattern compare with those produced by the other teams in the class?

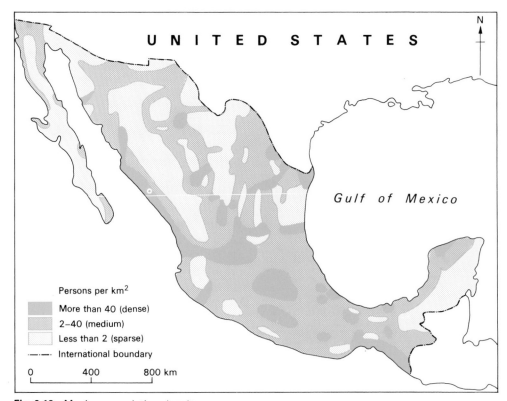

Fig. 9.18 Mexico: population density

Persons per km²
- More than 40 (dense)
- 2–40 (medium)
- Less than 2 (sparse)
- — · — · International boundary

0   400   800 km

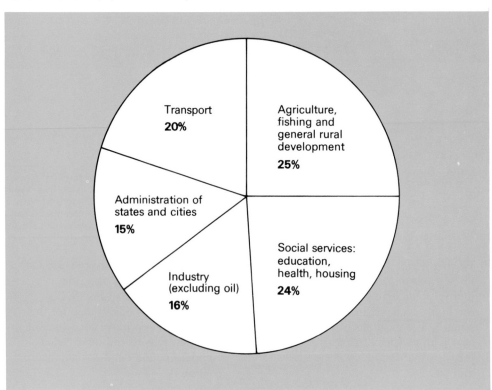

Transport **20%**

Agriculture, fishing and general rural development **25%**

Administration of states and cities **15%**

Industry (excluding oil) **16%**

Social services: education, health, housing **24%**

Fig. 9.19 How the Mexican government intends to spend its surplus oil income

Tourism in the Caribbean

More and more people are taking holidays abroad. In the late 1970s the number of international tourists each year was about 250 million, ten times the total in 1950. Cheaper air travel and package holidays have led to the continual development of new holiday areas, many in developing countries. Tourism can provide them with a valuable source of income and employment, especially if they are unsuited to the establishment of manufacturing industries. The islands of the Caribbean are a very good example of this trend and tourism there has expanded rapidly since 1960. The attractiveness of individual islands depends very much on their physical characteristics which can be divided into three main types:

1 Low-lying limestone islands with off-shore coral reefs and long white beaches, e.g. the Bahamas, Anguilla, Antigua, Barbados, Tobago.

2 Mountainous volcanic islands with higher rainfall and fewer hours of sunshine, e.g. Grenada, St. Lucia, Martinique, Dominica.

3 Larger islands, similar in structure to the volcanic islands but with a wider variety of landscapes, e.g. Jamaica, Haiti and the Dominican Republic, Puerto Rico, Trinidad.

6 a Locate the islands mentioned above on an atlas map of the Caribbean. Where are the three types of islands situated in relation to each other?

  b What aspects of the islands are likely to attract tourists most?

7 a Plot the figures from Fig. 9.20 for each island as a separate line on the same graph, with months on the horizontal axis and percentages on the vertical axis. Use a different colour for each line so that you can distinguish the pattern for each island.

Fig. 9.20 Monthly tourist arrivals on three Caribbean islands (percentages)

	Barbados	Martinique	Curacao
January	8·0	9·0	8·5
February	10·5	11·0	9·0
March	11·0	12·0	9·5
April	9·5	9·0	9·0
May	6·0	7·5	6·0
June	5·0	7·0	5·5
July	8·5	6·5	8·0
August	10·5	8·0	9·0
September	5·0	6·0	7·0
October	6·0	5·5	8·5
November	9·5	9·0	10·0
December	10·5	9·5	10·0
	100·0	100·0	100·0

  b Which times of the year are the busiest for tourism? Can you suggest reasons for this pattern? What disadvantages might this have for people working in the tourist industry?

  c Which island has the greatest seasonal variation in its tourist traffic?

Fig. 9.21 A calypso band plays for tourists at a Jamaican hotel

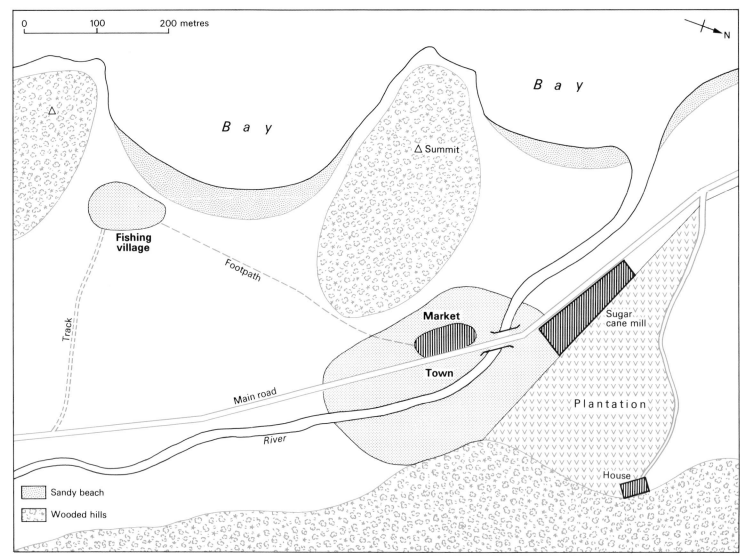

Fig. 9.22 Imaginary site for a tourist development on a Caribbean island

Tourism in the Caribbean reaches a peak between January and March, when the region is experiencing its hot dry season. This is also the time when tourists from North America and Europe want to escape the northern winter. There is a second peak in July and August which coincides with the main holiday period in the developed countries. The pattern of arrivals for each island varies according to the type and origin of its visitors. Puerto Rico, for instance, has a steady flow of visitors throughout the year made up chiefly of American businessmen attending conferences.

The seasonal nature of the tourist trade has important effects on the islands' economies. During the off-season many hotel rooms are unfilled and since room charges are also lower at this time some hotels find it difficult to operate profitably. Large numbers of staff are laid off during slack periods, adding to the already sizeable pool of permanently unemployed. Taxi drivers also suffer from the lack of business and some even migrate temporarily to the United States to maintain their income.

In spite of these drawbacks tourism is a crucial part of the Caribbean economy and

on some islands it is more important than agriculture. Many types of business benefit from tourism, particularly hotels, taxi and car-hire firms, the building industry, airlines, domestic services, and charter yachting. Wages paid to employees will also be spent locally on goods and services, providing a further boost to the economy. Since the hotels are very luxurious they require a large number of staff: more than one employee per room on average. However, because the hotels are frequently owned by foreign firms, the higher paid managerial jobs are not available to local people.

Fig. 9.23 Tourist chalets in a Caribbean holiday resort

Summary

Most industry in the developing world is concerned with primary products, which are then exported to the industrial nations. However, some countries, such as Brazil and India, have a highly developed industrial sector with substantial secondary and tertiary industries. Small-scale traditional industries form a valuable source of employment, but are vulnerable to competition from larger industrial organizations. Western nations have sometimes encouraged the developing countries to invest in high-technology factories which offer little employment. Labour intensive methods of production are much more suitable since they provide a large number of jobs and may well be cheaper. Appropriate technology encourages this type of industrial development. At present the world trading system makes it difficult for developing countries to sell their industrial products abroad. There need to be important reforms so that the developing world has access to wider markets.

8 Study Fig. 9.22. It is your job to plan a major tourist centre in this area. Facilities you should include in your plan are:

a large hotel with a swimming pool;
an area of small residential chalets;
guest houses run by local people;
a quay for boats used in water skiing and fishing;
a theatre for entertainments;
a tourist trail through the old town and market;
a footpath to a local vantage point, where a hilltop bar can be established;
closed areas of the beach where tourists can sunbathe and swim;
facilities for tourists to visit the old plantation house;
car parks and access roads where necessary.

a On a copy of Fig. 9.22 fill in the features of your plan and write a short explanation of the reasoning behind it.

b Now consider the response of the local people to this development. What reaction would the following individuals have to your plan?

a trader in the local market;
a fisherman in the village by the bay;
a worker on the sugar-cane plantation;
a local farmer producing fruit and vegetables;
a garage mechanic in the town;
an unemployed youth;
a school child;
a wife in the fishing village.

One less fortunate aspect of tourism in the Caribbean is the resentment it creates among some islanders. This may reflect the historic association of the region with slavery and colonialism. It is also a natural response to the obvious wealth of the visitors, in comparison with the poverty that afflicts many local inhabitants. This is a problem that has no easy solution and may well get worse.

Chapter **10** The divided world

The Brandt report

In 1980 a vitally important book called *North–South: a programme for survival* was published. It was the report of the Independent Commission on International Development Issues, which consisted of eighteen leading politicians from all parts of the world and was headed by the former German Chancellor, Willy Brandt.

The message of the report is clear: developed and developing countries must act together to resolve their differences and face the common threats to mankind. The words of the report stress the urgency of the situation: 'The future of the world can rarely have seemed so endangered . . . We see a world in which poverty and hunger still prevail in many huge regions; in which resources are squandered without consideration of their renewal; in which more armaments are made and sold then ever before; and where a destructive capacity has been accumulated to blow up our planet several times over.'

The report gives two overwhelming reasons for the developed countries to help the Third World. Firstly, there is a moral responsibility to solve the problems of the poor countries and remove the injustices that have prevented their development in the past. Secondly, since the two are dependent on each other economically, the future prosperity of the developed countries relies on development in the Third World. The threats posed by unemployment, the arms race, environmental decline, and dwindling resources can only be tackled through worldwide co-operation.

Fig. 10.1 Willy Brandt

Fig. 10.2 The future world?

SCENARIO FOR THE 1990s

FOLLOWING WIDESPREAD CROP FAILURE AND CITY RIOTS, THE INDIAN CHAPTER OF THE TERRORIST '*SOUTHERN JUSTICE ARMY*' SEIZES CALCUTTA AND BOMBAY, AND GRAIN SHIPS OFFSHORE. RISINGS ARE BRUTALLY SUPPRESSED FOLLOWING A LEFT-WING MILITARY COUP.

INDIAN AND BANGLADESH ARMIES INVADE RICHER PARTS OF PAKISTAN AND BURMA, BUT A CHINESE ULTIMATUM FORCES WITHDRAWAL.

THE OPPRESSED MUST **UNITE** IN STRUGGLE AGAINST THE PLUNDERING SUPERPOWERS OF IMPERIALISM

INDIAN EXPEDITIONARY FORCE OCCUPIES TWO SMALL GULF OIL STATES, DEFYING NUCLEAR THREAT BY IRAN. MOST OIL WELLS SABOTAGED. MEANWHILE THE '**UNITED AFRICA ARMY**' BESIEGES CAPE TOWN REDOUBT: BRITAIN AND HOLLAND RELUCTANTLY TAKE ITS WHITE REFUGEES.

INDONESIANS MOUNT RAMSHACKLE INVAS WESTERN AUSTRALIA. THE UNITED STAT TEMPTED TO RETREAT TO '*FORTRESS AM* SAN FRANCISCO AND NEW YORK ATTACKED AMERICAN GUERRILLAS. JAPAN SEIZES SOUT WITH RUSSIAN BLESSING, LEADING TO RENEW SOVIET BORDER CO

MEANWHILE BACK IN BRITAIN . . . TWENTY-SEVEN PER CENT UNEMPLOYMENT. NEWS CENSORSHIP ALMOST COMPLETE, BUT BAN ON POLITICAL ACTIVITY PERSISTENTLY BREACHED. RIGOROUS POPULATION POLICY. UTILITY STANDARDS FOR HOUSING, CONSUMER GOODS ETC. FUEL AND FOOD STRICTLY RATIONED. WHISKY-SIZE TAX ON MOST MEATS. CABINET STILL SPLIT OVER PLAN TO REOCCUPY IRELAND FOR ITS FOOD SURPLUS.

CRISIS 01.14 HRS — SUDDENLY BRITISH P.M. RECEIVES 36-HOUR ULTIMATUM FROM 'SOUTHERN JUSTICE ARMY' SUICIDE SQUAD WHO THREATEN TO EXPLODE NUCLEAR DEVICE AT SOUTHAMPTON UNLESS 43 TERRORISTS ARE GIVEN SAFE PASSAGE WITH 40 TONS OF GOLD BULLION.

RUSH EVACUATION ORDERED OF WHOLE SOUTHAMPTON REGION. ROADS QUICKLY CONGESTED. PANIC SPREADS. ARMOURED VEHICLES WITH NUCLEAR DETECTOR UNITS STOPPED FROM MOVING IN BY TERRORIST THREAT TO DETONATE BOMB AT ONCE.

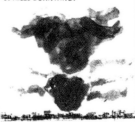

NEXT DAY: 13.16 HRS P.M. URGED TO GIVE IN TO TERRORISTS — 50,000 PEOPLE STILL STRANDED — BUT DECIDES SURRENDER WOULD ONLY ENCOURAGE FURTHER THREATS. EXPLOSION DEVASTATES CITY. FALLOUT SPREADS 60 MILES DOWNWIND.

NATO AND WARSAW PACT COUNTRIES DEEPLY DIVIDED ABOUT PROPOSED '**NORTHERN STOCKADE**' DEFENCE PACT TO MEET GROWING DANGER OF SOUTHERN 'WAR OF REDISTRIBUTION' LED BY CHINA. SUDDENLY ISRAEL, ABANDONED BY THE WEST, THREATENS ITS NUCLEAR CARD AGAINST CAIRO AND DAMASCUS. THE WORLD WAITS AS THE SUPERPOWERS DECLARE LAST STAGE 'RED ALERT'.

1 Study the strip cartoon 'Scenario for the 1990s' (Fig. 10.2).

   a How many different areas of conflict does the story refer to?

   b What are the main reasons for these conflicts?

   c How likely do you think the events suggested in the story are?

   d What do you think are the greatest threats to mankind?

The main recommendations of the Brandt report could all be made to work from a practical point of view: the crucial question is whether the political willingness exists to achieve the changes they require.

1 *Transfer of resources.* The developed countries should invest more in the Third World and help its countries to process their raw materials before export. This would give them a higher, more reliable income from their foreign trade.

2 *Industrialization.* The developing countries must be encouraged to industrialize, concentrating on the industries that suit them best. The developed world must be prepared to buy their products and accept the competition that they offer. Industrial countries should change their industrial structure to emphasize the high-technology goods that are rarely produced in the Third World.

3 *Codes of practice.* New rules should be laid down to govern all aspects of international business and to control the operations of multinational corporations, particularly limiting their influence in developing countries.

4 *Disarmament.* A commitment to disarmament is essential both for its own sake and so that military spending can be curbed and funds diverted to development. World military spending each year is over twenty times the amount devoted to international aid.

5 *Food.* Increased efforts must be made to improve world agricultural production and to build up emergency food stocks. Poor countries which have to import food should receive special investment to help them meet their own requirements.

Fig. 10.3 How one cartoonist sees the North-South issue

6 *Energy.* Oil should be used more economically but supplies need to be reliable and to change price predictably. Exploration for new sources of oil and gas should be increased and coal and hydro-electric power supplies need to be developed further. Research into other types of energy, e.g. solar power, should be speeded up.

7 *Money.* A new world monetary system must be agreed upon to fight inflation and remove the injustices of the present arrangements. The developing countries should have more say in the workings of the International Monetary Fund. Lending by the World Bank should be increased through the provision of additional funds by the developed countries.

8 *International taxes.* Revenue for development programmes could be raised automatically by the introduction of a worldwide tax system which would relate the amount of tax paid by a country to its overall wealth.

9 *International aid.* All developed countries should meet the target of giving 0·7 per cent of their gross national product as official development assistance by 1985. The quality of this aid should be improved so that more is untied and available to the poorest countries.

10 *World Development Fund.* A new organization, which might be called the World Development Fund, should be set up. This would co-ordinate the financing of development programmes and would provide the opportunity for all countries to co-operate on a more equitable basis.

2 What aspects of the Brandt report do you think Fig. 10.3 refers to? Write a paragraph explaining the meaning of the cartoon in your own words. Can you think of a suitable title for the cartoon?

3 a Read through the twenty statements in Fig. 10.4 and note down whether you agree or disagree with each one.

b Then award yourself marks according to the following scheme:
odd numbered statements—
 1 mark if you agreed,
 0 marks if you disagreed
even numbered statements—
 0 marks if you agreed,
 1 mark if you disagreed

c Total up your marks and see what your score indicates.
0–10 marks. You tend to be pessimistic about the future. The lower your score the more pessimistic you are. You have considerable doubts about the way the industrial economy operates and the encouragement of materialism. You are more concerned with the quality of life and the need for greater community spirit. You believe that we place too much faith in science and technology. You are worried about the effects that man's activities are having on the environment. You are probably more sympathetic towards the needs of developing countries.
11–20 marks. You have an optimistic view of the future. The closer you are to 20 the more optimistic you are. You believe in the principles of our industrial society: competition, rewards for success, economic growth. You have great faith in technology and its ability to produce a better world. You do not anticipate problems with the environment and approve of man's widespread exploitation of natural resources.

d What was the average score for your class? Does the class tend to be optimistic or pessimistic? Which statements did most people in the class agree with and disagree with?

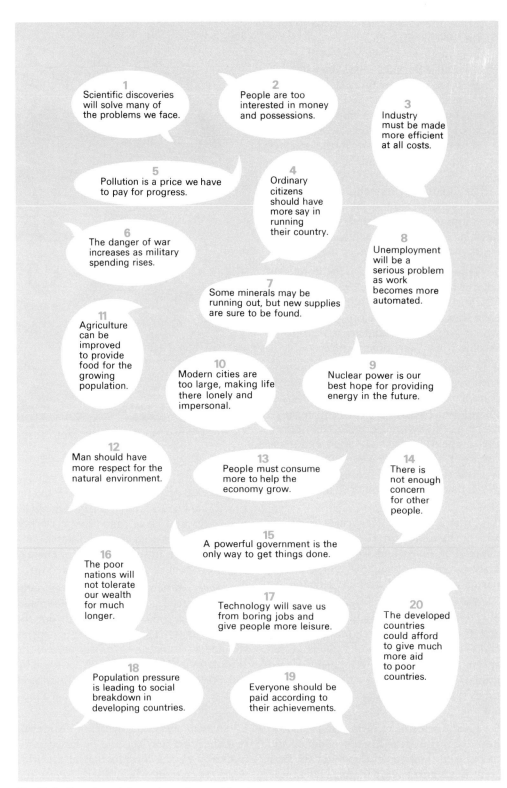

Fig. 10.4 Twenty opinions about the world today

Arms: the unnecessary burden

Worldwide spending on arms doubled between 1970 and 1980. Half of that total was devoted to stocking the arsenals of the two superpowers, the USSR and the USA, and the arms race between them continues to increase the danger of a major war as well as representing an enormous waste of resources. The industrialized nations spend a hundred times as much on defence as the less developed countries, yet two-thirds of the world trade in arms goes to the Third World. Deals are negotiated through the governments of the main suppliers—the United States, USSR, France, and Britain.

There are four types of goods involved in this trade: major arms such as ships, aircraft and tanks; small arms such as rifles and machine guns; non-lethal equipment like computers, electronics and communications systems; and back-up services providing spares, maintenance and training. Since the Second World War rapid developments in technology have made weapons increasingly lethal and costly, especially in the major arms category. Few countries have the expertise and industrial facilities to manufacture major armaments, so that they must be imported at great expense. The less developed countries can ill afford to have the burden of a major arms bill, but in some countries spending on defence can represent one-third of the total budget.

Governments in the Third World buy arms for a variety of reasons, which include rivalry with neighbouring countries, national prestige, corruption, and pressure from the armed forces within the country. Sometimes major world powers encourage the less developed countries to expand their armies so that they can fight their own wars.

Although the arms trade is only one of many influences on development it can have far-reaching effects. When a country decides to expand its armed forces it gets caught in a web of spiralling costs which affect its balance of payments. As well as the initial cost of purchasing the arms money must also be found to pay for the continuing programme of maintenance and spares, and for all this the country must use foreign exchange (currency which is acceptable on the world market). The only way it can accumulate foreign exchange is by exporting its own goods or by getting a

Fig. 10.5 A submarine which will carry nuclear missiles is launched in France

Fig. 10.6 The aftermath of a clash between guerrillas and the national guard

Fig. 10.7 A guerrilla squad assembles for early morning training

loan, which will have to be paid back with interest.

To increase its exports the government has to place emphasis on the production of cash crops or minerals. Sometimes tourism or the movement of migrant labour abroad will bring further capital into the country. This leads to a replacement of the traditional subsistence economy by commercial activities, particularly farming for export. Consequently less land is available to provide food for home consumption and food prices rise. Since farmers become dependent on the sale of food abroad for their income they suffer if there is a slump in world food prices. In general the prices paid for Third World commodities have declined in relation to the cost of goods imported from developed countries.

The move away from a subsistence economy in the Third World leads to increasing poverty among the bulk of the population and the rise of a privileged minority. Poverty in turn encourages political unrest, which can be dealt with by either reform or repression. Since the wealthy minority wants to preserve its advantage it has to rely on the army to control the unrest, which involves the purchase of more arms. Often the ruling class will welcome the arrival of Western businesses and their products, leading to further expensive imports. This creates further foreign exchange problems and the need for more loans. Sometimes the army uses its strength to seize power and a military government takes over, but this type of government is even more likely to favour the purchase of increased armaments.

4 Look at Fig. 10.8. Think of a caption for the cartoon and then write a paragraph explaining the points it is making about arms and the Third World.

5 Using the figures in Fig. 10.9, draw a line graph with the years on the horizontal axis and spending on the vertical axis. What pattern does the graph show about the rate of Third World spending on arms?

Fig. 10.8 Arms and the Third World

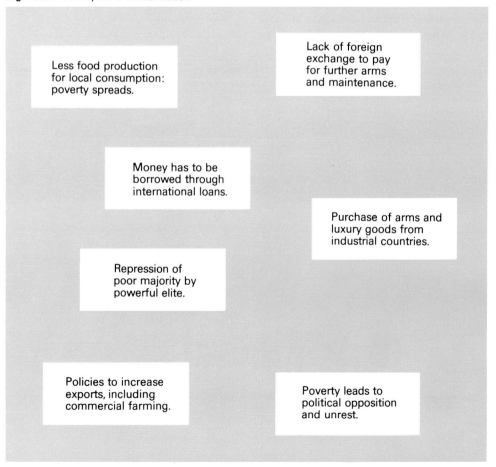

Fig. 10.9 Third World military spending (constant 1973 prices)

Year	Index	Year	Index
1957	100	1967	215
1958	110	1968	235
1959	110	1969	255
1960	115	1970	285
1961	120	1971	335
1962	130	1972	350
1963	150	1973	390
1964	155	1974	450
1965	180	1975	515
1966	200	1976	580

Fig. 10.10 The cycle of militarization

6 Fig. 10.10 shows a sequence of events that might affect a Third World country. Arrange them in a circular pattern to demonstrate how the cycle of militarization develops.

7 Study Figs. 10.6 and 10.7 which show two scenes in the Central American country of El Salvador.
  a How can you tell the dead man is a guerrilla?
  b What age do you think he is?
  c How might he have got his rifle?
  d Who might have supplied the armoured car to the national guard?
  e Whereabouts in El Salvador would you expect the guerrilla bases to be situated?
  f What political beliefs might the guerrillas be fighting for?
  g Which political group is the national guard likely to support?
  h Write an account of a clash between guerrillas and national guardsmen from the point of view of
  i) a western journalist living in secret with the guerrillas,
  ii) a government observer reporting for the national information service.

Less food production for local consumption: poverty spreads.

Lack of foreign exchange to pay for further arms and maintenance.

Money has to be borrowed through international loans.

Purchase of arms and luxury goods from industrial countries.

Repression of poor majority by powerful elite.

Policies to increase exports, including commercial farming.

Poverty leads to political opposition and unrest.

South Africa and apartheid

South Africa is a wealthy nation with thriving industries and agriculture, but most of the money is concentrated in the hands of the White minority. The South African population consists of 18 million Blacks, 4½ million Whites, 2½ million Coloureds, and 0·75 million Asians. The Blacks are Bantu people who originated in central Africa and migrated southwards over a period of several hundred years. The Whites are the descendants of European settlers, mainly Dutch, German and British, who colonized South Africa from the seventeenth century onwards. The Coloureds are people of mixed race, found chiefly in the Cape Province while the Asians are predominantly Indians who came to work as labourers in colonial times.

In 1652 the Dutch established the first European settlement at the Cape of Good Hope. When the British took over the Cape

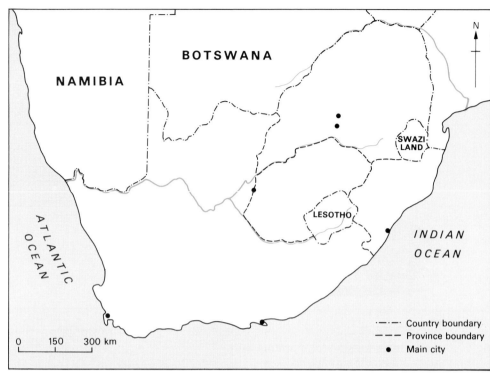

Fig. 10.11 Outline map of South Africa

Fig. 10.12 Crossing the South African veldt in the late nineteenth century

Colony in the early nineteenth century, large numbers of Dutch peasant farmers (Boers) migrated inland to the north and east. As a result of this journey, known as the Great Trek, the Dutch set up the republics of Natal, the Orange Free State, and the Transvaal. This led to a persistent conflict between the Europeans and the Bantu tribes as they competed for land, a struggle which was eventually won by the Whites. The discovery of diamonds at Kimberley and gold on the Witwatersrand attracted British settlers from the Cape, causing great friction with the Dutch farmers already living there. This finally resulted in the Boer War of 1899–1902, which gave Britain control of the whole of South Africa.

8 Make a copy of Fig. 10.11. Use an atlas to identify the following geographical locations and label them on your map.
 a The four provinces: Cape Province, Natal, Orange Free State, Transvaal.
 b The main cities: Cape Town, Port Elizabeth, Durban, Johannesburg (on the Witwatersrand), Pretoria, Kimberley.
 c The Cape of Good Hope and the rivers Orange, Vaal, and Limpopo.
 d The Kalahari desert.
 e Draw in two arrows in different colours to show the movement of the Dutch settlers eastwards from the Cape and the Bantu tribes southwards from East Africa. Label them accordingly.
 f Show diamonds and gold by symbols at the appropriate locations.

As industry began to develop in the late nineteenth century, particularly around Johannesburg, there was a serious shortage of labour. This problem was solved by the employment of Bantu men, who were attracted away from their tribes by the prospect of paid work. Large settlements of Blacks grew up around the industrial towns as the men brought their families to live

Fig. 10.13 Drilling for platinum on the Witwatersrand

with them. But the South African state that developed in the twentieth century was a White state and the Blacks were not considered a part of it. The Whites had all the political and economic power: they controlled the government and held all the skilled, well-paid jobs. Blacks were limited to the unskilled trades and the dangerous work in the gold and diamond mines.

In 1948 an all-white Afrikaner government came to power (the Afrikaners were the descendants of the Dutch-speaking colonists). This government introduced a policy of apartheid, or separate development for each racial group in South Africa. In practice this meant that Whites and Blacks were segregated from each other in virtually every aspect of their daily lives. The government built special residential areas known as townships, where all black people were forced to live. Every Black African had to carry a pass, stating where he lived and worked.

The Afrikaners have kept a tight hold on the country by establishing a police state. Any outbreaks of political unrest are dealt with ruthlessly. Anyone can be imprisoned

Fig. 10.14 Discrimination on a public footbridge

without trial for as long as the authorities like. The Afrikaners justify their policy of apartheid by claiming that the Blacks have simply come to work in South Africa and have no right to live there permanently. To support this argument the government has established ten homelands, or Bantustans, where the various tribal groups are supposed to live. In the mid 1970s two of them, Transkei and Bophuthatswana, became independent states, though South Africa was the only country that recognized them.

It is not hard to see why other countries refuse to give the homelands official recognition. For example, Bophuthatswana has no marked frontier and its capital, Mmbatho, consists of just a garage and a hotel. The following description of the Transkei should give you an idea of how 'independent' the homelands are.

It has the plausibility of occupying a large and beautiful territory—not large, perhaps, in relation to the rest of the Cape Province, of which it used to be part, let alone in relation to South Africa as a whole, but nevertheless unfragmented and recognizable. It is inhabited by people who speak a common tongue (Xhosa) and recognize a certain kinship with one another, despite tribal divisions among them. It has a capital, by the name of Umtata, which is graced by a tiny parliament building with columns in front and a dome above, a holiday inn, and a new university of which phase one is being constructed. It has an unspoilt coastline of astonishing intricacy and splendour, and hence has a small tourist industry catering for White South African holiday-makers. It has the K. D. Matanzima airport, named inevitably enough after its prime minister.

But it is bone-poor. So poor that most of its adult males have to spend their working lives in the cities and farms across the frontier, where they are treated like any other Blacks. So poor that the government is almost as dependent on South African handouts as that of Bophuthatswana. The wide, fenceless spaces of the country, profusely dotted with traditional round huts of mud and thatch, give an impression of serenity and changelessness. In fact, the place is overpopulated, overgrazed, eroded, and disease-ridden.

Fig. 10.15 Farms in the Transkei countryside

Fig. 10.16 New building in Umtata, capital of the Transkei

The people we met were, on the whole, no friendlier in their demeanour than Blacks elsewhere in South Africa. But some of them spoke frankly to us: one young man who despised Matanzima and his government, said of the 'independence' of the country, 'It's like cutting off a man's arm—and then telling the arm that it is independent'.

(from 'Behind the sham of the homelands' by Dan Jacobson, *Observer Magazine*, December 1978)

9 Study Fig. 10.17.

a Rank the Bantustans from one to ten, in descending order of size, by making a rough estimate of the total area that each homeland covers.

b How many separate pieces of land does each homeland consist of?

c Why do you think they are so fragmented? What problems do you think this fragmentation would cause if they became independent states?

The homelands make up 13 per cent of South Africa's total area, yet in theory they are meant to support 72 per cent of the population. They are among the least developed parts of the country and could not possibly support the 18 million Blacks who are supposed to live there. The whole basis of the homelands is that a large proportion of their populations will be working in White South Africa. This is because there is little or no work available in the homelands. The vast section of the country allocated to the Whites contains all the main mining and industrial areas, as well as the best farming land.

To back up its homelands policy the government has forced many Blacks to be re-settled in their tribal Bantustans. Since 1960 3 million people have been relocated in this way. Many of them were the old and the young, the sick, and mothers who had several children to look after. Some had been living in areas that were declared 'White', while others had broken the pass laws by living somewhere without permission. The resettlement camps are in iso-lated districts where there is no hope of employment. The land is dry and infertile, making farming extremely difficult. It cannot grow enough food to provide an adequate supply for the growing population. Disease is rife and over half the children suffer from malnutrition. Infant mortality rates are as high as 250 per 1000, compared with 15 per 1000 for White South Africans.

The situation in the homelands forces most adult males and some women to apply for jobs as migrant workers. If a man wants a job he must apply to the labour bureau in his homeland. He is issued with a contract which allows him to go and work for eleven months in White South Africa. His contract will be for a specific job as a mine labourer or an unskilled worker in a factory. At the end of his work period he must return to his homeland to get another contract. His pass is stamped to give him permission to live in a men's hostel in a black township near his place of work. Living conditions are spartan and overcrowded and there is little in the way of entertainment. The migrant worker has no hope of securing a better job or of improving his working conditions since trade union activity is made very difficult. What changes that have occurred have been the result of

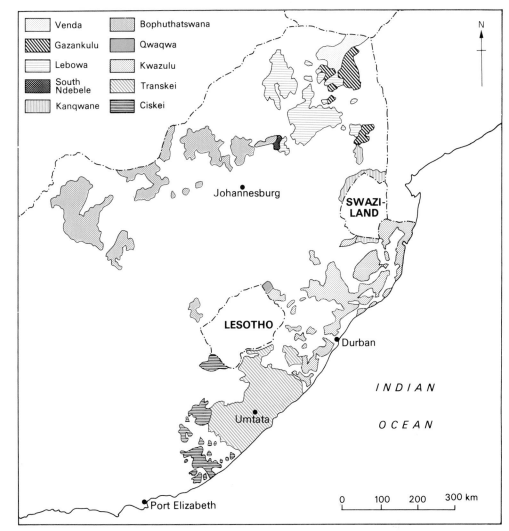

Fig. 10.17 South Africa's Bantustans

Legend:
- Venda
- Gazankulu
- Lebowa
- South Ndebele
- Kanqwane
- Bophuthatswana
- Qwaqwa
- Kwazulu
- Transkei
- Ciskei

Fig. 10.18 Migrant workers waiting to present their papers at a Johannesburg mine

Fig. 10.19 Standardized housing in the township of Soweto

violent demonstrations, when the frustrations of the workers have finally boiled over, but most migrants become dispirited and lose their self-respect, resigning themselves to the exhausting, monotonous, and badly paid work.

The effect on the families of the migrant workers is equally destructive. Since the able-bodied men are absent, farming is left to women, children and old folk. They find it very hard to carry out the physical labour involved and consequently productivity is very low. The families generally rely on money sent back by the men or women working in the towns.

Naturally there has been a good deal of opposition to apartheid from the Blacks themselves. Many have disobeyed the regulations and set up shanty towns where they can live together as families. Much discontent is concentrated in these shanty towns and also in the townships near the main cities. Probably the best-known centre of Black opposition is the township of Soweto near Johannesburg. The word township gives the wrong impression, since it is really a city of 1·5 million people, many of whom live there illegally. It consists of endless rows of small houses, which are sweltering hot in summer and freezing cold in winter. Only about one-fifth of the houses have electricity, but generally living conditions in the townships are rather better than the shanty towns. As one Black politician said: 'Why should our homes be compared with shanties in African states? We compare them to the luxury homes in White suburbs in our own country. We helped to create this wealth and we want a share in it.'

Apartheid is stifling the economic growth of South Africa. The country has a severe shortage of skilled labour because it cannot attract enough White immigrants from the developed world. Yet it is not prepared to let Black people be properly trained to take over these skilled jobs. As long as South Africa continues to hold back its Black majority the future of the country will be dangerously uncertain.

Aid

International aid is the transfer of money, goods, and expertise to assist the development of the world's poor countries. The main source of this aid is the developed nations of the Western World, though the communist countries also have aid programmes.

The first major aid scheme was the Marshall Plan, by which the United States helped to finance Europe's recovery after the devastation of the Second World War. The success of this programme led America, and later other developed nations, to direct money towards the Third World. This was intended to stimulate trade and industry, but was also seen as a way of gaining favour with the governments of poor countries. In the last twenty years there has been a growing split between the rich and poor nations, the North versus the South. Now the South is demanding a fairer share of the world's wealth, through increased aid and better trading terms.

In 1980 the total amount of official aid transferred to the developing countries was £18 000 million. Of this £13 500 million came from the developed nations of the West, £3500 million from the OPEC countries, and £1000 million from the Soviet bloc and China. Although OPEC countries are themselves essentially developing countries, their massive oil incomes have allowed them to become involved in aid schemes. The Russians justify their small contribution by claiming that they have no obligation towards developing countries since they did not exploit them as colonies. Chinese aid is usually associated with small-scale projects in countries that are sympathetic to Chinese political ideas.

Western aid is organized in several different ways. A basic distinction is between bilateral aid, which is given by a single country, and multilateral aid, which is funded jointly by the developed nations and tends to be distributed more evenly. Multilateral aid is co-ordinated by the many different agencies which operate under the umbrella of the United Nations.

Fig. 10.20   A debate on development at the United Nations headquarters in New York

Fig. 10.21   Literacy class in Mali funded by the World Bank

The United Nations also co-operates with the independent charities in relief operations and fieldwork. The charities vary considerably in their approaches. Some are associated with the church, such as Christian Aid, while others, like Oxfam, have no religious links. Some concentrate on providing money to relieve suffering during emergencies, while others prefer to invest in the long-term improvement of conditions in developing countries.

Fig. 10.22 shows the various channels through which a developed country can distribute aid. It is provided either by government bodies (official flows) or by businesses and voluntary agencies (private flows). The most valuable part of the official flows is official development assistance (ODA). This represents the aid that is given as grants (i.e. gifts), loans on favourable terms, or technical assistance. Frequently money is only given as long as certain conditions are met: this is known as tied aid. A common condition is that the money must be spent on products or services from the donor country.

Until the late 1960s much aid was tied to particular projects. Ideas on development at that time encouraged investment in large-scale industrial schemes. It was hoped that by improving industrial productivity the benefits would 'trickle down' through the economic system to help everyone. In reality project aid supported a wealthy minority in the main cities and did nothing for the poor, rural peasants. The developed countries liked this type of aid because it allowed them to sell advanced technological equipment and made it easier to provide technical assistance. They could also keep close control over the way in which the aid was spent.

Since then there has been a swing away from large projects and an increasing emphasis on rural development. Although this is more complicated to administer and carries less prestige it benefits a much greater proportion of the population. The move towards non-project aid means that a donor gives money to a total investment programme.

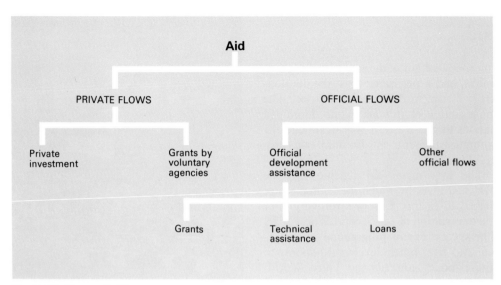

Fig. 10.22 Types of aid

Fig. 10.23 Official development assistance given by the main donor countries in 1980

Country	Value (£ million)	ODA as percentage of GNP
United States	3570	0·27
France	2025	0·62
West Germany	1760	0·43
Japan	1650	0·32
United Kingdom	890	0·34
Netherlands	790	0·99
Canada	520	0·42
Sweden	460	0·76
Italy	335	0·17
Australia	330	0·48
Belgium	290	0·49
Denmark	235	0·72
Norway	235	0·82
Switzerland	125	0·24
Austria	85	0·22
Finland	55	0·22
New Zealand	35	0·32

There have been various attempts to get western governments to commit themselves to giving a certain amount of aid each year. A recommendation that countries should give 0·7 per cent of their gross national product as official development assistance has never been agreed upon. Fig. 10.23 shows the situation in 1980.

10 a Rewrite the list of countries in Fig. 10.23 with their rank order according to the percentage of gross national product given as ODA.

b Using this rank order, draw a bar graph of the value of each country's contribution as a percentage of gross national product. (Netherlands will be highest with 0·99 per cent and Italy will be lowest with 0·17 per cent.)

c How does the order shown by your graph compare with the order in the table, based on the absolute value of aid given? Which countries have the biggest differences in their rank positions?

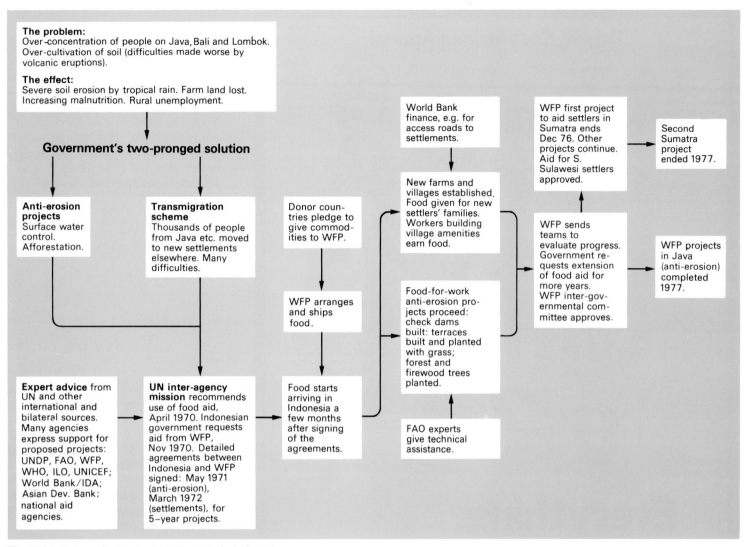

The problem:
Over-concentration of people on Java, Bali and Lombok. Over-cultivation of soil (difficulties made worse by volcanic eruptions).

The effect:
Severe soil erosion by tropical rain. Farm land lost. Increasing malnutrition. Rural unemployment.

Government's two-pronged solution

Anti-erosion projects
Surface water control. Afforestation.

Transmigration scheme
Thousands of people from Java etc. moved to new settlements elsewhere. Many difficulties.

Expert advice from UN and other international and bilateral sources. Many agencies express support for proposed projects: UNDP, FAO, WFP, WHO, ILO, UNICEF; World Bank/IDA; Asian Dev. Bank; national aid agencies.

UN inter-agency mission recommends use of food aid, April 1970. Indonesian government requests aid from WFP, Nov 1970. Detailed agreements between Indonesia and WFP signed: May 1971 (anti-erosion), March 1972 (settlements), for 5-year projects.

Donor countries pledge to give commodities to WFP.

WFP arranges and ships food.

Food starts arriving in Indonesia a few months after signing of the agreements.

World Bank finance, e.g. for access roads to settlements.

New farms and villages established. Food given for new settlers' families. Workers building village amenities earn food.

Food-for-work anti-erosion projects proceed: check dams built: terraces built and planted with grass; forest and firewood trees planted.

FAO experts give technical assistance.

WFP sends teams to evaluate progress. Government requests extension of food aid for more years. WFP inter-governmental committee approves.

WFP first project to aid settlers in Sumatra ends Dec 76. Other projects continue. Aid for S. Sulawesi settlers approved.

Second Sumatra project ended 1977.

WFP projects in Java (anti-erosion) completed 1977.

Fig. 10.24 International co-operation to help Indonesia

d If the UK has a population of 56 million, how much aid did we give per head in 1980?

e How does this compare with the following countries: United States (220 million), Sweden (8 million), Japan (113 million), Australia (14 million), West Germany (60 million)?

f On your bar graph mark in with a horizontal line the average percentage of gross national product given as ODA by the seventeen countries.

11 a How many different organizations are involved in the aid programme shown in Fig. 10.24?

b Identify each organization and find out what sort of work it specializes in.

c List all the different ways in which foreign assistance helped this programme.

12 Take a recent newspaper or magazine and cut out all the charity advertisements that appear in it. Compare the style and content of the advertisements.

a How many of them are raising money for use i) in Britain, ii) in the Third World?

b Which advertisements would you expect to be most successful and why?

Fig. 10.25 An Oxfam newspaper advertisement

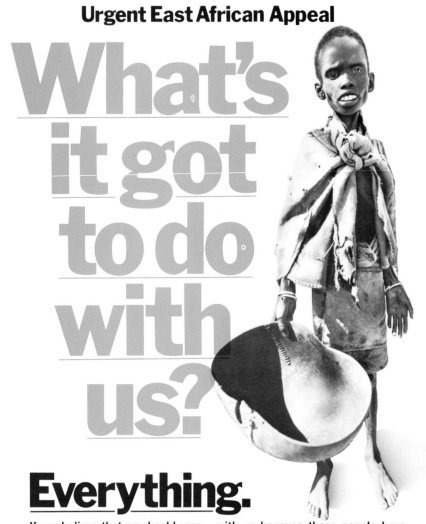

Urgent East African Appeal

What's it got to do with us?

Everything.

If you believe that we should care about the suffering of others, then it is everything to do with us. And, thank goodness, there are thousands who have responded to the needs of the drought stricken and the refugees of East Africa.

But this is one of the biggest and cruellest disasters of the century. And more, much more help – such as food, medical teams, transport and other vital supplies – is needed.

At this very moment, mothers are helplessly watching their children starve to death. Sadly, the problems in Africa, particularly Eastern Africa, are especially acute and our help will be needed for a long time yet.

This disaster is everything to do with us because these people have nothing – and we have so much.

Please help us to help stop the suffering. Don't delay even for a moment. Do it now.

And thank you. For everything.

I enclose £_____ as my contribution to the Oxfam African Emergency appeal.

Name_____

Address_____

_____

Oxfam, Room XXXX, 274 Banbury Rd., Oxford OX2 7DZ.

13 Study Fig. 10.25.
  a In what ways does it appeal to the conscience of people in Britain?
  b Do you think it is an effective advertisement? How would you expect other people to react to it?
  c How much of their money should charities spend on advertising?

Summary

In this final chapter we have considered the major issues and problems that face the world today. The developing countries are demanding a fairer distribution of the world's wealth. The main way of achieving this would be by changes in the world trade and monetary systems. International aid should be stepped up and spent more carefully. If the developed nations are reluctant to share their prosperity this will lead to increased tension between the North and the South. Racial conflict and prejudice can only make the situation worse. Since spending on arms and defence is rising rapidly in the Third World the danger of war increases all the time. Even if wars are localized political commitments mean that the superpowers will always be involved to some extent.

If man is to overcome the threats posed by hunger, disease, pollution, dwindling resources, the arms race, overcrowded cities and intolerance, then the main solutions he must find are political ones.

Index